LINKING THEORY TO PRACTICE

Framed by an overview of theories that guide student affairs practice, the cases in this book present a challenging array of problems that student affairs and higher education personnel face, such as racial diversity, alcohol abuse, and student activism. The revised edition has 30 new cases, with content on issues that reflect the complexity of today's environment at colleges and universities, including the expanded use of social networking, the rise in mental health issues, bullying, study abroad, and athletics. This fully updated edition includes new references, expanded theory with an increased emphasis on race, ethnicity, and sexual orientation, and three entirely new chapters on admissions, student identity, and campus life. An excellent teaching tool, this book challenges students to consider multiple overlapping issues within a single case study.

Features include:

- A two-part structure that sets the stage for case study methods and links student affairs theory with practical applications
- Cases written by well-known and respected contributors set in a wide variety of institution types and locations
- Over 35 complex case studies r⟨   ⟩ıdent affairs professionals face in to⟨

Frances K. Stage is Professor of Highe⟨   ⟩New York University.

Steven M. Hubbard is a Clinical Assistant Professor of Management and Director of Student Affairs at the McGhee Division, New York University.

LINKING THEORY TO PRACTICE

CASE STUDIES FOR WORKING WITH COLLEGE STUDENTS

Third Edition

Edited by

Frances K. Stage
Steven M. Hubbard

Routledge
Taylor & Francis Group

NEW YORK AND LONDON

Third edition published 2012
by Routledge
711 Third Avenue, New York, NY 10017

Simultaneously published in the UK
by Routledge
2 Park Square, Milton Park, Abingdon, Oxon OX14 4RN

First edition published 1993
by Routledge
Second edition pubished 2000
by Routledge

Routledge is an imprint of the Taylor & Francis Group, an informa business

© 1993, 2000, 2012 Taylor & Francis

Library of Congress Cataloging-in-Publication Data
Stage, Frances K.
Linking theory to practice : case studies for working with college students / Frances K. Stage and Steven M. Hubbard. – 3rd ed.
p. cm.
Stage's name appears as principal author on first edition.
Includes bibliographical references and index.
1. Student affairs services–United States–Case studies. 2. College student personnel administrators–Training of–United States. I. Stage, Frances K. II. Hubbard, Steven M. III. Stage, Frances K. Linking theory to practice. IV. Title.
LB2342.9.S73 2012
378.1'946–dc23
2011042460

ISBN: 978–0–415–89871–3 (hbk)
ISBN: 978–0–415–89870–6 (pbk)
ISBN: 978–0–203–19741–7 (ebk)

Typeset in New Baskerville
by Keystroke, Station Road, Codsall, Wolverhampton

Printed and bound in the United States of America
by Edwards Brothers, Inc.

Contents

Preface

This book is the third edition of the original *Linking Theory to Practice: Case Studies for Working with College Students*. As with the second edition, cases in this book are updated to ensure student affairs coverage of immediate campus issues. We have 30 new cases, as well as nine cases from the second edition that reviewers mentioned as classroom favorites. We have also included a new chapter on identity to address growing challenges surrounding that topic on college campuses. In addition, we have included cases involving study abroad, social media, bullying, and athletics. Our goal is to provide a comprehensive and realistic set of classroom challenges for aspiring student affairs professionals to prepare them for the increasingly complex college environment.

Chapter 1, The Role of Theory in a Practical World, has been updated. Chapter 2, Theory and Practice in Student Affairs, serves as a general reference for theories, and includes a table for quick reference. The chapter has been completely rewritten to include descriptions of a broad array of theories to reflect changing student affairs practice. Student development theories are separated into: cognitive development, psychosocial, and typology. The chapter includes theories of the college environment, impact and outcomes; and organization and administration. Finally, this chapter provides a summary of critical analyses that will give the reader new insights on how to better apply theory and ask important questions for our profession and use of theory. Chapter 3, Analyzing a Case, again provides a rubric for analysis of case studies. The chapter includes analysis of a new case, Take Back the Night: A Gauge of the Climate for Women on Campus, by Jillian Kinzie and Patricia Muller. The detailed analysis can be used as a guide for the facilitator as well as the student in using the remainder of the book.

We have included an index specific to the case studies, divided into a case-by-case reference and a subject reference, in addition to a more typical book index. Faculty and workshop facilitators can use the index to quickly identify cases covering issues and institutional characteristics that are of interest to them. Students and faculty are cautioned however, that we only identified the most salient and obvious issues for each case. More sub-issues likely exist and will need to be identified and analyzed for a thorough case analysis. Once again, we expect a future demand for even newer case studies reflecting emerging campus issues that we have yet to envision. Therefore we again solicit your comments now on this book as well as suggestions for issues to be included in a future volume.

This book is intended to be used to supplement other reading materials within student affairs preparation courses. It might also be used as material for workshops for student affairs professionals and paraprofessionals. While Chapter 2, Theory and Practice in Student Affairs, includes an expansive overview of theories guiding student affairs practice, complete and comprehensive coverage is impossible here. Other materials that cover these important topics, especially those referenced in these chapters, should be used in conjunction with this book.

The second part of the book contains the cases. The cases themselves are divided into six chapters, based on areas of work within student affairs: Organization and Administration, Admissions, Advising and Counseling, Academic Issues, Identity, and Campus Life. One of the first things the reader may notice is the lack of discreteness of cases organized into these arbitrary chapters. Cases in Advising and Counseling sometimes overlap into Identity issues. Admissions and Academic issues might be entwined. Nearly every case is related to Organization and Administration. This is the reality of today's complex college campus.

The case study authors present a challenging array of problems to be tackled. Cases include setting, characters, and a statement of the events of the case. A few cases also have a list of facts. In each case, professionals are faced with an array of short-term as well as long-term issues. Topics of cases within sections vary across such current issues as study abroad, the use of social media, campus violence, and student activism. The campus environments vary as well; settings for cases include large research universities, community college campuses, minority serving institutions, proprietary schools, and residential liberal arts colleges. The professionals involved in the dilemmas described range from vice presidents for student affairs to fresh student affairs hires in their first weeks on a job.

The 42 authors of the cases in this book have collective campus experience, by a conservative estimate, of over 300 years. We are fortunate to have their expertise to help with such an important aspect of student affairs preparation—the translation of academic learning from the classroom into the practical realities of the college campus.

Fran Stage and Steve Hubbard

Chapter 1

The Role of Theory in a Practical World

Frances K. Stage

Theories focusing on college students have grown in number and have become well defined and differentiated in recent years (Bilodeau & Renn, 2005; Ferdman & Gallegos, 2001; Kerwin & Ponterotto, 1995; Kim, 2001; Mayhew, 2004; Ortiz & Rhoads, 2000). Nevertheless, in student affairs literature authors describe the difficulties of linking day-to-day issues on a college campus to theory and the related research to practice (Bensimon, 2007; Evans, Forney, Guido, Patton, & Renn, 2010; Hurtado, 2007; Love & Guthrie, 1999; Pope, Reynolds, & Mueller, 2004; Torres, Howard-Hamilton, & Cooper, 2003; Upcraft, 1998). This remains true despite an explosion of knowledge about student development, campus environments, organizations, and characteristics of diverse college students. While these are all requisite components in the education of student affairs workers (Komives, 1998; McEwen & Talbot, 1998), professionals also require practice applying this newly acquired knowledge to the reality of a college campus.

In the past, individuals with a variety of educational backgrounds who liked the campus atmosphere and who liked working with students decided to enter the student affairs profession. Usually, they were given entry-level jobs in which they worked closely with administrators and learned the ropes. Under the protective environment, the fledgling administrator was shielded from making serious professional errors and—perhaps with occasional minor slipups—was guided along under the watchful eyes of his or her mentor.

Today few student affairs divisions have the luxury of providing new employees with this kind of mentoring. Given the state of postsecondary education budgets, such a luxury won't return. Instead, the expectation is that new professionals, even at the lowest levels, will have the ability to work independently and solve complex issues knowledgeably and with skill and integrity, resulting in the movement of student affairs from an apprenticeship type of profession to one with a strong educational base. Increasingly, professionals in student affairs have graduated from a student affairs preparation program.

Some of the difficulties in applying theory stem from difficulties inherent in studying concepts in the abstract atmosphere of the classroom or meeting room. Therefore, student affairs preparation programs typically include components of practical application. Internships, practica, and graduate assistantships all contribute to the increased sophistication of today's new professional. Nevertheless, most students have only a limited amount of such experiences. Additionally, such preprofessional experiences are necessarily limited to only one or two types of campuses. There is no guarantee that those campus settings will closely match that of the new job setting. Case-study analysis can provide an additional and necessary method of linking the student affairs knowledge base with practicality across a broad range.

Additionally, within student affairs curricula, in sessions at professional association meetings, and in staff training, the focus is on developmental theories, campus environments, organizational theories, and student characteristics—usually one theory at a time. Interactions of a particular student at a certain stage of development for a given theory in a specific campus setting are considered. Rarely, however, are aspiring professionals given the opportunity to consider and choose from many theories, possibly in combination, within a general, more holistic and honest context. Later translation of those theories by practitioners in the work setting leaves gaps between theoretical intention and administrative action (Komives, 1998).

Finally, litigation concerning students on college campuses is growing. As U.S. citizens became more consumer-oriented and more willing to litigate, so too became the college "consumer" as well as his or her parents. Now, student affairs professionals often are involved in a legal defense of them-selves and their colleges. Student affairs professionals must continually weigh decisions in light of the culpability of themselves and their institutions. Case-study analysis can provide a format for considering the legal implications surrounding campus decision issues.

Case-study analysis provides a means for consideration of the interactions between many elements of campus life and beyond. The broad perspective of a case study gives students and administrators a realistic opportunity to use theory in action before attempting to apply it in the work setting. In addition to considering students, the case-study analyst must take into account interrelationships between faculty, administrators, and community members in particular campus settings with specific histories, traditions, norms, and values. The idealism of the classroom is suspended while the analyst vicariously enters the college environment of the case study.

This chapter presents case-study analysis as a useful tool for connecting discrete theory and topics studied in student affairs classes to the aggregate reality of the college campus. This book is not intended to be used in lieu of other materials on college students, their growth and development, organizations, and campus environments. Rather, it is intended as a supplement to be used with other sources for education of those who work or who hope to work with college students. In the remainder of this chapter, some of the difficulties of applying theory in practice are discussed. Then, an argument is made for the use of case studies to link classroom learning with the realities of various campus settings.

A GAP BETWEEN THEORY AND REALITY

A hypothetical example illustrates how creation of theory and resultant research can result in a paradox:

Professor Thompson wants to learn about student experiences in the first year of college. She writes a proposal and is awarded a modest amount of money to conduct a qualitative study of students at the end of their first year of college. From her research she develops a theory of college student satisfaction.

She conducts two, hour-long interviews with 40 students. The format is open-ended with a handful of questions forming the basis for information gathering: "What were the most positive aspects of your year on campus?" "What were the most negative?" "If you could choose all over again, would you still choose this college?" "Would you tell a friend to come to school here?" "What would you change about this campus if you could?"

As a result of her study, Thompson has a wealth of information about college students. Consider elements gleaned from three interviews:

Marcus was the first in his family to attend college. Early in the semester he had trouble with his roommate. He now has a new one and they get along fine. He thinks his family doesn't really understand how hard college is and how time-consuming the homework can be. He relies on his friends and resident assistant for support. He makes friends easily and particularly enjoys talking to faculty after class about things in which he is interested. Toward the end of the semester he started running out of money and got a job to cover expenses. His grades went down because he couldn't spend as much time as he needed studying.

Katharine is a basketball player majoring in chemistry. At the beginning of the year she had a hard time making ends meet but began working at the local community Girls' Club. A month after she came to school her ten-year-old cat died. She almost left college then. Sometimes she feels out of place in her classes full of mostly men, especially when she has to go to lab right before practice and has her warm-ups on. First semester, she had a lab instructor who seemed to like her and who encouraged her to "stick it out" when she was thinking of quitting college. Though she enjoys basketball and has lots of close friends on the team, her athletic obligations take time from her studies. After a rocky start, she earned a higher GPA than she expected first semester.

Chris is a Black student who was admitted to an historically Black college but he decided instead to go to the state university that was closer to home. Sometimes, especially at first, he felt lonely when he was in a class or at an event and he was the only Black student. He soon learned that other Black students were friendly, even if they didn't know him. He got in the habit of looking for them whenever he was in a new setting. After the first month of school Chris joined a service club. Now, when he is not studying, he is usually involved in community projects like working with kids at a Community Center. The advisor of the club was helpful to him when he needed someone to talk to and didn't want to worry his parents. He is thankful that his parents provide him with 100% financial support; he has other friends who struggle to pay their expenses. Sometimes, however, his parents expect him to go home on weekends for family occasions and special events at his church. Then he has trouble catching up with his work. He is proud of the fact that he earned a B+ average first semester.

In formulating her theory, Professor Thompson examined what she learned from these students and from 37 others. She looked for commonalities among the findings and carefully noted similarities in students' descriptions of their first year. Not surprisingly, she developed a theory that revolved around four elements: grades, finances, friends, and relationships with faculty and student affairs professionals.

The process in this research project is not dissimilar to the ways in which many theories of college student behaviors, experiences, and interactions are formulated. The researcher or theorist asks a variety of students to talk about the aspects of college life that were important to their satisfaction, intellectual growth, or other successes. In this case four common elements were mentioned by students over and over again and emerged to form the basis of a theory that would be generalized to all college students. Individuals reading the report would agree that Thompson's four elements were important to college success. However, readers also would have to agree that important elements of these individual students' college lives were missed.

The job of the theory builder and some kinds of researchers (like Professor Thompson) is to ignore the finer details of students' lives. However, the student affairs professional's job typically is not to ignore these details. This discrepancy is a major cause of the gap between the researchers and theorists and the practitioners.

In addition to the discrepancy described above, student affairs professionals must deal with relatively discrete bodies of knowledge (student development, campus environmental and organizational theories, and college student characteristics) derived almost exclusively from two disciplines—psychology and sociology. Differences in assumptions across the two disciplines also makes theory-based practice difficult. While these obstacles to applying theory in practice are formidable, they are not necessarily overwhelming. Case-study analysis provides one means for overcoming these difficulties.

Case-study analysis can provide student affairs staff and students in professional preparation programs with experience in weighing such contextual considerations. Diverse characteristics of students along with other particulars such as characteristics of a specific institution, personalities, and considerations all play a role. Efforts to reach a decision take you, the analyst, from the abstract realm of the classroom or workshop to the concrete domain of reality.

BENEFITS OF CASE-STUDY ANALYSIS

Case-study analysis benefits student affairs administrators as well as students in professional programs in four ways: by providing challenges to conventional habits of administrative thought and action, by promoting consideration of multiple perspectives, by promoting consideration of unique campus environments, and by manipulating problems with realistic legal, institutional, and political constraints. Lessons learned along each of these dimensions provide an advantage to the professional who uses theory.

Challenging Habits of Administrative Thought and Action

Administrators cannot easily change their habits of action. Argyris (1976) called such habits, the underlying guides to professional behavior, "theories in use." Earlier in this chapter was a discussion of some of the difficulties of translating formal theories and newly acquired knowledge into theories in use or personal theories of action. A second difficulty is simply habit. For some administrators, habits of action become second nature. In a crisis situation they react almost without thinking in a manner that has served them well or adequately in the past. These administrators may not even recognize their behaviors as habits. Beyond that, changing those reactions, even when one wants to, can be difficult (Argyris, 1976). Case-study analysis is an ideal way to begin to challenge and modify theories of action or, in the absence of theories of action, to cultivate positive ones.

An individual's consideration of a case, examined thoroughly alongside the analyses of others, reveals the value of flexibility in approaching issues. Through rehearsal, student affairs professionals develop the characteristics of a responsive administrator (one who listens to others and "reads" the environment) rather than developing into a reactive administrator.

For example, suppose in a case study an advisor to the student senate is presented with a decision issue. A Pro-Life group of students has sought funding for their organization, and it appears that the request will be voted down. The Dean of Student's Office has received several calls from politicians and community members who are in favor of the organization. One parent threatened to sue the university if the organization is denied funding.

Perhaps the case-study analyst's own typical approach in advising student groups is "hands off" except to advise on institutional policy and procedural matters. The analyst, however, must weigh his or her typical response or habit of action (hands off) against the other reasonable alternatives from other analysts that might be more responsive to the campus environment.

Questions that may help challenge negative habits and create positive responses to issues include the following:

What is my first impulse on this issue?

What are the positive implications of that first impulse?

What are the negative implications of that first impulse?

Are any theories available that might apply to the situation?

By working through issues in several cases, the analyst will gain practice holding impulses or habits of action in check. As such, that habit or impulse will become just one of many options weighed for a more deliberate, less reactive style of administration.

Considering Multiple Perspectives

A student affairs professional advancing to increasingly responsible positions of administration experiences ever-expanding realms with which to be concerned. At the earliest levels, a student affairs administrator is most often concerned with students, a few subordinates, peers, and supervisors. Moving up the hierarchy, he or she experiences not just more people, but more complex relationships.

At the middle levels of administration, one moves further away from links with students, and becomes more focused on the student affairs division and the web of peer administrators at other campuses. Supervisors remain important and, as a manager, the professional recognizes broader, campus-wide implications of administrative decisions. A chief student affairs officer must consider, in addition to students, not only a host of subordinates and institutional peers (the chief academic and business officers, academic deans, and those in other parallel positions), but also a cadre of regional and national chief student affairs officers. Finally, the president, board of trustees, and key politicians must not be forgotten.

The case study can give the analyst, as a beginning or mid-level administrator, practice thinking about these constituents and their sometimes contrasting influences. When the analyst eventually finds himself or herself in a position serving a wide variety of conflicting constituents, he or she will then be better prepared.

In addition to the changing relationships that bureaucratic advancement brings, with the multicultural nature of today's college campus an important point is for administrators to be able to view issues from many perspectives. Case-study analysis can provide practice considering issues from the perspective of a minority student, a faculty member, a returning student, or a concerned citizen. With enough practice, taking the time to consider multiple perspectives can become second nature to any skilled administrator.

For example, in the sample case analysis presented in Chapter 3, analysts deliberate about issues surrounding gender issues, campus diversity, conflict between student organizations, and concern about the institution's image.

The case-study analyst becomes accustomed to seeking multiple views by asking the following key questions for every case:

Who are the actors in the case?

What roles do these actors play?

What is the view of each actor on the issues?

Which of the actors are also decision makers?

What would be each of their decisions?

Would some "invisible" actors be affected by the decision?

What would be their perspectives?

In working through issues of each case, an analyst will foster habits of an administrator who listens to others' voices. The case-study analyst will try to remove himself or herself temporarily from a limited perspective to consider others' views more fully. The analyst may also learn to shift from looking for answers to examining ideas (Wassermann, 1994). Finally, the analyst will gain practice listening to the weakest as well as the most powerful of those voices.

Considering a Wide Range of Campus Environments

While great diversity exists within the student and staff population on nearly every college campus, great diversity also exists across campus environments (Brazell, 1996). Lessons learned in a student affairs class or in an institutional training session typically reflect the environment of that campus setting. In studying theories or thinking of examples for application, professors tend to draw on their own limited repertoire of campus environments. Such provincialism can limit vision and stifle creativity.

Up until the last quarter of the twentieth century, many student affairs administrators could afford to be somewhat provincial. Institutions were relatively homogeneous and, typically, administrators did not move from location to location. A thorough knowledge of one campus environment would be adequate to ensure success in administrative decisions. Now, however, the student affairs profession is more mobile. Administrators may move from large residential universities to commuter campuses to small liberal arts colleges as they progress in the profession.

Additionally, college environments are less homogeneous than they once were (Brazell, 1996; Stage & Manning, 1992). Many liberal arts colleges now offer professional programs such as nursing and teaching to draw people from their local communities and bolster enrollments. International students make up sizable portions of many colleges' student bodies. Some colleges engage in entrepreneurial efforts in conjunction with business or industry from their local communities. More frequently student affairs divisions are becoming heavily involved in fundraising. Case-study analysis can provide vicarious experiences in a variety of campus situations, giving student affairs professionals more flexibility in viewing their own campus settings. In essence, they contextualize problems and the abstract ideas and theories we bring to bear on those problems (Miller & Kantrov, 1998).

For example, suppose that you are an administrator at a small liberal arts college. Additionally, you attended a liberal arts college as an under-graduate. In a workshop utilizing case-study analysis you are asked to consider the problems of an urban commuter campus experiencing dwindling enroll-ments. As part of the analysis of the case you must consider the needs of commuter students as well as adult students who work full-time. This population may be invisible (existent, but not in great numbers) on your own campus. Hopefully, as a result of your work on the case, future administrative decisions you make might include consideration of the needs of these students. Of course, such change will not occur unless one is willing. Perhaps experience with case-study work can provide the catalyst for pro-fessional growth.

Case-study analysis can force you, your facilitator, and your classmates out of the comfort of your own home campus environment and into one that presents new and greater challenges. You, as case-study analysts, are chal-lenged within the supportive classroom environment in a way that fosters flexibility and creativity in everyday decision making.

Environmental questions that can help you broaden your institutional perspective include the following:

What is the history of the institution?
What is the history of student affairs at the institution?

What is the relationship of the student affairs officer to superiors/
subordinates/faculty/other stakeholders in the institution?
What is the relationship of the campus to the local community?

By working through a variety of campus settings presented in cases, the
case-study analyst can develop flexibility. The analyst will gain vicarious
experiences that can make him or her a more knowledgeable student affairs
administrator. Finally, the practical knowledge can help analysts become
more creative administrators in their present campus environment.

Considering a Variety of Legal, Institutional, and Political Constraints

The classroom or workshop environment tends to be idealistic. There, it is
easy for armchair administrators to generate lists of "shoulds" and "oughts"
when speculating about ways of administering. The reality of the college
campus, however, presents a totally different situation.

In solving an actual campus problem, analysts must not forget to consider
the legal implications of their actions. Additionally, decisions made must fit
within established institutional processes and procedures. Finally, analysts
may have difficulty as new professionals in envisioning and reconciling
conflicts between a supervisor's desires and professional values.

Through analyzing case studies, one attends to descriptions of restrictions,
limitations, and the facts of the case. This additional information presents a
greater challenge for learning to apply classroom knowledge. Additionally,
these details, delimited within a case, will help the analyst become accustomed to seeking similar information in dealing with issues on his or her own
campus.

For example, suppose you are an administrator embroiled in a campus
controversy. Students in a residence hall intend to show X-rated movies in
order to raise money for intramural teams and social activities. The students
and their law student advisor maintain that no one will be offended; it will
not be a public showing since people must pay to get in. Others argue that
university property should not be used to display pornographic materials.
Someone notified the county sheriff who promised to check the situation
out. As an administrator dealing with this issue, you should consult with the
university's attorney. How do local standards for pornography affect your
decision? Is such entrepreneurship encouraged at your institution? Have you
briefed your superiors and the university president on this issue? What are
their opinions?

Through analyzing case studies, idealism about a college campus can be
tempered with reality. In an increasingly litigious society, it is important to

consider the legal ramifications of any decisions made. One must not run afoul of institutional governance practices. Positive relationships with other campus constituents should be cultivated. Finally, politics must go beyond merely understanding the perspective of others.

Questions that can be used to identify constraints for a given institution include the following:

What is the mission of the institution in question?

What are the legal ramifications of possible solutions?

Are there particular aspects of institutional governance that must be considered?

Does the president (a trustee, a key politician) have any particular interest in this issue?

Could resolution of this issue cause bad press for the institution?

As the case-study analyst views a smorgasbord of case studies, he or she will see a variety of constraints affecting administrators' flexibility in decision making. The analyst will gain practice in balancing the ideals of the classroom with the realities of today's complex college environment. As a result, solutions to campus issues can be tempered in ways that meet multiple demands.

CONCLUSION

The case study can serve to blend the separate elements of student development, campus environments, organizational theory, and student diversity into ways of decision making on the college campus. Within a classroom or workshop one learns *what* an administrator should do, yet within the classroom one rarely learns *how* to do it. Through vicarious analysis of realistic cases, the administrator or future administrator can practice with the theoretical tools of the trade. While case analysis cannot replicate a sense of danger or urgency (no one will lose a job for a weak analysis of a case), it can provide useful practice for future administrative decision making. Sharing perspectives on a case in a workshop or classroom setting can provide not only a challenge but also a deepened and enriched learning experience.

REFERENCES

Argyris, C. (1976). Theories of action that inhibit individual learning. *American Psychologist*, 31, 638–654.
Bensimon, E.M. (2007). The underestimated significance of practitioner knowledge

in the scholarship on student success. *The Review of Higher Education*, 30(4), 441–469.

Bilodeau, B.L. & Renn, K.A. (2005). Analysis of LGBT identity development models and implications for practice. *New Directions for Student Services*, 111, 25–39.

Brazell, J.C. (1996). Diversification of post secondary institutions. In S.R. Komives, D.B. Woodward, Jr., and Associates (Eds.), *Student services: A handbook for the profession* (3rd ed.) (pp. 43–63). San Francisco: Jossey-Bass.

Evans, N.J., Forney, D.S., Guido, F.M., Patton, L.D., & Renn, K.A. (2010). *Student development in college: Theory, research, and practice* (2nd ed.). San Francisco: Jossey-Bass.

Ferdman, B.M. & Gallegos, P.V. (2001). Latinos and racial identity development. In C.L. Wijeyesinghe & B.W. Jackson III (Eds.), *New perspectives on racial identity development: A theoretical and practical anthology* (pp. 32–66). New York: New York University Press.

Hurtado, S. (2007). Linking diversity with the educational and civic missions of higher education. *The Review of Higher Education*, 30(2), 185–196.

Kerwin, C. & Ponterotto, J.G. (1995). Biracial identity development. In J.G. Ponterotto, J.M. Cass, L.A. Suzuki, & C.M. Alexander (Eds.), *Handbook of multicultural counseling* (pp. 199–217). Thousand Oaks, CA: Sage.

Kim, J. (2001). Asian American identity development theory. In C.L. Wijeyesinghe & B.W. Jackson III (Eds.), *New perspectives on racial identity development: A theoretical and practical anthology* (pp. 129–152). New York: New York University Press.

Komives, S.R. (1998). Linking student affairs preparation and practice. In N.J. Evans & C.E. Phelps Tobin (Eds.), *State of the art preparation and practice in student affairs: Another look* (pp. 177–200). Lanham, MD: University Press of America.

Love, P.L. & Guthrie, V.L. (1999). Understanding and applying cognitive development theory. *New Directions for Student Services, Vol. 88*. San Francisco: Jossey-Bass.

Mayhew, M. (2004). Exploring the essence of spirituality: A phenomenological study of eight students with eight different worldviews. *NASPA Journal*, 49(1), 40–55.

McEwen, M.K. & Talbot, D.M. (1998). Designing the student affairs curriculum. In N. Evans & C.E. Phelps Tobin (Eds.), *State of the art preparation and practice in student affairs: Another look* (pp. 125–156). Lanham, MD: University Press of America.

Miller, B. & Kantrov, I. (1998). *A guide to facilitating cases in education.* Portsmouth, NH: Heinemann.

Ortiz, A.M. & Rhoads, R.A. (2000). Deconstructing whiteness as part of a multicultural educational framework: From theory to practice. *Journal of College Student Development*, 41(1), 81–93.

Pope, R.L., Reynolds, A.L., & Mueller, J.(2004). *Multicultural competence in student affairs.* San Francisco: Jossey-Bass.

Stage, F.K. & Manning, K. (1992). *Enhancing the multicultural campus environment: A cultural brokering approach.* San Francisco: Jossey-Bass.

Torres, V., Howard-Hamilton, M.F., & Cooper, D.L. (2003). *Identity development of diverse populations: Implications for teaching and administration in higher education.* ASHE-ERIC Higher Education Report, 29(6). San Francisco: Jossey-Bass.

Upcraft, M.L. (1998). Do graduate preparation programs really prepare practitioners? In N. Evans & C.E. Phelps Tobin (Eds.), *State of the art preparation and practice in student affairs: Another look* (pp. 225–237). Lanham, MD: University Press of America.

Wassermann, S. (1994). *Introduction to case method teaching: A guide to the galaxy.* New York: Teachers College Press.

Chapter 2

Theory and Practice in Student Affairs

Steven M. Hubbard

Theories play a significant role in the work of student affairs professionals. They describe characteristics of our student population, demonstrate differences in the learning process, give us a deeper understanding of the campus environment, and help us navigate the politics of academic administration. Theories provide a road map for professionals to evaluate problems and reach best practice solutions.

With today's increased concerns over shrinking budgets in higher education, theories play an even more important role when working with college students. Theories are a reference point for the student affairs professional who needs to assess learning outcomes or provide rationales to keep programs alive under threatening budget cuts. They are also useful in the planning process of new programs and ideas. A strong background in the theoretical knowledge of college students and the campus environment is critical to being a successful professional in the field.

This chapter provides a brief summary of relevant theories that will help the reader explore and respond to the cases in this book. The chapter first covers student development theories, which are separated into three subsections: cognitive development, psychosocial, and typology. The chapter then explores theories of the college environment, impact and outcomes, and organization and administration. The chapter also provides a summary of critical analyses that will give the reader new insights on how to better apply theory and ask important questions for our profession and our use of theory. Finally, the chapter concludes with a table of theories and studies that the reader may use as a quick reference when searching for research and theoretical frameworks to assist in solving cases in this book (Table 2.1).

STUDENT DEVELOPMENT

Student development theories are the cornerstone of the student affairs profession. Their origins began in the progressive movement of the 1920s (Strange, 1994). Since then, the student population in higher education has grown and become more diverse. Research in the profession has responded with an evolving palette of theoretical frameworks to help the practitioner serve their student population.

As Stage, Downey, and Dannells (2000) noted, all student development theories encompass Sanford's (1962) concepts of *challenge* and *support*. Without challenges, students will not experience the dissonance needed to progress further in their intellectual and identity development. Without support, students do not have the resources or services to respond to challenges and sustain their development. Theories from three categories of student development are described below: cognitive development, psychosocial, and typology.

Cognitive Development

The intellectual development of college students is an important process within academia. Both faculty and student affairs professionals are concerned about how our students learn and develop intellectually. Cognitive development theories rely heavily on psychology and the work of Piaget (1952). These theories primarily focus on the intellectual growth of students, how students understand knowledge, and the frameworks they use to solve ethical decisions and understand difficult problems (Evans, Forney, Guido, Patton, & Renn, 2010; King, 1978).

Many of the cognitive development theories introduced in this chapter assume that students progress through a natural order of stages—sometimes also referred to as positions, levels, and categories. They also assume that cognitive development is not age-related. Some researchers and theorists have criticized that the predominant paradigm used to develop cognitive theories comes from a hierarchical approach (Moore, 1994). Therefore, cognitive development theories have evolved to include a variety of frameworks to address the intellectual development of college students.

Historically, two cognitive development theories in the student affairs profession are often referred to and highly respected: Perry's (1970) Scheme of Intellectual and Ethical Development and Kohlberg's (1977, 1981) Stages of Moral Development. The concepts introduced from both theories are often used in the professional vernacular. Some have criticized the use of these two theories because they do not adequately reflect the diversity of today's student population (Stage, Downey, & Dannells, 2000). However, both theories were used as seminal works in the development of new approaches to the college student cognitive development—demonstrating their heuristic value (Evans et al., 2010).

Perry described cognitive and ethical development as a series of nine positions that were subdivided into four categories: *dualism, multiplicity, relativism,* and *commitment to relativism* (Perry, 1970). *Dualism* is the initial category of Perry's scheme. At this level, students recognize knowledge that comes from authority, and students at this level often view the world dichotomously (Perry, 1970). Knowledge is either right or wrong, and it is defined by authority figures and by absolutes. Many times in college (and often before college), students will find that experts and authority figures often disagree. This occurrence is called *cognitive dissonance,* when students are challenged with conflicting ideas or points of view (Evans et al., 2010).

As students experience cognitive dissonance, they move to the next level, *multiplicity.* In this category, students recognize that there are multiple ways to understand a problem or an issue (Perry, 1970). In this category, you may hear a student express that everyone has a valid opinion and a right to that opinion (Evans et al., 2010). Rarely are opinions or points of view defended with facts or logic. In the next category, *relativism,* students begin to understand that some opinions are more defendable than others (Perry, 1970). Relativistic thinkers also recognize that knowledge and answers to problems are context-bound—which means that answers/opinions are dependent on complexities like the environment, situation, and other factors.

The final level, *commitment to relativism,* is the most complex and controversial category of Perry's scheme (1970). As individuals move from relativism to commitment to relativism, they begin to make commitments to ideas, values, and individuals. They also begin to have a deeper understanding of their identity and responsibility to others in the world.

King and Kitchener (1994) critiqued Perry's scheme and found that the last stages mixed intellectual development with ethical decision making. Building on Perry's theory, King and Kitchener developed the Reflective Judgment Model. In this theory, King and Kitchener investigated how individuals make a decision on their beliefs about a *vexing problem,* which is a complex and sometimes controversial problem. Their model has seven stages, grouped into three categories: *prereflective thinkers, quasireflective thinkers,* and *reflective thinkers. Prereflective thinkers* do not recognize the uncertainty of knowledge, usually justify answers in a simple fashion, and often refer to authorities for answers. *Quasireflective thinkers* recognize there is uncertainty when finding answers to vexing problems, but these thinkers have difficulty making conclusions and developing an argument for their opinions. *Reflective thinkers* understand that knowledge and opinions need to be substantiated with facts and data. In addition, they recognize that knowledge is individually constructed (King & Kitchener, 1994).

Other theorists critiqued Perry's work on college student intellectual and ethical development and developed their own theories. Using the work of Perry (1970), Gilligan (1982), and a feminists' framework, Belenky, Clinchy, Goldberger, and Tarule (1986) developed Women's Ways of Knowing, which is a theory that focused on the epistemological development of women. Women's Ways of Knowing is grouped into five epistemological perspectives. The *silence* perspective is characterized as powerlessness (Belenky et al., 1986). Here women are often subject to external authority and often socially and economically deprived. *Received knowledge* is a perspective where the individual typically lacks self-confidence and seeks knowledge/truth from others. *Subjective knowledge* is a perspective where truth and knowledge are determined by the individual. The *subjective knowledge* perspective is similar to Perry's multiplicity. Knowledge from the *procedural* perspective focuses on how the individual uses formulas/systems to receive and convey knowledge. The fifth perspective is the *constructive knowledge* perspective, where individuals develop their own authentic voice by using both subjective and objective knowledge. From this perspective, the individual constructs their own truth and knowledge (Love & Guthrie, 1999).

Baxter Magolda (1992) also developed a cognitive development model that focused on gender. Her model outlines four stages of epistemological reflection. These stages include: *absolute knowing*—the ability to receive and master knowledge; *transitional knowing*—individuals recognize that knowledge is sometimes certain and sometimes uncertain; *independent knowing*—knowledge is recognized as uncertain, belief that everyone has their own opinion; *contextual knowing*—knowledge is constructed based on evidence and context. Baxter Magolda (1992) found gender differences in epistemological development. Women tend to favor received, interpersonal, and interindividual knowing (Evans et al., 2010). However, she also found more similarities than differences between men and women in their epistemological perspectives.

Another track of cognitive development theories when working with college students are theories that focus on moral decision making. Lawrence Kohlberg's (1977) work on Moral Development outlines how individuals make moral decisions. Kohlberg's model is a six-stage model that is divided into three levels: *preconventional, conventional,* and *postconventional.* At the *preconventional* level, individuals make moral decisions based on how the decision serves the self. At the *conventional* level, the individual establishes moral decisions based on how the decision serves important others (e.g., friends, family, government). Finally, the individual at the *postconventional* level bases moral decisions on a social contract and serves anonymous others (King & Mayhew, 2002).

Interestingly, Kohlberg did not conduct research on the moral development of women (Evans et al., 2010). Carol Gilligan (1982), a student of

Kohlberg, critiqued this weakness and developed an alternative view of moral and ethical decision making. In her research, she saw women tended to adopt a *"voice of care"* over a *"voice of justice."* Those adopting a *"voice of care"* perspective strive for strengthening relationships, equality, and reciprocity. The *"voice of justice"* values autonomy, rights, values, and rules. Her research challenged the conventional paradigm used in developing cognitive theory, and she inspired others to develop new theories that challenged the conventional approach to student development (e.g., Belenky et al., 1986).

Spiritual development theories are a group of developmental theories that can fit in both cognitive and psychosocial categories. Since many of these theories rely on the work of Piaget, Perry, and other cognitive development theorists (Fowler, 1981; Parks, 1986), they were placed in this section. Fowler's (1981) Theory of Faith Development is a six-stage theory that outlines the spiritual development of an individual through the life span. Stages one through two are stages that primarily focus on young children (*intuitive-projective faith* and *mythic-literal faith*). Stage three, *synthetic-conventional faith*, typically occurs in the teenage years. In this stage, an individual is interested in conformity. Similar to many cognitive theories, the individual seeks assurance and understanding from external sources. The fourth stage is *individuative-reflective faith*—which typically occurs during young adulthood. This stage is characterized by a deeper understanding of faith. Here the individual develops their own system of belief and way to make meaning (Evans et al., 2010). In the fifth stage, *conjunctive faith*, the individual enhances their understanding of their own belief systems, but they also become more aware of their own personal actions (Fowler, 1981). The final stage is *universalizing faith* which is characterized by establishing universal values. It is rare for an individual to reach this stage (Evans et al., 2010).

Cognitive development theories provide the student affairs professional ways to strengthen the learning outcome of in-class and out-of-class experiences. They are also useful when working with student governments, judicial councils, and honors organizations. Finally, these theories may prove useful when working with faculty or discussing the student affairs relevance to the academic mission of the institution.

Psychosocial

As the name suggests, these theories concentrate on the psychological and social development of students. In addition, these theories typically focus on the development of one's identity and relationships with others. Often, these theories focus on the life cycle of the individual, and the stages tend to be sequential and age-related (Stage, Downey, & Dannells, 2000).

Theories of psychosocial development draw upon the work of Erik

Erikson's Stages of Development. This theory outlined eight challenges/ tasks individuals must face based on their age and stage in life (Widick, Parker, & Knefelkamp, 1978). Arthur Chickering built upon Erikson's work and focused on the fifth stage of the model—Identity vs. Identity Diffusion— the recognized stage of a traditional college student. Chickering and Reisser (1993) identified seven tasks (vectors) that students accomplish to further their identity development: *Developing Competence, Managing Emotions, Moving through Autonomy toward Interdependence, Developing Mature Interpersonal Relationships, Establishing Identity, Developing Purpose,* and *Developing Integrity.* As individuals progress through these vectors, they enhance their ability to handle new relationships, assumptions, routines, and roles in life. Since Chickering and Reisser (1993) recognized the fluidity of identity development of college students, he identified these seven tasks as "vectors" to highlight the fact that development may not be a "straight line."

Chickering's Seven Vectors of Identity is probably the most recognizable theory and the one most often used by student affairs practitioners. Since it broadly encompasses the many challenges college students face, the theory is useful in developing wide-ranging programs. Similar to other student development theories, researchers have criticized Chickering's work because it does not reflect the diversity of today's college student (Stage, Downey, & Dannells, 2000). In addition, the theory instills assumptions for the student affairs professional (Widick, Parker, & Knefelkamp, 1978; Evans et al., 2010).

Using the work of Marcia (1966), Josselson (1987) developed the Theory of Identity Development in Women which identified four identity groups: *foreclosure, identity achievement, moratorium,* and *identity diffusions.* These groups are defined by the individual's experience with identity exploration and ability to make identity commitments. For instance, women in the *foreclosure* group have made identity commitments, but they did not explore or experience an identity crisis. Josselson called this group *Purveyors of Heritage.* They made commitments about their identity based on childhood experiences and influence from parents. Women in the *identity achievement* group were identified as *Pavers of the Way.* These women progressed from identity exploration to identity commitment. They made identity commitments that were separate from their childhood experiences. Josselson's (1987) third group is referred to as *moratorium: Daughters in Crisis.* This group is experiencing an identity crisis or exploring their identity, however they have not made a commitment. Many in this group may move to the *identity achievement* group, while others will remain without making an identity commitment. Finally, Josselson identified the *identity diffusion* group— referred to as *Lost and Sometimes Found.* Women in this group lack experience with identity exploration and to make an identity commitment. Typically individuals in the group avoid decisions and withdraw from relationships. They also may have problems in the college environment.

Also using the work of Marcia (1966), Phinney (1990) proposed a Model of Ethnic Identity Development. This theory focused on how students from minority ethnic groups are influenced by their experiences with family and the community around them. Similar to Marcia (1966) and Josselson (1987), Phinney developed the model by using identity exploration/crisis and commitment to achieve a healthy identity. In Phinney's (1990) model, the first stage is *diffusion-foreclosure*, characterized by an individual who has not explored their attitudes and assumptions about ethnicity and race. In the second stage, *moratorium*, an individual becomes aware of ethnic identity issues. They awaken to the significance of ethnicity in their identity development and often experience anger and emotional intensity toward the dominant group. They may also experience feelings of guilt for their previous lack of knowledge on race and ethnicity. For the final stage, *identity achievement*, an individual achieves a healthy identity that has explored and made commitments to their identity in terms of race and ethnicity (Phinney, 1990).

In addition to ethnicity, student development theories also address identity development of African Americans. Cross's (Cross & Phagen-Smith, 1996) Model of Psychological Nigrescence addresses the socializing process of an individual moving from a non-Afrocentric to an Afrocentric viewpoint. The model has five stages. The first stage is *pre-encounter*—the individual views race as unimportant and constructs a worldview from a Eurocentric background (Cross & Phagen-Smith, 1996). In the second stage, *encounter*, the individual experiences events that cause disequilibrium and powerfully impact a person's identity. The individual sheds his/her old identity and commits to change in the third stage, *immersion-emersion* (Evans et al., 2010). In the fourth stage, the individual resolves identity conflicts and gains more self-confidence in being Black. Finally, in the last stage, the individual outwardly commits to their identity and becomes involved with activities that address concerns of African Americans and other minority groups (Cross & Phagen-Smith, 1996).

Cross's model is seminal to the work on race and identity development developed by other theorists. For instance, Ferdman and Gallegos (2001) developed the Model of Latino Identity Development. It proposed six orientations of Latino identity that reflect the diversity of this population and their cultural background. Their orientations include the following: *undifferentiated/denial*, where race is viewed as unimportant; *White-identified*, where race is viewed in terms of Black and White; *Latinos as others*, where Whites are viewed negatively; *sub-group identified*, where an individual identifies with their sub-group (e.g., Columbian, Dominican, etc.) and race is viewed as secondary; *Latino identified*, where being Latino is seen positively and broad; and *Latino integrated*, where race is viewed as socially constructed (Ferdman & Gallegos, 2001; Gallegos & Ferdman, 2007).

Kim (2001) proposed a model of Asian American Identity Development. This theory identified five stages of Asian American development. In the first stage, the model identifies that children will learn about their ethnic identity from their families. Therefore, they begin with the *ethnic awareness* stage. Once a child starts school, he or she becomes aware of their feelings of being different than the majority culture—the *White identification* stage. Through the next stage, *awakening of social and political consciousness*, the individual recognizes that there is a social structure that perpetuates racism and becomes aware that they are members of an oppressed group. Through the next stage, *redirection to an Asian American consciousness*, the individual begins to focus on their personal experiences and express feelings of pride toward their identity. The Asian American identity and other identities are blended and combined in the final *incorporation* stage (Kim, 2001).

Helms (1993) formulated the White Identity Model which describes the process of a white individual moving toward a nonracist White identity. The theory has two phases, with three statuses in each. In Phase 1: *abandonment of racism*, an individual starts with a naive and simplistic view of race and racism. However, through contact with a racial dilemma, an individual begins to grapple with their own White identity while seeking reassurance and trying to lessen the feelings of guilt of being White in a social environment that perpetuates racism (Evans et al., 2010). Through Phase 2, the individual first develops an intellectualized White identity that superficially questions the ways Whites have perpetuated racism. Next, the individual begins to replaces stereotypical assumptions about people of color and discovers a new deeper, internalized identity that accepts accurate information about race and racism in our social environment (Helms, 1993).

In addition to race and gender, identity development theories also explore the identity formation of lesbian, gay, and bisexual (LGB) individuals. The most widely known theory of LGB development is Cass's (1979) model of Homosexuality Identity Formation. This psychosocial stage theory describes a linear process of "coming out" from first awareness of same-sex attraction to an integrated identity. However, negative resolutions through these stages may lead to identity foreclosure. In the first stage, *identity confusion*, the individual first becomes aware of their homosexual thoughts and feelings. Next, in the *identity comparison* stage, an individual may become confronted with alienation as they begin to admit to the possibility that they are gay, lesbian, or bisexual. Through the *identity tolerance* stage, the individual begins to "tolerate" or bear their identity as an LGB individual. As they increasingly acknowledge their identity and "come out" to friends and family as gay, lesbian, or bisexual, the individual develops an *identity acceptance*. In the next stage, *identity pride*, the individual becomes proud of their sexual identity and may actively participate in LGB rights and community events (Stage, Downey, & Dannells, 2000). Similar to other identity theories, the last stage—*identity synthesis*—is characterized by an integration of the individual's sexual orientation with other aspects of their life.

In recent years, other theorists have developed models of LGB identity (Bilodeau & Renn, 2005; D'Augelli, 1994; McCarn & Fassinger, 1996). These theories have recognized that identity formation of sexuality is often more complex than the linear model presented by Cass (1979). For example, Queer Theory (Turner, 2000) is a perspective of human sexuality and gender that has reflected the complexity of identity and sexuality. Queer theory is a multidisciplinary approach that explores why society categorizes sexuality and gender. It is also a theory that recognizes the many culturally marginalized sexual self-identifications. This theory provides a critical lens to discover how society influences and develops power structures by categorizing others (Turner, 2000).

Typology

Typology theories in student affairs describe and explain personality types, learning styles, and how students interact with their environment. These theories are different from developmental theories (i.e., cognitive and identity). Typology theories use complex descriptions and statements to describe frameworks, outcomes, differences, and similarities of environments. Unlike developmental theories, however, typology theories do not describe progression from one stage to the next.

Typically used in career planning and development, Holland's (1966) Theory of Vocational Personalities and Environments hypothesizes that students choose their work and academic environments based on their life history and expression of their personality type. An individual expresses their personality by conveying their motivations, preferences, abilities, and assumptions. The environments are created through a collective effort by the individuals in the environment. In the academic and work environments, behaviors are rewarded and reinforced for the individual's "acquisition of the attitudes, interests, and abilities of the analogous personality types who dominate them" (Smart & Umbach, 2007, p. 184). In other words, congruence is reached when the individual's personality type "fits" with the collective environment. Holland (1966) outlined six different personality types and environments: *realistic, investigative, artistic, social, enterprising,* and *conventional.* These personality and environment types are used by student affairs professionals to help students explore and identify their interests (academic and career) while also describing the type of environments they will encounter in their academic and work experiences.

Another theory that describes personality types is the Myers Briggs Type Indicator (MBTI). This theory and popular assessment tool were created by

Isabel Myers and Katherine Briggs. The MBTI uses Jung's research on personality, and it identifies 16 different personality types, based on eight functions within four preference scales (Myers, 1980). For instance, an individual will have a preference on how they focus their attention. They will either focus their attention on *extraversion*—outer world activities. Or, they will prefer *introversion*—focused on their inner world (Myers, 1980). The theory also includes dichotomous preferences on how the individual gathers information (*sensing* vs. *intuition*); how the individual makes decisions (*thinking* vs. *feeling*); and how the individual interacts with the world (*judging* vs. *perceiving*). An individual's personality type is described and identified by assessing a person's preference in these four dimensions (Stage, Downey, & Dannells, 2000). Student affairs professionals use the MBTI in mediating conflicts (both group and individual), describing career interests, and developing leadership skills.

Student affairs professionals work closely with college learning environments both inside and outside the classroom. Since students learn from experience, many professionals use Kolb's (1984) Experiential Learning Model—a typology theory—to help describe both an individual's learning style and their learning process. To describe the experiential learning process, Kolb identified four stages that students progress through to maximize learning outcomes. After the initial *concrete experience*, a student *reflects* on the observations they encountered through discussion, writing, visualization, etc. After reflection, a student will internalize the learning process and develop *abstract concepts* about their experience. Next, the student will test the hypothesis and concepts developed in the previous stage and conduct *active experimentation* (Kolb, 1984). After this stage, the experiential learning cycle begins again with *concrete experiences*. Student affairs professionals use this theory to help plan educationally purposeful programs and learning opportunities for the college student. Kolb's model, however, is also a typology theory, because it identified preferences in learning styles. Using the four stages described above, Kolb identified the four different learning styles: *accommodators* (feeling and doing); *divergers* (feeling and watching); *assimilators* (thinking and watching); and *convergers* (thinking and doing). Kolb's (1984) Experiential Learning Model is helpful in both planning focused interventions on campus and identifying the teaching methods needed to reach all learning styles.

Another typology that is focused on learning is Gardner's (1983) theory of Multiple Intelligences which identified seven intelligences: *logical-mathematical, linguistic, musical, spatial, bodily-kinesthetic, interpersonal,* and *intrapersonal*. On most college campuses and learning environments, the *logical-mathematical* and *linguistic* intelligences are often favored over the other five. However, a growing movement in academia and the student affairs profession is beginning to understand the importance of enhancing learning opportunities in all seven of Gardner's Multiple Intelligences (Stage, Downey, & Dannells, 2000).

COLLEGE ENVIRONMENT THEORIES

In the book, *Education and Identity*, Chickering and Reisser (1993) outline several key environmental influences that impact student development on campus. For instance, *clear and consistent institutional objectives* help establish a powerful environment for student learning and can maximize student engagement both inside and outside the classroom. As Boyer (1987) noted, an institution without purpose is caught, "scrambling for students and driven by marketplace demands" (p. 3). Chickering and Reisser (1993) also noted that *institutional size* is an important environmental factor that impacts student development. Smaller schools typically have clearer and more consistent institutional objectives and develop a stronger institutional ethos and sense of community to encourage student development.

Environments that encourage *student–faculty relationships* were also identified factors by Chickering and Reisser (1993) that influence student development. Student–faculty interactions outside and inside the classroom significantly contribute to student learning and development (Kuh, Schuh, Whitt, and Associates, 1991). *Curriculum* also has an impact on student learning and development. An institution's core and general education programs promote the institution's purpose and mission as well as increase learning and developmental opportunities for students. Chickering and Reisser (1993) also outlined other factors that contribute greatly to the learning environments of college students, including *teaching, friendships, community, programs, student services,* and the *integration of work and learning.*

In addition to Chickering and Reisser's (1993) work on college environments, Strange (1994) described four propositions of campus environments that influence college student development. In proposition 1, a campus's *physical space* can both limit and facilitate student learning and development. For proposition 2, the *human aggregate* on the campus environment influences student development through collective characteristics that encourages conformity. In proposition 3, campuses defined as *organized environments* and goal directed "influence certain behaviors and sustain certain organizational milieus, from the dynamic to the static" (Strange, 2003, p. 303). In proposition 4, *constructed environment* models recognize that the influence of the environment is a function of how people perceive, evaluate, and differentiate the environment.

Theories on college environments can give the student affairs professional a context of how the problem or issue started and how it can be resolved. These theories can provide a framework to give the professional tools to give a bigger picture of the problem and allow the professional to redefine the problem and discover alternative solutions.

COLLEGE IMPACT AND OUTCOMES RESEARCH

Following the seminal work of Feldman and Newcomb (1969), Pascarella and Terenzini (1991, 2005) studied student outcomes by using meta-analysis of research on college students. Student outcome studies are different than the social and psychological college student developmental theories presented previously in this chapter. These studies focus primarily on outcomes from the college experience. The work of Pascarella and Terenzini (1991, 2005) summarized the broad changes that occur during the college experience. From the first year to the senior year, evidence demonstrates that students will increase in their learning and cognitive abilities. Their values and attitudes shift toward more intellectual and cultural pursuits. Students will also experience psychosocial changes with increased self-esteem, autonomy, interpersonal relationships, and maturity. Pascarella and Terenzini (1991, 2005) also found that living on campus and working on campus maximized the developmental and learning opportunities for college students.

Astin (1993) found similar results in his extensive research on college students. Using his input-environment-outcome (I-E-O) model, Astin (1993) identified that student involvement maximized learning opportunities. His model determined that student characteristics before entering college (input) and the personal interactions students experience in college (environment) will impact the characteristics of students after graduation (output). Astin (1993) proposed a "theory of involvement" which explained that the more students interacted with their peers, professors, and campus environments the higher student satisfaction and personal growth intellectually and socially. Astin's (1993) basic and significant concept of involvement is an important assumption for the student affairs profession. The theory highlights the impact that the many interventions and programs (e.g., student organizations, activities, learning communities, student–faculty events, etc.) have on the college student experience.

College impact studies are significant because they demonstrate the importance of the work we do as student affairs professionals. Student development theories are used to describe the developmental and learning process, and college impact studies provide the evidence that our efforts do make a difference.

ORGANIZATION AND ADMINISTRATION THEORIES

In addition to the student developmental process, learning outcomes, and campus environments, student affairs professionals need to understand the organizational and administrative structure of the institutions. These theories simply describe *how colleges work* (Birnbaum, 1988). From his book with the same title, Birnbaum (1988) outlines models of organizational functioning within the college environments: *collegial, bureaucratic, political,* and *anarchical.*

Typically found in liberal arts institutions, the *collegial* model is characterized by little (or no) hierarchy. Interactions between faculty and administrators of the organization are often informal. Major decisions are often slow and need thorough discussion by members of the organizational body. Often, a consensus must be reached for most major decisions.

The *bureaucratic* model is the very opposite of the *collegial* model. It is characterized by the hierarchy in place and is demonstrated through the institution's organizational chart (Birnbaum, 1988). The organizational structure, lines of communication, and authority are clearly defined. Roles of the administration are clearly defined by job descriptions and institutional rules and regulations. The organizational structure of this type of institution is very clearly displayed and executed. Many community colleges use a bureaucratic organizational model.

The *political* model of organization is characterized by acquiring, maintaining, and using power. All higher education institutions have politics, however the political model recognizes that change can only happen through power and conflict resolution (Kuh, 2003). From a political model perspective, the creation of policy is used as a means to encourage change. In addition, sub-groups of the institution become important as groups work with each other to influence decision making.

The *anarchical* model was first described by Cohen and March (1974), and is typically found in large institutions. In this model, decision making at the institution is often characterized as "organized anarchy." Autonomy is valued in this model. Therefore, "each individual in the university is seen as making autonomous decisions. Teachers decide if, when, and what to teach. Students decide if, when, and what to learn. Legislators and donors decide if, when, and what to support" (Cohen & March, 1974, p. 33). Kuh (2003) identified several advantages of this type of model, for it resonates with the values of academia—autonomy, loose supervision, and individual choice. The model also provides a full description of an organizational structure in higher education that is not likely to be found in other types of organizations. Kuh (2003) also identified several challenges from the anarchical perspective. For example, information is not always clearly communicated to those who need it to make decisions. It also encumbers rapid responses to institutional crises.

CRITICAL ANALYSIS WORK

The theories presented in this chapter have their critics. As noted, many student development theories were constructed based on research of White males of traditional age. Therefore, these theories do not reflect the diversity of today's student population (Pope, Reynolds, & Mueller, 2004; Torres, Howard-Hamilton, & Cooper, 2003). Student affairs professionals have responded by focusing on issues of multiculturalism and diversity on campus. There is a growing body of research on how campuses can handle complex issues relating to diversity (Hurtado, 2007; Ortiz & Rhoads, 2000; Stage & Hamrick, 1994).

In her Presidential Address to the Association for the Study of Higher Education, Bensimon (2007) discussed the dominant paradigm that is often expressed in student affairs and higher education theory and research. She stated that the dominant paradigm of "student success is based exclusively on personal characteristics of students that have been found to correlate with persistence and graduation" (p. 443). Research and theoretical understandings in student affairs usually focus solely on the student. The theories summarized in this chapter focus mostly on the student experience in the college environment. However, Bensimon (2007) pointed out that we rarely conduct research on the practitioner and their impact on student success, development, and education. How do the assumptions, beliefs, education, interactions, and interests of the student affairs practitioner impact the success and development of the college student? Bensimon maintained that our profession and researchers cannot ignore the fact that student affairs practitioners and faculty have an enormous impact on college students, their development and success in college. For example, Bensimon (2007) highlighted how student engagement and involvement is an important theoretical concept for our profession. The more students stay engaged and involved on campus; the more likely they will persist and succeed in college (Astin, 1993). This is a significant theoretical concept for the student affairs profession. However, as researchers and practitioners, we rarely specify how some forms of engagement have more significant social and economic impact than other types of experiences. In addition, she also proposed that the quality of the engagement may differ based on race, class, and gender (Bensimon, 2007). Her analyses provide some critical questions we must ask about the theories we use and the way we use these theories.

Table 2.1 *Summary of Theories and Research for Working with College Students*

Theory or Research	Theorist	Category
Theory of Cognitive Development	Piaget (1952)	Cognitive – Intellectual
Scheme of Intellectual and Ethical Development	Perry (1970)	Cognitive – Intellectual and Ethical
Reflective Judgment Model	King & Kitchener (1994)	Cognitive – Intellectual and Moral
Women's Ways of Knowing	Belenky, Clinchy, Goldberger, & Tarule (1986)	Cognitive – Intellectual
Model for Epistemological Reflection	Baxter Magolda (1992)	Cognitive – Intellectual
Stages of Moral Development	Kohlberg (1977, 1981)	Cognitive – Moral
Model of Women's Moral Development	Gilligan (1982)	Cognitive – Moral
Stages of Faith Development	Fowler (1981)	Faith and Spiritual
The Faith Development Theory	Parks (1986)	Faith and Spiritual
Stages of Psychosocial Development	Erikson (1968)	Psychosocial – Identity
Seven Vectors of Identity Development	Chickering & Reisser (1993)	Psychosocial – Identity
Identity Status Theory	Marcia (1966)	Psychosocial – Identity
Theory of Identity Development in Women	Josselson (1987)	Psychosocial – Identity
Model of Ethnic Identity Development	Phinney (1990)	Psychosocial – Ethnic Identity
Model of Psychological Nigrescence	Cross & Phagen-Smith (1996)	Psychosocial – Race and Identity
Model of Latino Identity Development	Ferdman & Gallegos (2001); Gallegos & Ferdman (2007)	Psychosocial – Race and Ethnic Identity
Hispanic Identity Development	Cass & Pytluk (1995)	Psychosocial – Race and Ethnic Identity
Asian American Identity Development	Kim (2001)	Psychosocial – Race and Identity
White Identity Model	Helms (1993)	Psychosocial – Race and Identity
Biracial Identity Development	Kerwin & Ponterotto (1995)	Psychosocial – Race and Identity
Homosexual Identity Formation	Cass (1979)	Psychosocial – Sexual Orientation and Identity

Theory/Model	Author(s)	Category
Model of Lesbian, Gay, and Bisexual Development	D'Augelli (1994)	Psychosocial – Sexual Orientation and Identity
Theory of Vocational Personalities and Environments	Holland (1966)	Typology – Career and Personality
Myers Briggs Type Indicator	Myers (1980)	Typology – Personality Type
Experiential Learning Model	Kolb (1984)	Typology – Learning Style
Multiple Intelligences	Gardner (1983)	Typology – Learning Style
Four Propositions of Campus Environments	Strange (1994)	Four Propositions of Campus Environments
Theory of Involvement	Astin (1993)	Impact and Outcomes Research
Higher Education Models of Organizational Functioning	Birnbaum (1988)	Organization and Administration
Leadership and Ambiguity	Cohen & March (1974)	Organization and Administration
Five Characteristics of Academic Organizations	Baldridge, Curtis, Ecker, & Riley (1977)	Organization and Administration
Fostering Campuswide Development of Multiculturalism	Stage & Hamrick (1994)	Diversity and Multicultural
Multicultural Education Framework	Ortiz & Rhoads (2000)	Diversity and Multicultural
SPAR (Services, Programs, Advocacy, and Resources)	Jacoby (1993)	Diversity and Multicultural

CONCLUSION

This chapter provides a brief summary of theories for the student affairs professionals. There are many others theories that were not included. To provide a quick reference for you when solving the cases in this book, Table 2.1 below lists the theories mentioned in this chapter as well as other theories that you may find useful. The theories in this chapter and the case studies in this book will provide you the opportunities to hone your skills in applying theory to practice.

REFERENCES

Astin, A.W. (1993). *What matters in college?* San Francisco: Jossey-Bass.

Baldridge, J.V., Curtis, D.V., Ecker, G., & Riley, G.L. (1977). Diversity in higher education: Professional autonomy. *The Journal of Higher Education*, 48(4), 367–388.

Baxter Magolda, M.B. (1992). *Knowing and reasoning in college: Gender-related patterns in students' intellectual development*. San Francisco: Jossey-Bass.

Belenky, M.F., Clinchy, B.M., Goldberger, N.R., & Tarule, J.M. (1986) *Women's ways of knowing*. New York: Basic Books.

Bensimon, E.M. (2007). The underestimated significance of practitioner knowledge in the scholarship on student success. *The Review of Higher Education*, 30(4), 441–469.

Bilodeau, B.L. & Renn, K.A. (2005). Analysis of LGBT identity development models and implications for practice. *New Directions for Student Services*, 111, 25–39.

Birnbaum, R. (1988). *How colleges work: The cybernetics of academic organizations and leadership*. San Francisco: Jossey-Bass.

Boyer, E.L. (1987). *College: The undergraduate experience in America*. New York: Harper.

Cass, J.M. & Pytluk, S.D. (1995). Hispanic identity development: Implications for research and practice. In J.G. Ponterotto, J.M. Cass, L.A. Suzuki, & C.M. Alexander (Eds.), *Handbook of multicultural counseling* (pp. 155–180). Thousand Oaks, CA: Sage.

Cass, V.C. (1979). Homosexuality identity formation: A theoretical model. *Journal of Homosexuality*, 4, 219–235.

Chickering, A.W. & Reisser, L. (1993). *Education and identify* (2nd ed.). San Francisco: Jossey-Bass.

Cohen, M. & March, J.G. (1974). *Leadership and ambiguity: The American college presidency*. New York: McGraw-Hill.

Cross, W. & Phagen-Smith, P. (1996). Nigrescence and ego identity development. In P.B. Pedersen, J.G. Draguns, W.J. Lonner, & J E. Trimble (Eds.), *Counseling across cultures* (pp. 108–123). Thousand Oaks, CA: Sage.

D'Augelli, A.R. (1994). Identity development and sexual orientation: Toward a model of lesbian, gay, and bisexual development. In E.J. Trickett, R.J. Watts, & D. Birman (Eds.), *Human diversity: Perspectives on people in context* (pp. 312–333). San Francisco: Jossey-Bass.

Erikson, E.H. (1968). *Identity: Youth and crisis*. New York: Norton.

Evans, N.J., Forney, D.S., Guido, F.M., Patton, L.D., & Renn, K.A. (2010). *Student development in college: Theory, research, and practice* (2nd ed.). San Francisco: Jossey-Bass.

Feldman, K. & Newcomb, T. (1969). *The impact of college on students.* San Francisco: Jossey-Bass.

Ferdman, B.M. & Gallegos, P.V. (2001). Latinos and racial identity development. In C.L. Wijeyesinghe & B.W. Jackson III (Eds.), *New perspectives on racial identity development: A theoretical and practical anthology* (pp. 32–66). New York: New York University Press.

Fowler, J.W. (1981). *Stages of faith: The psychology of human development and the quest for meaning.* San Francisco: HarperCollins.

Gallegos, P.V. & Ferdman, B.M. (2007). Identity orientations of Latinos in the United States: Implications for leaders and organizations. *The Business Journal of Hispanic Research,* 1(1), 26–41.

Gardner, H. (1983). *Frames of mind.* New York: Basic Books.

Gilligan, C. (1982). *In a different voice.* Cambridge, MA: Harvard University Press.

Helms, J.E. (1993). Toward a model of white racial identity development. In J.E. Helms (Ed.), *Black and white racial identity: Theory, research and practice* (pp. 49–66). Westport, CT: Praeger.

Holland, J.L. (1966). *The psychology of vocational choice.* Waltham, MA: Blaisdell.

Hurtado, S. (2007). Linking diversity with the educational and civic missions of higher education. *The Review of Higher Education,* 30(2), 185–196.

Jacoby, B. (1993). Service delivery for a changing student constituency. In M.J. Barr (Ed.), *The handbook of student affairs administration* (pp. 468–480). San Francisco: Jossey-Bass.

Josselson, R. (1987). *Finding herself: Pathways to identity development in women.* San Francisco: Jossey-Bass.

Kerwin, C. & Ponterotto, J.G. (1995). Biracial identity development. In J.G. Ponterotto, J.M. Cass, L.A. Suzuki, & C.M. Alexander (Eds.), *Handbook of multicultural counseling* (pp. 199–217). Thousand Oaks, CA: Sage.

Kim, J. (2001). Asian American identity development theory. In C.L. Wijeyesinghe & B.W. Jackson III (Eds.), *New perspectives on racial identity development: A theoretical and practical anthology* (pp. 129–152). New York: New York University Press.

King, P.M. (1978). William Perry's theory of intellectual and ethical development. In L.L. Knefelkamp, C. Widick, & C.A. Parker (Eds.), *Applying new developmental findings* (New Directions for Student Services, No. 4) (pp. 35–51). San Francisco: Jossey-Bass.

King, P.M. & Kitchener, K.S. (1994). *The development of reflective judgment in adolescence and adulthood.* San Francisco: Jossey-Bass.

King, P.M. & Mayhew, M.J. (2002). Moral judgment developing in higher education. Insights from the Defining Issues Test. *Journal of Moral Education,* 31(3), 247–270.

Kohlberg, L. (1977). *Recent research in moral development.* New York: Holt, Rinehart, Winston.

Kohlberg, L. (1981). *Essays on moral development, vol. I: The philosophy of moral development.* San Francisco: Harper & Row.

Kolb, D.A. (1984). *Experiential learning: Experience as the source of learning and development.* Englewood Cliffs, NJ: Prentice-Hall.

Kuh, G.D. (2003). Organizational theory. In S.R. Komives and D.B. Woodard, Jr. (Eds.), *Student services: A handbook for the profession* (4th ed.). San Francisco: Jossey-Bass.

Kuh, G., Schuh, J., Whitt, E., and Associates. (1991). *Involving colleges: Successful approaches to fostering student learning and development outside the classroom.* San Francisco: Jossey-Bass.

Love, P.L. & Guthrie, V.L. (1999). *Understanding and applying cognitive development theory* (New Directions for Student Services, No. 88). San Francisco: Jossey-Bass.

Marcia, J.E. (1966). Development and validation of ego-identity status. *Journal of Personality and Social Psychology, 3,* 551–558.

McCarn, S.R. & Fassinger, R.E. (1996). Revisioning sexual minority identity formation. A new model of lesbian identity and its implications for counseling and research. *The Counseling Psychologist,* 24(3), 508–534.

Moore, W.S. (1994). Student and faculty epistemology in the college classroom: The Perry scheme of intellectual and ethical development. In K.W. Prichard & R.M. Sawyer (Eds.), *Handbook of college teaching: Theory and application* (pp. 43–67). Westport, CT: Greenwood Press.

Myers, I.B. (1980). *Gifts differing.* Palo Alto, CA: Consulting Psychologists Press.

Ortiz, A.M. & Rhoads, R.A. (2000). Deconstructing whiteness as part of a multicultural educational framework: From theory to practice. *Journal of College Student Development,* 41(1), 81–93.

Parks, S. (1986). *The critical years: Young adults and the search for meaning, faith, and commitment.* New York: HarperCollins.

Pascarella, E.T. & Terenzini, P.T. (1991). *How college affects students* (1st ed.). San Francisco: Jossey-Bass.

Pascarella, E.T. & Terenzini, P.T. (2005). *How college affects students, Vol. 2: A third decade of research.* San Francisco: Jossey-Bass.

Perry, W.G., Jr. (1970). *Forms of intellectual and ethical development in the college years.* New York: Holt, Rinehart, & Winston.

Phinney, J.S. (1990). Ethnic identity in adolescents and adults: Review of research. *Psychological Bulletin,* 108, 499–514.

Piaget, J. (1952). *The origins of intelligence in children.* New York: International Universities Press.

Pope, R.L., Reynolds, A.L., & Mueller, J. (2004). *Multicultural competence in student affairs.* San Francisco: Jossey-Bass.

Sanford, N. (Ed.) (1962). *The American college.* New York: Wiley.

Smart, J.C. & Umbach, P.D. (2007). Faculty and academic environments: Using Holland's theory to explore differences in how faculty structure undergraduate courses. *Journal of College Student Development,* 48(2), 183–195.

Stage, F.K. & Hamrick, F.A. (1994). Diversity issues: Fostering campuswide development of multiculturalism. *Journal of College Student Development,* 35, 331–336.

Stage, F.K., Downey, J.P., & Dannells, M. (2000). Theory and practice in student affairs. In F.K. Stage & M. Dannells (Eds.), *Linking theory to practice: Case studies working with college students* (pp. 17–39). New York: Brunner Routledge.

Strange, C. (1994). Student development: The evolution and status of an essential idea. *Journal of College Student Development,* 35(6), 399–412.

Strange, C. (2003). Dynamics of campus environments. In S.R. Komives and D.B. Woodard, Jr. (Eds.), *Student services: A handbook for the profession* (4th ed.). San Francisco: Jossey-Bass.

Torres, V., Howard-Hamilton, M.F., & Cooper, D.L. (2003). *Identity development of diverse populations: Implications for teaching and administration in higher education.* ASHE-ERIC Higher Education Report, 29(6). San Francisco: Jossey-Bass.

Turner, W.B. (2000). *A genealogy of queer theory.* Philadelphia: Temple University Press.

Widick, C., Parker, C.A., & Knefelkamp, L. (1978). Erik Ericson and psychosocial development. In L. Knefelkamp, C. Widick, & C.A. Parker (Eds.), *Applying new developmental findings* (New Directions for Student Services, No. 4) (pp. 1–18). San Francisco: Jossey-Bass.

Chapter 3

Analyzing a Case

Frances K. Stage and Steven M. Hubbard

While many day-to-day decisions made by administrators have quantitative elements (dollars spent, students served, staff hired), the solutions evaluated in case study analysis tend to be qualitative. What makes an incident a case study is that it presents a problem with no clear-cut solution. In other words, the issues fall between the cracks of regulation and expected campus behaviors. The broad campus issues presented in a case usually entail emotional involvement of the actors and conflicts in values that must be taken into account in the resolution. From a range of solutions that can be generated for a case, some will be more feasible than others. This feasibility can be ascertained through consideration of numerous factors including costs involved, ease of implementation, availability of resources, personalities of key characters, and fit with the mission of the college. While many of the elements for weighing the feasibility of a solution have no fixed numerical value, they can be evaluated against the similar elements of an alternative solution for the same case.

To gain the most as a case-study analyst, one needs to have direction in sifting through these multiple qualitative and quantitative elements. The purpose of this chapter is to provide an algorithm of sorts, a general guide to aid in the analysis process. The analysis presented here is by no means perfect, and the questions generated are not necessarily exhaustive or definitive. However, it represents an organized approach to case-study analysis that is used in sorting multiple considerations. Later in the chapter, a case study and sample analysis are presented to provide guidance to the novice analyst.

STEPS IN ANALYSIS

Every case study, like every major campus issue, has many possible solutions. A set of very general questions must be answered every time a case is analyzed:

1. What are the decision issues presented in the case?
2. What facts are essential for understanding and dealing with the issues?
3. What additional information must be collected?
4. Who are the principal decision makers and what roles do they play?
5. Are there any theories that might be relevant to the decision issues?
6. What alternatives are available to the principal decision makers?
7. What are the advantages and disadvantages associated with each alternative?
8. What course of action (short-term and long-term) will be taken?

These eight questions form the basis for an approach to case study that can be used to analyze the cases in this book.

Analysis of the Problem

The first question applies in any analysis of a campus problem or issue. What are the decision issues faced by the actors in the case study? Usually, the major issues seem obvious. Frequently, short-term issues might mask long-term issues, such as absence of campus policies and procedures. Practice identifying decision issues helps keep the case-study analyst from being too shortsighted or narrow in resolving campus dilemmas.

Essential Facts

In the second step you are looking for information that is essential in dealing with the issues discovered above. This step involves practice recognizing important facts and separating them from those that are merely colorful and that help to make a good story.

Additional Information

This step follows directly from the above step; is any additional information needed? Envision yourself in the role of the case professional; is there anything else you need to know? Are there any documents or facts usually available on a college campus that are relevant and were not provided here? What are the legal precedents for actions that may be taken? To whom might you need to talk to gather further information? Remember that decision makers seldom have all of the information they want or need, and often they must make reasonable guesses or assumptions about certain key facts. This step reminds the analyst to be explicit about his or her assumptions.

Key Actors in the Case

The next step requires the identification of key actors in the case. Of course the administrator or professional who is caught in the dilemma is included. Additionally, usually one or more of his or her supervisors are involved, if only from the standpoint of judging the outcome. In some case presentations, the principal decision makers must be ferreted out from within the body of the case. They include those who will likely take some sort of action or react to the action you take in resolving the case. Other key players, sometimes called stakeholders, may include powerful persons who may not be directly involved but seem to have strong opinions on ways to resolve the issues. Identifying the decision makers and stakeholders and verbalizing the roles they play gives the analyst practice considering a variety of perspectives for decision making.

Relevant Theory or Theories

The fifth step, identifying relevant theory, is the most individual of those in case-study analysis. Anyone familiar with some of the myriad theories discussed in Chapter 2 will have their favorites. At this stage, the case-study analyst attempts to link a theory (or theories) to the case. Sometimes more than one theory may be appropriate. At any rate, no one theory is necessarily the theory to be used; application of a theory is very personal. A theory that works for one person may not be helpful to others. In the resolution of the case presented later in this chapter, several theories are applicable. In any class or workshop, differences of opinion will occur as to which is most helpful and relevant.

Alternative Solutions

The greatest creativity in case-study analysis comes in the sixth step. Here the analyst, informed by the intervening steps, generates alternative solutions for each of the issues described in Step 1. At this stage the analyst is free to let his or her imagination roam. In the next step, the seventh, the constraints on the solutions are addressed.

Advantages and Disadvantages of Alternatives

In answering the seventh question—what are the advantages and disadvantages of each alternative?—the analyst must be mindful of several considerations. Possible reactions to the alternatives by each of the major characters must be assessed. Support by external as well as internal campus constituents must be considered. Legal responsibilities of the institution cannot be ignored (Kaplin & Lee, 1997). The mission statement of the institution or future visions of the campus could be factors. And, of course, the availability of resources must be realistically weighed.

Course of Action

Finally, a course of action, one that includes resolution of both short-term and long-term issues, must be selected in light of the work from the previous steps.

PRESENTATION OF SAMPLE CASE

The presentation of the following case provides information that allows you to enter a new campus setting. The case is described as realistically as possible and in as detailed a manner as is practical. First you, the analyst, are provided with context, characters, and facts about the case. Through this information you enter the scene of the problem or issue. Next, you are provided a chronological unfolding of events presented as a problem to be resolved or a goal to be achieved.

In the remainder of this chapter, the case will be presented and then analyzed according to the steps presented here. Jillian Kinzie and Patricia Muller's "Take Back the Night: A Gauge of the Climate for Women on Campus" describes conflicts both across and within gender groups regarding campus violence. Following the presentation of the case, it is analyzed according to the algorithm presented above. This analysis should provide a useful guide to instructors as well as students as they work on cases in the remainder of the book.

As you read the following case, you are encouraged to suspend reality for a while and to lose yourself in the reading of the events. Try to feel, as the administrator would, the urgency and the emotions of the situation.

TAKE BACK THE NIGHT: A GAUGE OF THE CLIMATE FOR WOMEN ON CAMPUS

Jillian Kinzie and Patricia A. Muller

Setting

Arlington University is a mid-sized, predominantly White, public university located in a traditional college town in the Northeast with an enrollment of approximately 15,000 undergraduates. Arlington is primarily a residential campus with 10,000 students living in university housing. Fraternities and sororities actively involve about 30% of the student population.

The ivy-covered buildings and beautifully maintained grounds, surrounded by a quaint college town projects the image of an idyllic college community. Indeed, part of Arlington's allure for prospective students and their families are the feelings of comfort and protection that the campus evokes. The occasional bike and unattended backpack thefts are the most frequently reported crimes. However, since Campus Crime Report Statistics have been made public, some students and their families were surprised to learn that last year 11 rapes were reported on campus.

In an effort to educate students about women's safety issues, the Women Students Association sponsored a number of events designed to heighten awareness. One such event, which has occurred annually at Arlington, is the nationally recognized Take Back the Night march (www.takebackthenight. org), to protest rape and violence against women.

Characters

Marissa Fields – Director of Student Activities.

Molly Tait and **Sonia Jenkins** – both juniors, are co-coordinators of the Take Back the Night event. They have been active in the Women Students Association since their first year at Arlington.

Pam Donlan – senior and president of the Women Students Association.

Rick Baldwin – member of a fraternity.

Letrece Brown – president of the Black Student Union.

Clare Vass – an untenured assistant professor in the chemistry department.

Joan Wainwright – professor and advisor to the Women Students Association.

Robin Chan – the Dean of Students.

Claude Penn – the director of Campus Police.

Case

On a warm evening in late September, more than 300 women students gathered at Lincoln Quad for the annual Take Back the Night march. Most of these students walked over from the nearby Pratt lounge where the Take Back the Night speak-out was held. The speak-out provided women the opportunity to speak publicly about their experiences with rape, sexual assault, or harassment. The accounts of date rape and sexual assault told by women during the speak-out were powerful. As the students assembled to begin their march, flyers with protest chants and details of the route, and candles are distributed. The dark quad is gradually illuminated as each candle is lit. Pam, the president of the Women Students Association addressed the group, emphasizing the importance of Take Back the Night to symbolically reclaim the night for women and promote women's empowerment. Molly, a coordinator of the event, informs the group of the national statistics regarding women's safety on campus. She then leads the group in a rehearsal of a few of the chants. By the second round of, "2–4–6–8, no more violence, no more rape!" the marchers' voices are reverberating off the neighboring buildings.

The marchers move out to their first reflection point, the site of an August campus assault on a first-year female student. They form a circle around the site and then a woman reads aloud the police report that depicts the incident and describes the attacker. The speaker leads the chant, "women unite, take back the night." As the group marches to their next stop, a fraternity house where a woman was raped by an acquaintance last spring semester, the crowd is assaulted by bottle rockets fired and obscenities shouted from the windows of a nearby residence hall. The marchers were instructed to ignore such encounters and to drown out distractions by increasing the volume of their chants. However, some marchers scatter as the bottle rockets begin to pop. The marchers stop in front of the fraternity house and a woman stands bravely on top of a stone pillar. She begins by reading the statistic that one in four college women have the chance of being a victim of date rape and ends with an empowering poem about women's safety. The march continues across campus, with two more stops at sites where assaults against women were attempted, and to various danger spots for women where lighting is particularly poor. These sites serve both as a somber reminder of women's victimization and, in the case of an unsuccessful assault, demonstrate women's ability to fight back.

You are Marissa Fields, director of Student Activities. On Monday, the day after the march, Molly enters your office. She excitedly tells you about the successful march. However, her enthusiasm is dampened by the flyer she found this morning on campus kiosks and on a bulletin board in the Political Science building. The flyer reads:

> Arlington men: who really deserves the night? Keep it for yourselves. Let's put those Take Back the Night feminazis in their place! March and rally Bell Tower, 8 p.m. Tuesday.

This flyer only adds to the anger she already feels in reaction to the obscenities and bottle rocket encounter of last night. Molly wants to know what action will be taken against the residence hall from which the bottle rockets were fired, and also wants to know how the administration will respond to the Tuesday rally, given Arlington University's policies barring gender discrimination, sexual harassment, and hate speech. Molly promises to return later in the day to find out what the university's official response will be to these incidents.

Meanwhile, Claude Penn reads over the police report of a few bottle rockets being fired out of a residence hall window last night. No persons were cited for the incident. After reviewing the report, Penn emails it to the director of residence life.

As Sonia heads out of her residence hall, she is stopped by one of the Resident Assistants (RAs). The RA hands her a copy of the police sketch flyer of the alleged perpetrator of the August assault on a new student. The flyer has been defaced with the words "give it up bitches" and "our hero." The RA says, "No big deal, probably just some guy threatened by the march last night."

As an action step of the Take Back the Night event, a sorority delivers more than 300 signatures collected on an online petition demanding increased lighting and a safety escort service on campus to Dean Chan.

Over lunch, Pam and Molly read the report of the march in the daily Arlington University News. They agree that the reporter did an accurate job covering the event but feel that the article downplayed the intensity of attacks on the marchers. On her way to her next class, Pam sees Rick Baldwin. She thanks him for honoring the request that men not participate in the march, adding "I liked your fraternity's display of candles on the porch as a sign of support. I only wish more fraternities took such an active stance in educating their members."

Professor Clare Vass notices the flyer announcing the Bell Tower rally on her way into her office. As one of three female faculty members in a 25-person chemistry department, Clare has been acutely aware of gender issues during her tenure at Arlington. She believes that some areas of campus are not safe for women at night and knows that some women students in her class are concerned about walking home after class ends at 8:30 p.m. Because this section has fewer women enrolled than her morning section she believes that women may avoid her section because they fear for their safety. Knowing that she restricts her own activities in the lab to times when others are in the building, Clare decides to talk with her department chair about the ways that fear of rape or assault limits women's educational opportunities.

Concerned about the rally advertised for Tuesday evening, Molly also contacts Joan Wainwright, faculty advisor to the Women Students Association to discuss how to respond.

Still angered by the incident during Freshman Welcome Week, in which an illicit scavenger hunt list was posted that commanded students to collect racially and sexually offensive items such as "a photo of a fat chick sitting on a toilet" and "impression of a girl's nipple in peanut butter," Professor Wainwright calls the dean of students to discuss what she sees as the latest in a series of incidents that are abusive to women. Professor Wainwright also discusses with Dean Chan the circumstances surrounding a student with excellent grades and stellar recommendations who was recently turned down for a campus scholarship because her grades dropped dramatically one semester. The predominantly male scholarship committee was aware that the student had been raped that semester but felt that she should have been able to handle it and maintain her academic status.

Dean Chan contacts you, concerned about the call he received from Professor Wainwright. The beginning of the year scavenger hunt incident resulted in a lot of negative national publicity for Arlington University, and Dean Chan wants to avoid further incidents that reflect poorly on the institution. The dean asks you to prepare a report detailing the current campus climate for women that can be used for public relations purposes and next week's Board of Trustees meeting to ease concerns. Before ending the phone call, Dean Chan tells you to make sure that "some men's rally" he heard about does not interfere with the campus tour activities occurring that evening for potential students, or "give the girls the wrong idea about Arlington."

During your phone conversation with Dean Chan you receive an email message from Letrece Brown, president of the Black Student Union. You check the message after ending your phone conversation with the dean. The message reads:

> Last night while walking across campus I heard women chanting "women unite, take back the night." After asking around I found out it was from the Take Back the Night March. It bothers me that the Black Student Union was not included in this event. So the event was in reality "Take Back the Night for White Women." As Black women on this campus our numbers may be small, but our issues should still be addressed. Women's issues are not just White women's issues.

Molly, Sonia, and Pam return to your office later on Monday. Molly asks what action will be taken against the residence hall from which the bottle rockets were fired and how the university will respond to the signs about the Tuesday rally. Molly presses for swift and deliberate action. However, Pam interrupts Molly to state that she believes there is more at stake here than just the men's rally and the bottle rocket incident. Pam advocates focusing on the larger picture rather than on these two incidents, stating that these incidents are just a symptom of a larger problem on campus that needs to be addressed. In fact, Pam thinks that responding to the men's rally will just unnecessarily add fuel to their fire. Molly and Sonia both strongly disagree. After presenting each of their perspectives, the three students wait for your response.

What will you say?

ANALYSIS OF THE CASE

In order for you to analyze the case, you must provide answers to the eight questions put forth at the beginning of this chapter:

1. What are the decision issues presented in the case?
2. What facts are essential for understanding and dealing with the issues?
3. What additional information must be collected?
4. Who are the principal decision makers and what roles do they play?
5. Are there any theories that might be relevant to the decision issues?
6. What alternatives are available to the principal decision makers?
7. What are the advantages and disadvantages associated with each alternative?
8. What course of action (short-term and long-term) will be taken?

Moving through this series of questions, you sort out the elements that allow you to arrive at a solution for the case.

Decision Issues

This case presents a complex set of decision issues, with various degrees of immediacy. Most immediate, of course, is the situation you, Marissa Fields, as Director of Student Activities are faced with: an answer to the young women leaders sitting in front of you, and a decision about the imminent march and rally "To put those Take Back the Night feminazis in their place." What will you do *now*?

You and Arlington University face myriad other, seemingly less pressing, but in the long run, even more important issues: How can the recent tensions across campus be addressed in a way that will lead to a community with greater appreciation and respect for women? What can be done to make the campus safer, given the reality of campus attacks on women? To what extent does the apparent attitude of the most vocal reactions against the "Take Back the Night" march reflect other more silent students' views both for and against? Nevertheless, the bottle rockets, the wording of the flyer for the counter-march, and the defacement of the police sketch flyer suggest, at the least, a hostile climate for women. These coupled with reported individual instances of gender bias must be dealt with over the long term.

Another set of issues surrounds the planning for the march. Did the women leaders consider inviting Letrece Brown and leaders of other cultural or ethnic groups to join them and express their concerns? Additionally, issues regarding the reputation of the campus regarding safety are a reality, given the importance of enrollments in these fiscal times. Finally, the coincidence of the planned Tuesday night men's march and the Tuesday visit of prospective students, followed a week later by a board meeting, add additional pressures.

What are the limits of free speech on campus? Does the current climate interfere with women's abilities to receive an equal opportunity for their college educations? Where does one draw the line between sophomoric humor and misogyny? What is the role of Campus Safety when peaceful demonstrations such as "Take Back the Night" occur on campus? Should campus security have been present during the march? What might be done in crafting university policy and staff development to improve the competence, confidence, and morale of the student affairs and other staff in relation to the climate surrounding gender issues at Arlington?

This set of questions frames the decision issues and forms a template for an analysis of the case. (Do you see other issues in the case that should be addressed?) By answering the remainder of the eight questions with which this section began, you develop solutions to the decision issues.

Essential Facts

Given the foregoing framing of the issues, what facts are essential for understanding and dealing with the case? Answers to this question typically can be found within the body of the case study. In this particular case, the facts are presented in chronological order. The "Setting" provides important history and background, including such salient facts as: this is a public, largely residential university. Arlington's administration is sensitive to external public relations and has already received negative publicity regarding violence against women. Women students' attempts to bring attention to the safety issue have resulted in negative pushback from some men on campus. Additionally, the Black Student Union, potential allies in the push for campus safety, were not notified of the march and felt disregarded. Finally, despite the advanced publicity for the "Take Back the Night" march, Claude Penn, the director of Campus Police, only learned of the bottle rocket incident by reading a report the following morning.

Additional Information

Examination of these facts leads directly to question number three: what other important information must be collected?

Given that you have few days before the planned counter-march, for you (Marissa Fields), other questions come to mind: To what extent are the

Campus Police equipped to deal with a large and boisterous group of marchers? If the march goes forward, should you put together a team of student affairs staff to be visible and active that evening? Is there a cohesive leader or group of leaders for the planned march? If you act to stop the march, what will be the implications for free speech claims at Arlington? Who was responsible for the Freshman Welcome Week scavenger hunt? (What other immediate questions run through your mind as you put yourself in Marissa Fields's place?)

Regardless of the events that will unfold in the following week, some other information would be useful to inform more long-term decisions. What is the true nature of the gender issues at Arlington that affect both faculty and staff? What is Arlington's commitment to providing women and all students a safe environment in which to live and work? Do the student affairs staff hiring and training procedures need to be revisited? What are the hiring procedures and training elements for Residential Assistant staff? What is the university's policy regarding sexual harassment? Does the university have a policy regarding gender equity issues? Do campus-wide and living group education programs address sexual assault and date rape? Finally, what is the relationship across campus groups representing race, culture, and identity and the other student groups on campus?

Key Actors in the Case

The fourth question asks who the principal decision makers are and what roles they play? In this case study, most of them are listed under the heading "Characters." You are cast in the role of Marissa Fields, Director of Student Activities, and the administrator most directly linked with the students and organizations involved in the issue. You also serve as a vital link to the campus administrators. You have an immediate decision, whether to take action to block the men's counter-demonstration on Tuesday, or to take measures to attempt to turn it into an educational event. Other critical decision makers include the named students in the case: Molly Tait, Sonia Jenkins, and Pam Dolan, organizers of the march; Rick Baldwin, supportive fraternity member; and Letrece Brown, president of the Black Student Union. Professors Clare Vass and Joan Wainwright represent women's concerns on campus. Your Dean of Students, Robin Chan, seems most concerned with appearance and publicity issues. Finally, Claude Penn, the director of Campus Police, will have to be involved in any efforts to make the campus a safer place for women.

In addition to the characters listed in the case, other actors and decision makers would likely include: the leaders of other racial ethnic and identity groups; sorority members who have already approached the dean with 300 signatures on a petition demanding increased lighting and a safety escort service on campus; the head of residence life; the Greek affairs advisor; the student government; the news media and those who attempt to influence it on behalf of Arlington; the editor of and the advisor to the campus newspaper; the president's advisory council; and, of course, the board that governs the university. Given the systemic and deep-seated nature of campus culture and the issues that surround campus safety issues, one might argue that virtually every member of the campus community is touched by, has a stake in, and will make individual decisions that will influence the long-term outcome of this case.

Relevant Theory or Theories

The fifth question asks whether any theories might be relevant to Arlington's decision issues. Several theories could be considered germane to the issues and might inform the decision made by the principal actors. Your handling of the immediate issues could be informed by literature on organization and administration.

In order to apply direction to actions and decisions in the days ahead consider consulting a practical model of managing a campus crisis like Duncan's (1993) or Cohen and March's (1974) which provide a convenient checklist of actions to be taken. Various environmental assessment theories (e.g., Strange, 1994) could help you and others better understand what is happening at Arlington in terms of the social climate of the campus.

You and the other university administrators could learn much from the literature on White students and underrepresented minority students' racial identity development (e.g., Helms, 1990; Kerwin & Ponterotto, 1995). Additionally, theories of cognitive development (Chickering & Reisser, 1993; Erikson,1968; Perry, 1970) and models that shed light on gender identity and women's perspectives (Gilligan, 1982; Josselson, 1987; Marcia, 1966) would be useful for understanding the issues and perspectives of male and female college students.

Arlington might consider the development of a comprehensive approach to addressing diversity on campus (Stage & Hamrick, 1994). To better understand and work with some of the key actors in the case, Torres, Howard-Hamilton, and Cooper (2003) would be useful. The legal and disciplinary issues in the case could be considered in light of the most recent law (Kaplin & Lee, 1997). Finally, Hurtado (2007) provides an excellent perspective on linking all members of a campus into its educational and civic mission.

Many theories, not just those suggested here, might be helpful to you as you contemplate the issues. However, it is best for you to settle on four or five theories with which you are most familiar rather than confusing the issues with an elaborate evaluation incorporating a dozen theories.

Alternative Solutions and the Advantages and Disadvantages of Each

Answers to the sixth question—what alternatives are available to the principal decision makers?—and the seventh question—what are the advantages and disadvantages associated with each alternative?—will be considered together.

With the planned counter-demonstration on Tuesday, you are faced with several alternatives. You could do nothing and let events run their course. This has the advantage of not making mistakes of commission, but also the disadvantage of appearing ineffectual and possibly even irresponsible to your superiors. You could ask your dean to ensure that campus security be present and active, which has the advantage of protecting university property and individuals from harm, should the crowd get out of hand, but may have the disadvantage of aggravating the situation if the security does not assume a low profile. You could ask your dean about the wisdom of notifying the president's cabinet of this issue. This has the advantage of giving the campus leadership a "heads-up" and can provide advice, but they may delay any efforts you might take to curtail Tuesday's demonstration.

You could rely on campus women to show up at the demonstration and voice their opposition to some of the sexist sentiments that will likely be displayed. This has the disadvantage of possibly creating an even more negative atmosphere between women who are concerned about campus safety and the men who are reacting to those concerns, resulting in a nasty confrontation. You could show up yourself at the counter-demonstration, address the leaders, and suggest a campus committee of the concerned women and representative men to deal first-hand with issues of campus safety. This kind of direct action might divert the kneejerk counter-demonstration into something more positive. It also runs the risk of simply inflaming the situation.

If Tuesday's demonstration happens as scheduled, the dean of students office and campus security must be available and prepared for any negative actions on the part of the student demonstrators. Additionally, the admissions office staff must plan for possible repercussions with their prospective students' visit scheduled for the same evening. Finally, the additional publicity likely to surround the counter-demonstration will only heighten concerns about campus security for women.

Beyond the counter-demonstration, Arlington and its principal decision makers will have many alternatives, depending largely on how seriously it takes the safety issues of the women on campus. It could use rhetoric to talk about the importance of public safety, offer evidence of attempts to make the campus safer, but invest no real resources into creating a safer campus. This may be attractive to an administration highly sensitive to bad press, but it may only delay and exacerbate safety problems. Alternatively, Arlington's leadership could immediately establish a committee to hear women's concerns and develop an action plan designed to make campus safe for women. Earmarking funding for this effort would send an even stronger message about the importance of this issue to the administration. This has the disadvantage of calling attention to the safety issue by the campus leadership, but it would have the advantage of allowing Arlington to be true to its mission and creating a safe environment for all.

Several mid-range alternative courses of action might be taken at Arlington. One relatively low-key and low-cost option would be to act on the petition that had been circulated by the sorority calling for increased lighting and a safety escort service on campus. That would send an important message to concerned women and go a long way toward making the campus safer. Additionally, it would create good publicity for the campus and would likely impress the parents of prospective students who are considering attending Arlington. A disadvantage is that it fails to address the broader issues of attitudes toward women in academic departments as well as among the student body.

Other decision issues require an analysis of alternative courses of action including: a lack of relationship among some student organizations resulting in the Black Student Union not being included in the planning for the Take Back the Night march. Another level of concern surrounds free speech issues and how far those may be taken on in a campus based on civil discourse and respect for fellow students. What alternative solutions do you see for these decision issues, and what advantages and disadvantages would you assign to each?

Course of Action to be Taken

Finally, the last question asks, what course of action (short-term and long-term) will be taken? To answer this, you must decide on the relative merits of the alternatives, weighing their advantages and disadvantages.

In the short term, Arlington's administrators as well as campus security should be alerted about the possible demonstration on Tuesday evening. Second those same parties should receive the context for the safety concerns of women, both students and faculty. Additionally, any campus safety concerns from staff members, about whom we've heard little in this case, should be solicited. In the likely event that the demonstration is allowed to go as planned, campus spokespersons will have to be prepared for eventual questions from press as well as visiting prospective students and their parents.

You decide to approach Letrece Brown directly and, after a lengthy conversation, ask her to aid you by playing a leadership role in the larger gender issues on campus. You promise to take a more active role in encouraging inclusion of all student groups in planning major events. Additionally, the issue of inclusion will be a part of future campus activity leadership development and training on campus.

The women's leadership group—Molly Tait, Sonia Jenkins, Pam Dolan, and Letrece Brown—as well as sorority women who organized the petition for campus safety and Rick Baldwin, the supportive fraternity member, and others could be part of a coalition working with you to put together a report for Arlington's administration. Additionally, any of those listed could be part of a longer-term campus-wide group focused on security concerns.

The counter-demonstration, the defacing of police flyers, and the seemingly harmless bottle rocket attack, have created a flashpoint at Arlington. The leadership team must be prepared to listen carefully to the concerns expressed by women on the campus and develop both a short- and a long-term strategy for addressing them. At issue is Arlington's commitment to making the campus a safe environment for learning for all students. The importance of a communication strategy to make public Arlington's plan for addressing the safety issues on campus cannot be over-emphasized.

Student affairs staff and Greek advisors, should focus intensively on gender issues as part of their programs for student leaders. The long-term plan should consider how gender issues are addressed in the training of RAs and other leaders on campus. Also, the student affairs division needs to consider how race and identity are part of training programs for student leaders. There are several resources in the student affairs literature on how to address these issues through leadership training and program planning (Hurtado, 2007; Stage & Hamrick, 1994).

CONCLUSION

An important point for users of this book to understand is that no single correct analysis of a case exists. Indeed, case analysis may be thought of as an art, as unique to the individual performing the analysis as decision making is to the campus administrator. The interplay among the various elements of the case will be weighed differently by each analyst. Hence, one of the values of analyzing cases in a group situation is that many alternative, equally valid and viable solutions are presented.

Unlike many case studies, those in this book do not end with a set of neatly described questions to be answered in the solution of the case. Instead, as in real life, cases end with the professional in the throes of a dilemma or attempting to follow a supervisor's instructions. Hopefully, again as in real life, the case study analyst will refer to the questions provided in this chapter to develop his or her own solutions.

Additionally, an important point to remember is that no attempt should be made to generalize from one case to another. The purpose of using the case-study approach to learning is that what works in one situation may not work in another. Finally, case-study analysis in class or another group setting reinforces the give and take of collegiality and team decision making in higher education. Much of our professional education helps us learn what one *should* do as a student affairs administrator. Let us now turn to the cases and begin to develop our own unique style for *how* to do it.

REFERENCES

Chickering, A.W. & Reisser, L. (1993). *Education and identify* (2nd ed.). San Francisco: Jossey-Bass.

Cohen, M. & March, J.G. (1974). *Leadership and ambiguity: The American college presidency.* New York: McGraw-Hill.

Duncan, M.A. (1993). Dealing with campus crises. In M.J. Barr & Associates (Eds.), *The handbook of student affairs administration* (pp. 340–348). San Francisco: Jossey-Bass.

Erikson, E.H. (1968). *Identity: Youth and crisis.* New York: Norton.

Gilligan, C. (1982). *In a different voice.* Cambridge, MA: Harvard University Press.

Helms, J.E. (1990). *Black and White racial identity: Theory, research, and practice.* New York: Greenwood Press.

Hurtado, S. (2007). Linking diversity with the educational and civic missions of higher education. *The Review of Higher Education, 30*(2), 185–196.

Josselson, R. (1987). *Finding herself: Pathways to identity development in women.* San Francisco: Jossey-Bass.

Kaplin, W.A. & Lee, B.A. (1997). *A legal guide for student affairs professionals.* San Francisco: Jossey-Bass.

Kerwin, C. & Ponterotto, J.G. (1995). Biracial identity development. In J.G. Ponterotto, J.M. Cass, L.A. Suzuki, & C.M. Alexander (Eds.), *Handbook of multicultural counseling* (pp. 199–217). Thousand Oaks, CA: Sage.

Marcia, J.E. (1966). Development and validation of ego-identity status. *Journal of Personality and Social Psychology, 3,* 551–558.

Perry, W.G., Jr. (1970). *Forms of intellectual and ethical development in the college years.* New York: Holt, Rinehart, & Winston.

Stage, F.K. & Hamrick, F.A. (1994). Diversity issues: Fostering campuswide development of multiculturalism. *Journal of College Student Development, 35,* 331–336.

Strange, C. (1994). Student development: The evolution and status of an essential idea. *Journal of College Student Development, 35*(6), 399–412.

Torres, V., Howard-Hamilton, M.F., & Cooper, D.L. (2003). *Identity development of diverse populations: Implications for teaching and administration in higher education.* ASHE-ERIC Higher Education Report, 29(6). San Francisco: Jossey-Bass.

Chapter 4

Cases in Organization
and Administration

Few crises on campus escape the attention of those responsible for the administration of the college. Additionally, a satisfactory solution of any problem within a subunit of the campus requires consideration of the total organization. The cases presented in this chapter focus on broad campus issues affecting the institution as a whole and student affairs divisions in particular.

In Katie Branch's "Less Drinking or Professional Sinking?" a young student affairs professional struggles for recognition and stature in campus meetings. A staff member is charged with salvaging a satellite campus that is draining funds from the main campus in "Strategic Program Planning: Retooling an Initiative to Reach Its Potential" by Paula Steisel Goldfarb. Ronald Williams and Tracy Davis describe an institution that must find ways to increase retention without changing admission requirements and is faced with increasing numbers of students with limited academic preparation in "Academic Preparedness and Degree Completion: West Tisbury State University."

Kim Yousey-Elsener describes a student affairs assessment director negotiation of a political minefield while conducting a research study on how students use their time in "Politically Driven Assessment Findings." A director of a college honors program faces a difficult decision when he receives outside information about a student while reviewing her application to the program in Bart Grachan's "Conflict of Interests: Using Information From Outside the Process." In "Student Dissent at Warren Community College," Florence Hamrick and Catrina Gallo describe a campus conflict over the naming of the building for a woman scientist who followed a questionable (by today's standards) line of research. In "American West Meets Assessment Woes" by Melissa Boyd-Colvin and Katie Branch a staff member encounters resistance rather than cooperation when leading a campus-wide assessment initiative.

As you work on this first set of cases you will get a view of the student affairs division as a whole, along with some current prevalent issues.

LESS DRINKING OR PROFESSIONAL SINKING?

Katie Branch

Setting

Premier University (PU) is known as the flagship institution in a southern state's higher education system. The total student enrollment at Premier is approximately 14,000 students (11,000 undergraduates, 3,000 graduate students). Nearly 55% of the undergraduate student population live in on-campus residential housing facilities. These facilities consist of 14 residence halls clustered in three residential areas, each with its own dining commons. Most of the remaining student population commutes to campus from within a 50-mile radius. PU is located in a small village and the state's fourth largest urban area is approximately 15 miles from campus.

Characters

James Porter, Director of Residence Life, has been working at Premier University for 15 years. He came to Premier immediately after earning a master's degree in College Student Personnel. Initially, James served as residence hall director. He was promoted to an area coordinator position after two years. In this position, which he held for five years, James supervised several residence hall directors and worked closely with the area's Facilities and Operations as well as Dining Services managers. While an area coordinator, James enrolled as a part-time student in Premier's Higher Education Administration doctoral program. When the associate director of Residence Life job opened up, James applied for and was selected for that position. After three years as the associate director, James not only had earned his Ed.D. but also was promoted to director of Residence Life upon the retirement of the incumbent. He has been in the director position for five years. James's leadership style is highly collaborative, and he is known for commitment to social justice and dedication to the students at PU. James reports to the vice president for Student Affairs.

William Stanford, Dean of Students, has been at Premier University for 28 years. During his senior year at a small, private, liberal arts college in the state, he served as the Student Body President. He began his career at Premier as the director of Student Activities, while also pursuing a master's in Public Administration at PU. Eventually, William's title also included "and assistant dean of students." Eighteen years ago, when the previous dean of students retired, William was promoted to this position. He has a no-nonsense management style coupled with a warm, friendly interpersonal style. He is well-known and liked by many students, staff, faculty and alumni. William, or Dean Stanford as he is known to most people, reports to the vice president for Student Affairs.

Paul Timmons, Director of the Student Health and Wellness Center, has been at Premier University for three years. He came to Premier after five years in a private medical group practice, although prior to that he worked for 12 years in University Health Services at a public institution of higher education that was located in a different geographic region. When his wife had a career opportunity in the urban area close to PU, they decided to move and he joined the private group practice. Eventually, the director of the Student Health and Wellness Center position at Premier became available and Dr. Timmons was recruited to fill the job. Although fairly new to his current position, Dr. Timmons has established himself as a collegial leader who operates with a community health perspective. He reports directly to the vice president for Student Affairs.

Michael Adams, Alcohol-Drug Education Services coordinator, has been in this position at Premier University for two years. He came to Premier after completing his doctoral work in Counseling Psychology, with a specialty in substance-abuse issues. In order to do outreach activities as well as hire additional staff (which includes graduate student interns with PU's Counseling and Consultation Services), Dr. Adams relies heavily on soft money, or grant, revenue. He is well-respected among his colleagues for his grant-writing abilities. Michael reports to Dr. Timmons.

Olivia Felds, Residence Life area coordinator, came to Premier University two years ago. Prior to this, she had served for three years as a complex director at a large public institution located in an urban area in a different geographic region. That job was the first professional position Olivia held after earning her master's in Student Affairs in Higher Education. During her two years at PU, Olivia has earned the respect of students and colleagues with her collaborative leadership style and commitment to social issues. She reports to James Porter.

Case

Within a month after the residence halls opened for yet another academic year at Premier, a number of the Residence Life hall staff members are showing signs of severe distress. This stress is primarily a result of dealing with several alcohol-related incidents that required the transporting of students with life-threatening blood alcohol concentrations to the nearest hospital. This hospital is about 14 miles from campus via mostly rural roads. It takes over 20 minutes by ambulance to get to the hospital, and the ambulance service is staffed by part-time Emergency Medical Technicians who receive training through PU's Student Health and Wellness Center. Statistics kept by the Office of Residence Life show there has been a steady rise in the number of such alcohol-related incidents at Premier over the previous three years.

The student newspaper, which has both print and electronic formats, has begun running stories on the number of drinking-related incidents that take place on campus and recently ran an editorial with the tone, "What do you expect when there's nothing else to do on this campus?" The stories and the editorial in the student newspaper are starting to attract the attention of the broadcast media from the nearby urban area. Humorous messages, which also may cast PU in a negative way, are being posted in Facebook and some unflattering tweets are circulating. These stories and electronic messages are starting to attract the attention of local and state politicians, many of whom graduated from PU.

On a bi-weekly basis, the two directors and the dean who report to the vice president of Student Affairs (i.e., Director of Residence Life/Porter, Dean of Students/Stanford, Director of the Student Health and Wellness Center/ Timmons) meet to discuss campus issues. Typically these meetings are held on a casual basis, such as over lunch. The men have decided that in their next meeting they will discuss strategies for addressing the increase in the number of alcohol-related incidents on campus. They have asked Michael Adams to join them. Also, they decided to meet in a room located in the student union so that they have use of a whiteboard as well as overhead and multimedia projectors, if needed. Dr. Timmons and Dean Stanford especially are interested in learning more from Michael about a webinar he participated in on using fines as a way of addressing this issue.

Two days before this scheduled meeting, James Porter learns he must attend another meeting. James asks Olivia Felds if she will attend the alcohol-related incidents meeting on his behalf. He specifically asks Olivia because he knows that she did field work with a community-based alcohol intervention program while earning her master's and has expertise related to judicial sanctioning. Olivia does indeed know the research and practices related to these areas, and she is pleased that she has been asked to represent the director of Residence Life in this meeting. Olivia prepares for the meeting by developing a list of possible intervention strategies for implementation at Premier.

When Olivia arrives at the meeting, Dr. Timmons and Dean Stanford already are present. They great her warmly, and Dean Stanford asks how her transition to Premier is going. She responds by saying that this year feels especially good to her since her first two years at Premier had been professionally rewarding and enjoyable. Michael arrives and the group begins to talk about the rise in the number of alcohol-related incidents on campus. Dean Stanford asks Michael to explain what he learned about fines in the seminar. Michael gives a brief presentation about the webinar and advocates using fines in Premier's residence halls. He proposes that fines be given as "immediate sanctions" when Residence Life staff members encounter blatant violations of alcohol policies. Basically, this means that Resident Assistants would write "tickets," and predetermined fines would need to be paid by those ticketed. There would be due process procedures established for appealing such tickets, and other sanctions might also be given to PU students during typical student conduct proceedings.

Olivia raises questions about placing paraprofessional students in such a role. Also, she explains that the research and practices that she is familiar with show highly variable results regarding the effectiveness of using fines to decrease the number of alcohol-related incidents, especially on a long-term basis. Dean Stanford says he has been in this line of work for a number of years and regardless of what the literature says, he thinks this a worthwhile approach to try at PU. Olivia brings up some studies that have shown other approaches to preventing and addressing alcohol-related incidents in college residence halls. Dean Stanford says to Olivia, "Just write down the information about fines and make sure Porter receives it." Neither Dr. Timmons nor Michael seem to take any particular notice of this comment and the men continue to discuss the fining idea. Olivia sits there stunned, and feels as though Dean Stanford has relegated her to the role of a note-taker. Although she occasionally comments during the remaining 20 minutes of the meeting, Olivia does not see an opportunity to present any more of her ideas.

Upon returning to her office, Olivia prepares a summary memo of the "facts" presented at the meeting for the director of Residence Life. As she types the memo, she becomes increasingly angry about the interpersonal dynamics in the meeting. She wonders why she seemed to be disregarded: Was it because the men seemed to know each other so well both professionally and personally? Was it because of her age or perceived lack of experience compared with others in the group? Was it related to her gender? The more she ponders the situation, the more upset she becomes; she thought that after five years of successful post-master's experience, she had established her credibility as a professional in Residence Life.

She prepares a summary memo that she emails to James and then goes by his office to drop off a hard copy. She attaches a note letting James know she would like to talk with him about the dynamics of the meeting. When she drops off the materials, James is in his office. He asks, "So how did the meeting go?" Olivia explains that she summarized the content of the meeting in a memo and adds that she did not feel as though her input was very welcome in the group. James says the group knows each other quite well and that is probably what she was sensing. He also requests that she continue to be his representative in that group until this issue is resolved, especially since he has just been assigned another major project that requires immediate attention. Olivia tells him that she would prefer to not be a part of future meetings of this group because the men seem to want his direct input. She does not mention the questions that she pondered regarding the personal dynamics in the meeting, especially since she is concerned that something be done as quickly as possible to reverse the escalating number of alcohol-related incidents among residential students. She fears that if something is not put in place soon, a student will die from alcohol poisoning. She asks James if she can have some time to think about whether she will continue to be the representative from Residence Life to this group. James suggests that they discuss it tomorrow morning during their prescheduled weekly meeting. Additionally, he wants to discuss her ideas for addressing the number and severity of the alcohol-related incidents on campus.

Olivia thanks James for listening and proceeds to her area staff meeting. As usual, she has a very full day ahead of her: a day that will leave little time for personal reflection. She knows, though, that she must make the time to decide what to tell James in the morning.

You are Olivia. What do you tell James in the next day's meeting?

STRATEGIC PROGRAM PLANNING: RETOOLING AN INITIATIVE TO REACH ITS POTENTIAL

Paula Steisel Goldfarb

Setting

University of the Midwest is a large, state university located in a city in the Midwest. It has a student body of 30,000 students, a large residential population, and brings in students mostly from around the state. However, it does draw a significant out-of-state population. University of the Midwest is a public institution, depending on state funds to survive despite its large population. It is highly regarded, offering both undergraduate and graduate programs. The faculty and administration are committed to the university's mission of educating the best and the brightest to bring talented students back into the region. The university has close ties to the community where it resides and is seen as an important part of the area's economic growth.

Characters

Shirley Moore, Associate Dean, Graduate Program Planning.

Mary Lauren, President of University of the Midwest.

John Carlson, Chief Financial Officer.

George Temple, Dean of the Graduate School.

Case

The dean of the graduate program has been charged by the president to generate ideas quickly to generate revenue for the university. The state has reduced funding to the university. It must create more self-sustaining revenue-generating programs in order to survive. The dean turns to the leadership of the graduate school to seek ideas for the university's growth. Given the financial and physical constraints of the university, the most reasonable proposal is to create a program that is in a different location at a minimal financial outlay for the university. Otherwise, the university faces serious hardship in the next five years. Time is critical and a satellite campus is the best option for addressing this revenue shortfall.

You are Shirley Moore, Associate Dean, Graduate Program Planning. Two years ago, Mary Lauren, President of the university, had made her mandate clear. It was a difficult economic time with state legislatures slashing school funding throughout the country. For a large public university these cuts would be devastating. How then could the University of the Midwest protect itself or even grow and thrive under these conditions? She gave her leadership team including George Temple, Dean of the Graduate School, the order to develop new ideas for generating revenue. He must come up with a successful idea in three months in order to save the university from massive layoffs.

Dean Temple sent out a communication to faculty and the senior leadership of the graduate school, calling for ideas. He mentioned this initiative at faculty meetings and meetings of his senior leadership team. After a few weeks, he received just a few responses and realized that the word just was not getting out. He decided to bring his senior leadership team together for an all-day meeting to discuss the seriousness of the situation and gave his team time to generate ideas away from the day-to-day work.

After spending the day together, Dean Temple could not get one of the ideas out of his head. He was so excited that he couldn't sleep that evening. The idea that caught his attention was to create a satellite campus for working students in a suburban area, close to some businesses, including one large consumer products company, and close to the homes of many young professionals.

Dean Temple decided to have the Associate Dean for Graduate Program Planning, Shirley Moore, create a taskforce to examine the feasibility of the idea. After a formal review of the idea was completed by the taskforce, two weeks later Dean Temple was presented with a feasibility study. The factors examined by the taskforce included demographic information, information on those interested in graduate studies, economic conditions in the area, current student demographics, and competitor information. The market looked like it was fertile ground to create a satellite campus.

The results indicated that this region was ripe for a satellite campus of the graduate studies program and all of the factors pointed to a potential success. In fact, Dean Temple could not believe that no other institution had developed a program in the area based on the data he reviewed.

Dean Temple presented the idea to President Lauren who ran it by the Board of Trustees at the next Board meeting. After a few questions, the Board agreed that this may be the solution that everyone was looking for in order for the school to generate more revenue. Based on the market analysis data presented, the Board approved the university move forward to create the satellite campus.

The Plan

The satellite campus would have some initial start-up operational costs, but the taskforce and Chief Financial Officer John Carlson believed that those would be minimal. The university owned a small building in the area already and the Graduate Studies Program was able to use the space for this satellite campus. Some construction was needed to bring the building up to code and create classrooms. Furniture was purchased and the building was assigned to the Graduate Studies Program. Operational costs included electricity and maintenance on the building. There were some additional marketing costs such as brochures and advertising but overall, the program was planning on filling an incoming class within a few months, making up for additional costs.

The plan was met with close to unanimous praise. The faculty and administration were all very excited about the satellite campus and alumni of the university were thrilled to hear about the university's plans for expansion. The new campus and the university both received extensive media coverage with the satellite campus's launch. The President of Midwest University was relieved that the Graduate Studies Program was able to develop a solution to the university's financial issues. All signs pointed to the satellite campus's success.

Implementation

However, there were some early signs of issues along the way. The faculty, generally located near the main campus, were reluctant to travel to teach at the satellite campus. Evening classes were already unpopular on the main campus, but traveling to teach them on a satellite campus was even more so. Because the campus was to cater to working students, a significant number of the courses were offered in the evening. Also administrators had difficulty managing the satellite campus from the university's central home. The overworked administrators made the new campus a second priority. The marketing campaign took longer than expected to generate interest and additional staff had to be hired to focus specifically on program management, development, and the recruitment of students. Unanticipated costs started to stack up.

The first incoming class started in the fall with fewer students than expected. The students had high expectations for their studies. However, the new campus was not well developed yet and the facilities were limited. Students were not able to check their email on campus and had difficulty accessing some of the central home university services, such as the library online. These services were critical to students, especially working students. Course offerings were limited since the student body was not as large as anticipated and students were disappointed with the quality of the programs. Also, turnover with on-site staff meant a lack of support and student service that a reputable university such as University of the Midwest ordinarily provided.

After almost two years, it seemed that the original projections had been overestimated and didn't take into account the actual costs of running the program. Additionally, retention issues surfaced since students who were working and had other commitments needed to have flexibility to start and stop their programs.

Now, two years later, Dean Temple, during his semi-annual review of the state of the graduate school, notices during Chief Financial Officer John Carlson's presentation, that the satellite campus—now 18 months old—is still much deeper in the red than original projections. He is concerned that the revenue-generating idea which should have saved the school is now bleeding the school's already constrained resources. He is worried.

Dean Temple is concerned about the program's success and wants to re-examine the program's market and potential. He has charged you with developing a plan for saving the program and presenting your findings to the President of the university and the Board of Trustees.

What will your plan look like? What other factors will you examine? What was missing from the original analysis? What will your budget for this program look like and what items would you include in it? Are there hidden costs (costs which are not determined) in generating a new program or satellite campus? What were these hidden costs in this situation? Are there other stakeholders that should have been consulted? Who else would you consult in developing this new satellite campus and why? What would you have done differently in this situation? How would you address the organizational issues raised above? Would you recommend closing the satellite campus? Why or why not?

ACADEMIC PREPAREDNESS AND DEGREE COMPLETION: WEST TISBURY STATE UNIVERSITY

Ronald C. Williams and Tracy Davis

Setting

West Tisbury State University (WTSU) is a public, regional, comprehensive university with two campuses. The institution serves approximately 15,000 students through its traditional, residential four-year campus in a rural community, with a population of 25,000 people, and its metropolitan commuter campus, in a populous area with over 450,000 people. There are five academic undergraduate colleges, the College of Engineering and Technology, College of Education, College of Business and Technology, College of Humanities and Fine Arts, and the College of Sciences and Mathematics. The university also has several departmentally based centers that generate significant interest, including the Center for Study Abroad Programs and International Studies, the Honors Program, and the Center for the Study of Men's Development where students may take courses for credit toward degrees, pre-professional degrees, and certificates. Although the institution places an emphasis on teaching, and focusing on the individual learner, scholarly research and service is becoming an integral part of the institutional culture.

WTSU has an annual budget of over $325 million and offers 86 undergraduate and 47 graduate degree programs. The institution is regionally accredited by an accrediting body that is recognized by the U.S. Department of Education and the Council for Higher Education Accreditation. WTSU has a student-to-faculty ratio of 17:1, the University's 772 full-time faculty members teach 95% of all undergraduate and graduate courses, in addition to courses in 20 pre-professional programs and 29 certificate programs. The academic programs with the highest enrollment are: Biological Sciences, Business Agriculture, Criminal Justice, Engineering, and Psychology.

Characters

Sonya Marechalneil Lapiratannagool is the Assistant Vice President for Academic Affairs. She reports to the Provost and Executive Vice President, and has served in this capacity for three years.

Kirk Relerford is the Assistant Vice President for Student Affairs. He reports to the Vice President for Student Affairs, and has served in this capacity for 12 years.

Meredith Collier Allen is the Director of Institutional Research and Planning.

Thomas Franzone is the Executive Assistant to the President.

Rebecca Fields is a 20-year-old junior in the physics engineering program.

Garrett Singley is the Director of the University Advising and Counseling Center.

Eunice Taylor is the Chairperson of the Department of Sociology and Anthropology.

Brandon Wilkes is the Director for Student Development.

Case

In recent years, the graduation and retention rates at WTSU have decreased significantly from a high of 86.9% to a low of 60.3%. Historically, the institution has maintained its original commitment to teaching and learning, with a special emphasis on research and scholarly inquiry.

This commitment has been expanded to serve underrepresented student populations in the past few years. Approximately 35% of the students who are currently enrolled at WTSU are eligible for Pell Grant financial aid assistance, and are classified as first-generation and low-income students (FGLI). Although the student-to-faculty ratio of 17:1 is relatively low, and faculty are actively involved in the educational process, seemingly, many of the incoming students are not academically prepared to be successful in a collegiate program of study.

WTSU has excellent academic programs; accomplished faculty, for the most part who are supportive of all students; and a mission that seeks to prepare students to become professionals who are equipped to lead in a diverse society. The faculty emphasize critical thinking, engaged learning, scholarly inquiry, and creativity in a challenging and supportive learning community. Students are engaged in academic environments that encourage collaboration with peers and faculty mentors. Currently, the male to female student ratio is 54% to 46%. Historically, more males have enrolled at WTSU due to the large number of males who select the popular majors at the university. The business agriculture, criminal justice, and engineering programs are predominately male. The institution's enrollment profile based on ethnicity is 86.1% White, 4.2% African American, 3.1% Asian, 1.1%

Latino, 0.1% Native American, 0.1% Pacific Islander, 3.1% two or more ethnicities, and 2.2% international.

For the past five years, unfortunately, over 45% of the incoming freshmen have tested into the developmental mathematics course offered by the university. The developmental mathematics course is essentially a review of high school level Algebra, and it is not taken for college credit. However, students must successfully complete this course prior to being admitted to Math 101, which meets mathematics competency for most majors. Typically, many of the students who are placed in the developmental course have difficulties meeting the mathematical competency requirement for graduation from the university. Reviews of random samples of high school transcripts reveal that many of these students were not required to take math courses during their last two years of high school. Therefore, this makes the task of preparing students for mathematical competency increasingly difficult for the faculty in the Mathematics department.

As a result of the lack of academic preparedness by incoming students, the graduation rates have suffered and continue to decline. Acting as Sonya Marechalneil Lapiratannagool, the Assistant Vice President for Academic Affairs, you have been charged by the institution's president to chair the Academic Advisory Committee (AAC). This committee is responsible for working with the Mathematics department, other faculty, and other stakeholders to identify solutions to problems with academic preparedness and degree completion. The president's cabinet expects a full report within three months that includes best practices and recommendations for improvement. Moreover, recommendations must have a limited fiscal impact on the institution's budget, due to challenging budgetary conditions.

Immediately, you select the individuals who will serve on the AAC, based on their roles and responsibilities at the university. Kirk Relerford agrees to serve as vice chair of the committee. Relerford is well situated to garner input from student affairs professionals—who have a pulse on student behavior and perceptions at WTSU. Per your request, Meredith Collier Allen agreed to join your meetings and provide the data and trends with respect to enrollment, graduation, and retention, as well as individual students who are not performing at optimal levels. This information will add to the discussion as the AAC members examine possible remedies to the problems that exist. Although the university has a strategic plan, it is dated and needs to be revised. Meredith was one of the primary authors of the plan, and she is able to provide valuable insight and perspectives that may help move the discussion in a positive direction during meetings.

While you are mainly focused on academic issues, during the first AAC meeting, you learn from others that the problem can generally be attributed to obstacles that many students from low socioeconomic backgrounds may experience. Additionally, you learn that the perceptions and the societal attitudes for many FGLI students' families may negatively impact students' abilities to successfully complete college and earn degrees. For example, students who work full-time to support themselves, and/or in some instances their families, while going to school full-time may have difficulties managing and prioritizing their time. This may affect their ability to apply themselves in school and to graduate within a six-year period. Additionally, many students who are FGLI do not have family members to help guide them through the higher education process. FGLI students are more likely to miss financial aid and scholarship deadlines, they may not join student organizations or fraternities and sororities, and they may not feel as if they are a part of the campus community.

Subsequent meetings with the AAC uncovers that many faculty are becoming disgruntled with teaching students who meet minimum standards for admission to WTSU. Eunice Taylor indicates that her faculty colleagues in the humanities have increasing elitist attitudes regarding higher education. In one instance, Eunice reports that an associate professor stated that, "I want West Tisbury to limit admission to students who have a 3.5 GPA and a 32 or better on the American College Testing (ACT) standardized examination." Eunice further reports that the associate professor stated, "I am an expert in my field, and I only want to teach the best and brightest students in the country. Why should I be bothered with teaching students with B and C averages?" Thomas Franzone from the president's office added that, "several university-wide committees, dealing with various issues, have brought back similar information from some faculty members." A close colleague, who holds tenure in the Department of Accountancy and Finance in the College of Business and Technology, finds it difficult to understand why some of your colleagues have taken an elitist view of higher education. Having been a member of the professoriate for several years prior to your administrative appointment, you took great joy in teaching all students without regard for any differences that may have existed. Your charge from the president was to identify solutions; however, thus far you have only learned of additional issues that are contributing to the problem.

Since the late 1990s, WTSU has received national recognition for successfully educating FGLI students who had marginal admission profiles. Until recent years, the institution was able to graduate a high percentage of FGLI students in six years or less. Many people on the AAC believe this was possible because of the university-wide commitment to the institution's values: academic inquiry, diversity, and environmental accountability. This commitment was paramount to cultivating an environment that is inclusive to all individuals. However, the sentiments that Eunice and Thomas shared from some of the faculty certainly do not support WTSU's commitment to equal opportunity and access.

Rebecca Fields, who is a junior in the physics engineering program in the Engineering department, indicated that she was the type of student the associate professor was speaking about. Although the average academic profile of an incoming WTSU student is a 3.0 GPA and a 22 ACT score, Rebecca was admitted through an alternative admissions program because she graduated from high school with a 2.7 GPA and scored a 19 on the ACT. As an FGLI student, she did not have an opportunity to take the appropriate courses in high school, which caused her to be academically deficient in several subjects. However, she has persevered, and is now a successful engineering student with a 3.8 GPA. As a result, she tutors students in mathematics at the University Advising and Counseling Center. Garrett Singley says that, "she is an excellent student with a great work ethic." He further stated that, "Rebecca is a primary example of why we need diversity on a college campus, and that she serves as a positive role model for all students, particularly students who may identify with her and/or her circumstances."

During the second to the last meeting before the AAC must prepare their recommendations for the president's cabinet, Brandon Wilkes suggests that alcohol may be yet another factor that deters students from earning degrees. Although WTSU has been providing relatively affordable and quality education for over 150 years, alcohol has become a large part of the institutional student-life culture. It is clear that the consumption of alcohol is not promoted by administrators, faculty, and staff. However, college students who are 21 years of age or older are eligible to drink alcoholic beverages, and sometimes this culture of drinking gets out of control, causing problems. The Office of Student Development provides information and workshops on the dangers of alcohol and examples of what can happen when it is not used responsibly.

For several months, the AAC meetings have yielded three prominent themes that may impact students' academic preparedness and degree completion. Themes include: 1) limited familial support and collegiate preparatory curricular opportunities for FGLI students when in high school; 2) negative faculty attitudes toward teaching FGLI students; and 3) alcohol consumption. You, along with the AAC, must identify solutions for increased degree completion (retention) and overcoming limited academic preparation for incoming students, without significantly increasing admission requirements and abandoning the institution's mission. Also, keep in mind that it is politically perilous to accuse faculty of being unwilling to teach students who are academically unprepared, from low socioeconomic backgrounds, or from other underrepresented groups. Therefore, this cannot be a formal part of your report to the president's cabinet, which will ultimately be released to the entire campus community.

How would you proceed? What recommendations would you make to increase the degree completion rates at your institution? Please explain your rationale.

POLITICALLY DRIVEN ASSESSMENT FINDINGS

Kim Yousey-Elsener

Setting

Metro University is a large private institution located in a mid-sized city in the midwestern United States. With just over 25,000 undergraduate and graduate students, this comprehensive university offers academic majors through its seven schools specializing in business, education, liberal arts and sciences, nursing, performing arts, law, and medicine. Students attending this institution pride themselves in being independent and often come to this city for opportunities outside the classroom.

The size of the institution, combined with a student body that tends to be highly independent as well as diverse in its backgrounds and interests means that it is often a challenge for the Division of Student Affairs to have a strong understanding of the needs, interests, and behaviors of its students. The 12 departments of the Division are led by the Vice President of Student Affairs, who has decided to embark on an assessment project that would provide information about how students spend their time, in order to more appropriately design co-curricular programs and services.

Characters

Boyd Jackson, Vice President of Student Affairs, considered the leader of this project, had a successful experience at his last institution studying students' time and strongly feels it would be a helpful project for this institution.

Abby Thompson, Director of Assessment, has been charged with creating and administering the time study project.

Sarah Wise, Director of Communication and Technology, has been charged with creating new technology to gather data from students about their use of time.

Vice President's Cabinet, made up of Directors from each department in the Division, has been charged with using the data once it is collected.

Institutional Review Board (IRB), made up of faculty and administrators from the institution, is charged with monitoring research projects being conducted at the institution to ensure that they abide by established ethical standards including ensuring confidentiality of the study participants and making sure participants are not coerced to participate. At this institution, the IRB must approve research projects which they define as any projects gathering data for the purpose of externally reporting on the findings via publications, conference proposals, post sessions, etc. Typically assessment projects completed for internal use only (e.g. data being shared within the department or division) do not require IRB approval.

[Note: Institutional Review Boards on each individual campus determine what types of projects (e.g. external or internal) should be reviewed and approved. Before conducting any research or assessment project, check with the IRB on your campus.]

Case

Abby Thompson was recently hired as the Director of Assessment for the Division of Student Affairs. While there are many priority projects, her highest priority is to design and administer a time-use study of undergraduate students at the university. A pilot study was conducted prior to her arrival that led to a need to completely redesign the technology used to gather information from students as well as the incentives involved in encouraging students to participate. In addition to administering this project, she is charged with ensuring that each department in the Division completes at least one assessment project by the end of the semester. In order to accomplish this, she meets with the director of each department to talk about their assessment plans. While meeting with them, she learns that most directors do not see a need for the time-use study and feel it is a drain on the Division's resources (both financial and human).

Prior to administering the survey, Abby first meets with Sarah about how to better design the online data-collection tools. Because the study requires students to enter their activity into a diary, existing technologies could not meet its needs. Therefore Sarah has been charged with creating a web-based diary tool that will meet the needs of the study. Sarah was active in administering the pilot and learned that the tool that was used required too many details and made it difficult to enter information. As a result, there was considerable drop-off in student participation in the one-week administration period.

Boyd was not deterred by the pilot's challenges and assigned Abby and Sarah a team, consisting of himself, two administrators, and four students to help design better technology, as well as determine the appropriate ways to ensure that participants complete a full week of the study. In addition, Boyd provided a significant amount of financial resources to invest in providing incentives to participants. Planning meetings were scheduled and within a few weeks new technology was developed that, when tested with students, appeared to solve many of the problems related to the pilot study.

Abby then applied to the IRB at the university in order to gain approval for the project. Because Boyd intended for the project to be used not only for internal use within the Division, but also as conference presentations and publications, obtaining IRB approval was essential in moving the project forward. After considerable review of the project, the IRB did not approve the project, based on two things. First, the data being collected was sensitive in nature and connected to the participant's name. Because participants were providing data about their behaviors, and may reveal illegal activities such as consuming alcohol under the age of 21, IRB ethic rules dictate that data should be collected without being connected to a student's name, email address, or student ID number. With data of this type, IRB wanted the data to be anonymous. While Abby tried to change the administration protocol to make the data anonymous, the planning team felt that the participants' names would be needed in order to provide incentives and to track participants in order to ensure they were completing their time logs. The IRB also rejected the project because of the incentives being offered. While reasonable incentives are normally approved by the IRB, the incentives for this project were so large that the IRB felt that it violated its standards and might make participants feel that they were being forced or required to participate. This again violates one of the major ethical standards, in that research participants should always feel that they are voluntarily participating in a survey. In this case, the IRB agreed that offering several thousands of dollars to participants coupled with sending them repeated reminders every day, may translate to some participants as being told they have to participate in and complete the study. Abby tried to explain to the planning team the IRB's concerns, but the planning team again felt that the incentives were absolutely necessary in order to make sure participants completed the study. After much discussion, it was decided by the planning committee and Boyd that the study would continue without IRB approval. Abby explained at that time that without IRB approval the information could only be used for internal decisions, and could not be presented at external conferences or in publications.

The project was set to be administered in February. A sample of 10,000 students was invited to participate with the goal of having 1,000 students complete the project. Students invited to participate were asked to log their time through an online diary each day for one week. The diary asked students to log their time every 15 minutes, using a drop-down menu with general categories such as studying/preparing for class, in class/lab, rehearsals, socializing, eating, sleeping, exercising, using technology (email/Facebook, etc.), etc. Every participant who completed the study received a T-shirt. In addition there were daily drawings for gift certificates and grand prize drawings at the end of the week. Incentives totaled several thousand dollars for the week.

As the project was being administered there was a growing buzz around campus about the project. Directors of departments and other staff within the Division began questioning the resources being used for the project and how the data would be used, given the limits placed on results by not having IRB approval. In addition, students participating in the study were challenged by keeping up with the diary and making sure it accurately reflected their time use. By the end of the week, slightly over 1,000 students completed the study and data analysis began.

Abby and Sarah took care not to reveal any data before it could be properly cleaned up (eliminating the students who did not complete the study) and transferred from the database attached to the online diaries into a form that could be analyzed statistically. With Boyd's interest in the results growing more intense each day and pressure from the Vice President's Cabinet members over whether the data would be useful, Abby worked diligently to make sure the data was analyzed quickly but accurately in order to avoid any challenges to the results after they were presented.

The day that the results were ready to share, Abby was met with several challenges. The first source of challenges came from the Vice President's Cabinet members, who questioned the results as whole. They felt that at best the results served as something "interesting" that could be talked about in casual conversation, as if an answer to Metro Trivia. At worst they felt the results did not lead to any actionable data that could be used to adjust programs or services. They were extremely disappointed in the waste of resources for this project and upset that the data could not provide any additional insights into students at their institution. While Boyd was the initial champion of the project, he left Abby to respond to the questions posed by the Cabinet and with the charge of finding ways to make the data actionable.

The second source of challenges was from Boyd, the Vice President, himself. While being the champion of this project from the beginning, the results were not what he expected in many areas. He was disappointed in the lack of statistical findings related to GPA and time spent studying as well as how low some of the hours spent were in relation to his initial expectations. He asked for the data to re-analyzed in the hopes of new numbers being discovered. In addition, Boyd requested that Abby begin preparing conference proposals and publication outlines for the study in the hopes of sharing the data more widely than within the Division/institution.

You are Abby. What do you do, considering the politics of "disappointing" results and lack of IRB approval?

CONFLICT OF INTERESTS: USING INFORMATION FROM OUTSIDE THE PROCESS

Bart Grachan

Setting

County Community College (CCC) is a mid-sized community college, with a full-time enrollment of 4,000, and an overall enrollment of nearly 9,000. It is in the northeast, settled in a busy suburban community very near a large urban center. The surrounding community is heavily middle-class, both blue-collar and white-collar in nature, and has historically maintained college-going rates for high school graduates that are higher than the national average, with about 70% of them going off to college. Where those students are heading is changing, however. Consistently until ten years ago, about 20% had gone to community colleges in the area, while the rest had gone to a mix of public and private institutions, with a few at the top-tier schools. Over the last decade, as the number of college-bound graduates had increased, particularly among the low-income students in the area, the percentage of students going to community colleges had grown to 25%. In the last two years, however, that percentage had grown to nearly 30%, and CCC's enrollment had increased by 15%, as the middle-class families of the area had started relying on two years of low-cost tuition at CCC as a means of saving money for the high-cost institutions that they were aiming for.

To accommodate the growing wave of students entering their institution with the express intent of transferring out, and to keep them at CCC through completion of the associate's degree (an important factor in the institution's state funding), an honors program had been created. This program awards scholarships, provides special honors sections of courses, provides specialized supports, activities, and advisement, and works articulation agreements with the surrounding four-year institutions. Students can apply to the honors program as part of the admission process, and in return, they are expected to enter transfer-designed programs (rather than applied degrees), take required honors classes, maintain a 3.5 GPA, and graduate.

Characters

Richard Payton, director of the honors program at CCC: Richard has been the director for 5 years. He is a full-time administrator who teaches some college orientation courses as an adjunct, but he is not on a faculty line and does not have tenure. He is responsible for reviewing applicants to the program and approving those who are ready as first-term students, as well as applicants from within the college.

Alicia Ibrahim, student applicant to the honors program: Alicia is a high school senior in a town near CCC; she has applied to CCC's honors program, along with a dozen other schools. She has been denied or admitted without sufficient financial aid to the four-year schools, however, and is relying on CCC and the honors program to get her over the top as a transfer applicant in two years.

Case

Richard sat reviewing the list of applicants for the honors program he oversaw at CCC. He heard a noise, then realized that it was him that was making it— he had groaned audibly when he got to her name. Alicia had been emailing him, not just regularly, but what Richard saw as compulsively; three and four times a day, about anything and everything. If he didn't respond within a few hours, it triggered a fresh round of "I'm not sure you got this, so I'm resending it . . ."

The list he was reviewing had come from the admissions office of the college. With the economy tanking and college costs skyrocketing, CCC's honors program had become increasingly popular with the high-achieving students from the immediate and surrounding areas, students who never would have considered CCC just a few years before. As a public community college, the costs were already extremely low for students, so even those not admitted to the honors program were still enrolling, having been drawn to the scheduling flexibility, the freedom to explore courses without "wasting" money, and the ability to triple their savings by living at home and working while in school.

The school benefited, both in prestige and in pedagogy, from having top-flight students enrolling, as expected, but other benefits were emerging. Arts, language, and literature classes, all courses that had been under-enrolled and in danger of being cut from the curriculum to make space for vocational training, were now fully enrolled with students who needed them for transfer purposes. Beyond that, these students were significantly more likely than other students to both complete their degrees and to transfer to four-year institutions, both important statistics for CCC and its funding. The honors program provided real benefits for its students, but many outside the program were benefiting just from its existence.

Richard glanced at the honors application Alicia had submitted. As a result of the dozens of emails she had sent him, it mimicked his responses, echoing what he, and thus the honors program, was looking for. Her transcript was stellar; her test scores high for many top four-year schools, off the charts for CCC. Alicia was a classic "almost" student—almost poor enough to qualify for a variety of state and federal grants, almost strong enough a student to get the big institutional scholarships . . . almost, but not quite. Alicia was looking at CCC to get her to the next level, and her desperation came through in every email, in her essay, in her short-answer responses, all of it. Too much so, in fact; it was a bit off-putting. The letter of recommendation from her counselor had been glowing, in addition to her stellar academic record, however, so Richard was fully prepared to approve her application and award the scholarship when he submitted his list the next day.

That night, Richard was out at a local restaurant when he saw an old friend as they waited for their tables. As they chatted, the conversation inevitably turned to work. The friend taught at a local high school, and on hearing that Richard was head of the honors program at CCC, the friend started to smirk.

"Oh, man. You must know Alicia then. I know she's applying for that—I have her in class, it's all she's talked about for two months."

Richard started to laugh. "Yep, I definitely know Alicia. She's relentless, isn't she? Is she this determined in her classes?"

At this, the friend glanced around the bar and leaned in. "A little too much so, actually. I gave her a C on a paper once, and spent the next two months in meetings because she called me a racist. I got cleared, but you can't un-ring the bell, man. She's pulled this kind of stuff with a bunch of us over the years; we're sexist, racist, we don't like her, whatever. She's a known quantity at the school, but she makes claims that they can't legally ignore. She plays any card she can think of to get what she wants. Be careful of that one." Richard's "FERPA" was flashing like a red alarm light in his mind. He knew he shouldn't discuss a student with anyone outside the college, but this was too close for him to ignore.

Deciding that he wasn't violating anything if he just listened, he asked his friend to elaborate, nodding the whole time. By the time he was at his table for dinner, he had made his decision. The next day, he submitted his list of students who were to be admitted to the honors program for the following fall. Alicia was not on the list. She was a headache that he simply didn't want to deal with for the next two years.

Two weeks later: "Mr. Payton, you can go in now." The president's administrative assistant opened the door to his office and Richard entered the office. The president, the provost, and the dean of academic affairs were all inside waiting. When notified of the decision to admit her to the college, but not to the honors program, Alicia had begun an intensive emailing and phone-calling campaign, sending copies of her application, transcripts, essays and recommendations to a dozen people on campus, including the three people in the room looking at Richard now.

"Richard, what can you tell us about this young lady? We're not usually called in to review applications, but this is a singularly determined young lady. She included copies of your email correspondence with her, showing that by all indications you thought she was a good candidate for the program. She's even sent a letter to the editor of the local paper, calling the program a scam and asking for a review of the racial, ethnic, and gender breakdowns of the program. He's on the school's board, so he's asked us to look into it before he publishes it. What was the basis for your not accepting her into the program?"

You're Richard. Is there a way to explain the situation? How could you have handled the situation to have avoided this conversation? What are the possible ways that this can go from here?

STUDENT DISSENT AT WARREN COMMUNITY COLLEGE

Florence A. Hamrick and Catrina Gallo

Setting

Warren Community College (WCC), now part of a state community college system in the northwestern United States, serves a principally rural and suburban 12-county area. Warren (pop. 100,000) is the largest city in the region. WCC was founded in 1948 as a technical institute to train workers for the region's industrial and manufacturing companies. Now, the majority of WCC's 14,000 students are enrolled in one of four programs: environmental sciences (ES), engineering technology (ET), computer science (CS), and general education (GE) to support transfer to baccalaureate degree programs at four-year colleges. Although all four programs remain strong, in recent years the general education program enrollments have boomed as costs at four-year colleges and universities have risen. The region's political climate has become more conservative over the last 15 years; some long-standing regional employers have opened facilities or outsourced portions of their production to manufacturers in other countries.

The majority (68%) of WCC students are men. Thanks to aggressive recruitment—particularly at the local high schools—enrollment by women students has almost doubled in the last ten years, growing from 18% to 32% while the proportion of students of color has remained steady at 18–20%. The mean age of students is 22 for women and 27 for men.

Characters

Dennis Austin is Senior Vice President of Instruction and Educational Services. Dennis joined the ES faculty 31 years ago and served as Environmental Sciences Dean prior to his current appointment.

Angela Reeves has been Dean of Students for eight years. She reports to Dennis Austin.

Jim Russell is Placement Director. He reports to Dennis Austin.

Adele Willis is Vice President for Information and Public Relations. Two years ago, she left a senior marketing position at a local company to join WCC.

Henry Larson is a 29-year-old part-time ES student employed at Regency Manufacturing.

Phil Connors is a 19-year-old GE student who plans to pursue a history degree at the state university. He is an officer in WCC's Humanities Club.

Brenda Fountain is a 20-year-old CS student and President of the Women in Science Club. She is an engineering technology student.

Jaime Ramirez is a 31-year-old CS student and Student Government President.

Case

As Angela Reeves, you are responsible for counseling and advising students, supervising the educational support and tutoring office, registering student organizations, planning student-family events, and advising student government. You also work closely with Jim to organize career-related events for alumni and current students.

You did not attend a community college, and when you applied for the WCC job you envisioned low levels of student engagement. Instead, you've been pleased by students' pride in WCC and by the evening and weekend events that attract large numbers of WCC alumni. You enjoy your work at WCC and suspect that your BS in Chemistry enhanced your initial credibility with WCC students and faculty. You have received the Outstanding Staff Member award and have just been nominated for WCC's Distinguished Service Medallion. In your eight years, you have earned a reputation as a level-headed student advocate and leader at WCC.

Declining state appropriations over the past ten years led to WCC's deferring a great deal of building maintenance, and some older buildings have fallen into serious disrepair. WCC's new President is completing his first year at WCC and has worked closely all year with the nine-member Board of Trustees to plan major fundraising efforts to support capital projects and student scholarships. The elected trustees are well-known business and community leaders from WCC's 12-county region, and they have charged the President with increasing the number of alumni donors in addition to securing corporate gifts.

During the year, the President has also discreetly approached prominent alumni and business leaders and secured commitments for a signature project to be announced at the kick-off dinner for the campaign. Since the dinner is this Friday—only four days away—speculations about the "surprise" announcement are regularly discussed on campus and in the community.

Rumor has it that the trustees unanimously approved a resolution that Grand Hall, a classroom and office building that dates to WCC's founding, be completely renovated and named Phillips Hall, in honor of the late Reverend Charles Phillips. After service in World War II, Charles Phillips entered WCC in 1948. Two years later he became the first African American graduate of WCC, and after working at Regency Manufacturing for ten years, he became an ordained minister and was President of the state's NAACP during the late 1960s and early 1970s. Serena Phillips, one of his daughters, completed WCC's GE program in 1975 and earned a Biology degree at the state university. A resident of Warren, Ms. Phillips has continued her father's community organizing and educational work, and Ms. Phillips is expected to be an honored guest at the Friday dinner.

The following day (Tuesday), Henry Larson sent an email to a number of WCC students and asked them to distribute it widely. Henry's brother Aaron, a recent graduate of the state university, had conducted research on Reverend Phillips as part of his senior honors thesis and discovered that he delivered a number of sermons toward the end of his life in which he argued that intelligent design was a defensible scientific theory. With Aaron's permission, Henry included excerpts from Aaron's honors thesis in the email message, along with Henry's own conclusion that Reverend Phillips's positions were incompatible with WCC's status as an academic institution with a strong reputation in science and technology fields. Henry's email concluded: "If we are serious about real science and WCC's being a credible institution, we can't let this building be named after someone who earned a degree here but came to espouse such ridiculous beliefs. The trustees have voted, but students must get this decision changed. There will be a meeting at 4 p.m. this Thursday in the Biology Building Conference room to talk strategy."

By Wednesday, Aaron's findings and Thursday's meeting have become the talk across campus. In your informal conversations with students on Wednesday, you hear a variety of reactions. During a meeting about an upcoming Humanities Club event, Phil Connors complained: "I'm not really sure what to think about all this. It was exciting to think that a building here would be named for a man who not only served our country but was also the first African American man to graduate from WCC. I don't agree with his personal beliefs about intelligent design, but who could deny the great contributions he's made to the community and the place in history he earned through his civil rights work? I think he deserves to be honored."

Brenda Fountain stopped by your office and remarked: "How could we let this happen? This new information on Reverend Phillips shows exactly what type of person he really was. His advocacy of intelligent design goes against everything that this institution stands for! WCC is going to be a joke if we honor a man who supported these ridiculous ideas. Don't we take pride in our science programs? This is unreal!" Angela emails Dennis with an offer to brief him on the situation, and the auto-generated reply reminds her that he's on his sea-kayaking trip with family members until Friday. Angela leaves a message on his cell phone asking him to call her as soon as he can.

Early Thursday morning, you get a call from Adele. She explains that the college's Twitter account (@WarrenCC) has become the target of angry "tweets" from across the state, and increasingly, across the nation. Adele says that the number of tweets about WCC is increasing steadily, and she reads two recent messages:

> From @HenryLarsonWCC: "@WarrenCC to name a building in honor of a creationist? #WCCisajoke. I may have to drop out anyway—no $$. Good riddance?"

> From @JebSmithUTP: "Intelligent design?!? Does @WarrenCC think April Fools Day came late this year? Yes #WCCisajoke."

Adele continued, "I had to explain what this all meant to the president earlier—that when other Twitter users mention @WarrenCC in their 'tweets,' our Twitter account will be notified. Also, I explained that anyone can create a 'hash tag,' with the pound sign, in hopes that other Twitter users will use the same hash tag and create a trending topic that attracts even more tweets. This is all fairly new to me, and I'm doing my best to compose and encourage positive and constructive tweets, but the account is still being bombarded with negative comments. And now, WCC's Facebook page is covered with a lot of really harsh wall posts too. I've identified three current WCC students thus far who have posted terribly negative and untrue things, and they will need to answer for that."

The next meeting on your calendar is with Jim Russell. You and Jim update each other on progress toward the Career Fair to be held next month, and then your conversation turns to Phillips Hall. Jim says, "I'm worried about this. On my follow-up calls to employers about the Career Fair this week, they're starting to hear the rumors about Reverend Phillips, and they're asking a lot of questions. The established companies around here—no problem. They know the high quality of our academic programs, and I can take their jokes. But some new companies that are just branching out to recruit in this area—well, this does influence how they see us, and it makes it more difficult to get past that and emphasize our strong programs and graduates. We need to maintain a certain image if we want our students' degrees to mean something. With these new people, perceptions are so much more important and this is shaping up to be a real threat to our reputation."

On the way back to your office after another mid-afternoon meeting, you run into Jaime, who said: "This is getting crazy. A lot of the students are outraged, and it's not just students. I bought groceries at the store down the street this morning and overheard a woman in the same check-out line talking on her phone. She said her daughter had joined some sort of Facebook group protesting the building naming. When I logged on today, I noticed several other new groups with similar names. Even if the college isn't interested in hearing from students, Facebook will make sure that our voices are heard. This is awesome."

A voicemail message from Adele is waiting when you get back to your office. In a flustered tone, she said, "You won't believe this. I've now seen more than one dedicated Facebook group that is spreading rumors and misinformation. And isn't Brenda Fountain one of our students? She created a group called—let me get this right—'What happened to real science at WCC?' that's been liked by over 2,000 people already. Every time I check the group, more people have joined, and the number is growing very fast! What can we do? I'm really worried that the trustees and dinner guests will be hearing about this soon, and of course I've already alerted the president."

You glance at the clock to see that it's 3:45 already. An engineering technology faculty member with whom you've worked knocks on your open door and steps in: "Hey, these are exciting times, right? My neighbor is good friends with two of the major corporate sponsors of the Phillips Hall renovation. Someone forwarded both of them the email that Henry Larson had sent around campus, and now my neighbor's kids have shown her some of the Facebook pages. You may know her—she's taught a class in evolutionary biology here as an adjunct, and she was furious that she hadn't known about Reverend Phillips's background. And this morning two of my students asked me to read a letter to the editor they've written for tomorrow's local newspaper. They did a good job—they cited passages from some of his sermons and argued their case for reconsidering the naming decision. Wow, students here are really running with this. What a great learning opportunity. I haven't seen anything like this in my 20 years at WCC."

Your cell phone rings, and the faculty member waves goodbye and steps out. You see that the call is from Dennis Austin. Dennis says, "We just got off the water and I saw your message. What's up?" You recap recent events and tell him that you are leaving in a few minutes to attend the 4 p.m. meeting. Dennis says, "This is bad. At the last meeting, the president and trustees agreed that the Phillips Hall honor was the right thing to do for a whole host of reasons. We have to back the president and smooth things out with the students. I'm counting on you to help the students see things differently—and that has to start now. My kids and I are still a day away from where the outfitters will pick us up and take us back into town. And I'm flying back tomorrow just in time to attend the dinner. I'll try to get in touch with the president now and let him know that we're working on this. Call me after the meeting's over. With luck I'll have cell phone reception where we're camping tonight."

What do you do?

AMERICAN WEST MEETS ASSESSMENT WOES

Melissa Boyd-Colvin and Katie Branch

Setting

American West (AW) is a medium-size baccalaureate institution that has catered historically to a population of approximately 8,500 undergraduates, with another 500 students enrolled in master's or professional degree programs. Conveniently located near the perimeter of a metropolitan area, AW boasted a 5% increase in admissions over the previous year, with a noted increase in applications from non-traditional undergraduates. The Office of Institutional Research attributes these increases, in part, to an articulation agreement that was solidified three years prior with a community college located within the same metropolitan area. Until recently, this community college was the only institution of higher education in the area meeting the federal definition of a Hispanic Serving Institution (HSI).

Priding itself on providing a high-quality liberal arts education while enacting a mission built upon a respect for diversity, American West also received recently the HSI designation. Campus data indicates that over 70% of the undergraduate population receives some form of financial aid and more than 47% of students report working at least 20 hours per week. Currently, the total Hispanic undergraduate enrollment is 28% and 56% of all undergrads self-identify as female.

Characters

Caleb Jackson, associate dean of Admission, has served in this role eight years. He has an Ed.D. from a nearby educational leadership program and is on AW's institutional assessment team. Known as a "doer" by campus colleagues, he has had success in leading committees with clear objectives and specific timelines for completion. Caleb reports to the vice president of Academic Affairs.

Christina Jacobs, a staff member for 16 years, has served as the American West Scholars Program (AWSP) director, for a decade. AWSP was created to recruit and retain first-generation and underrepresented students. As a first-generation college student herself and a former campus athlete at AW, Christine has a strong affinity for the institution and her students. She has an MBA and reports to Caleb Jackson.

Ana Beltran, director of Student Services, has served at AW for six years. Among her many duties and supervisory responsibilities, Ana is now charged with leading the newly established Assessment Committee for the Division of Student Affairs. Ana was appointed to this position by the vice president for Student Affairs who deemed her as the most qualified person in the division because of her experience assessing first-generation and underrepresented populations at her former institution. Leading this committee also fits well with Ana's research interests as a Ph.D. candidate in a higher education and student affairs program. Ana reports to the vice president for Student Affairs.

Jason Morgan, assistant director of Athletics, has been at AW for four years. Formerly in a similar job at a smaller institution, Jason accepted this position as an opportunity to work with a more established athletic program. Jason is responsible for assisting with compliance issues, supervising the coaching staffs and ensuring student-athlete academic success. As a leader and as a supervisor, Jason appreciates a collaborative approach with his primary focus on building solid relationships as a means to sustaining a quality program. Jason reports to the director of Athletics, who in turn reports to the vice president for Student Affairs.

Greg Samuels, coordinator of Student Involvement, reports to Ana Beltran. Greg is a new professional who earned a bachelor's degree in business and immediately entered a college student affairs program for his master's degree. Interested in gaining as much applied experience as possible during his graduate program, Greg sought opportunities to serve on both the Information Technology and the Student Affairs Learning Outcomes committees. As a new hire at AW, Greg brings enthusiasm. Responsible for overseeing more than 50 student organizations as well as Late Night Programs, Greg works closely with a significant number of students and is expected to voice their needs and concerns to campus administration.

Bryn Martinez, a 27-year-old Latina who transferred to AW as a psychology major after attending the community college that has an articulation agreement with AW, is a student employee in Student Involvement. Her work-study award allows her to be paid for approximately 15 hours per week. Because of care responsibilities for young children, Bryn tries to work in the afternoon and take evening undergraduate courses.

Victor Alvin, a 21-year-old senior who was recruited to AW through the AWSP, is the vice president of the Association of MultiEthnic Students (AMES). This group, which was the local affiliate of the Association of MultiEthnic Americans, is overseen by Greg Samuels. Victor is a full-time student and works about 25 hours per week at an off-campus job.

Case

After receiving the charge to chair an Assessment Committee for the Division of Student Affairs, Ana moved quickly to convene a group of stakeholders from units that comprise the division. She included students and also invited representatives from academic affairs. These individuals, inclusive of those described previously, attended the first committee meeting.

In an effort to inform attendees of the charge to the committee and to clarify the task at hand, Ana prepared a presentation to review with the group. The presentation was packed with detailed enrollment trends at AW from the past five years, demographic data from the region, the parameters set for HSI funding and limited divisional data from last year's annual reports that were submitted by unit heads. At the conclusion of Ana's presentation, the stakeholders from the units within the Division of Student Affairs were charged with presenting specifics as to how their departments or offices were supporting the goals of the division and addressing the institution's distinction of becoming an HSI. This information, with supporting data, was to be discussed at the committee's next two weekly meetings. The group then would prepare a report for the vice presidents of AW. Ana reassured the committee members that data would be used to focus on improvement and enrichment opportunities for students and would not be tied to unit or personnel performance evaluations. This is what she had been told when charged to lead this committee.

A few days after the Assessment Committee had reconvened and attendees had begun to share the requested information, unit heads received an email from the vice president for Student Affairs warning of potential fiscal cuts for the coming academic year. Thus, unit heads were asked to prioritize budget requests for the coming year and to show evidence of "value-added" outcomes from the previous year in order to access monetary funding available from HSI grants. Almost immediately, Ana received emails from some Assessment Committee members claiming that the purpose of the committee had been misrepresented and that they were no longer willing to share information in open forums. Ana noticed that two of these messages came from unit heads with staff known to be struggling with assessment initiatives.

Ana approached this situation by seeking guidance and clarification from the vice president of Student Affairs. She requested a meeting with the vice president but because of the vice president's travel schedule she was unable to get an appointment before the next scheduled Assessment Committee meeting. Ana offered to meet virtually, but this offer went unacknowledged.

Gathering Jason and Greg in a session to prepare for the upcoming Assessment Committee meeting, Ana wanted to discuss creating a unified approach to leading the meeting and the type of data that her unit would continue to share. Jason advocated for presenting data on student success initiatives that were collaborative across the division. Greg, who was utilizing a number of internet and smartphone-accessible programs capable of collecting campus involvement data (e.g., SurveyMonkey, SurveyGizmo, Facebook, Twitter), informed them that he already had forwarded data to the vice president of Student Affairs. Greg was eager to highlight late-night programming and to advocate for increased funds, per students' requests.

In the midst of their discussion, Ana was notified that Christina Jacobs was requesting to meet with her immediately. Although informed that Ana was in a meeting, Christina insisted on discussing "this assessment mess" before meeting with her own supervisor, Caleb Jackson, in the next hour. Asking Jason to take over the session with Greg and requesting that they prepare a draft agenda with some talking points for review, Ana met with Christina for 30 minutes. During this time, Christina indicated that Caleb might withdraw both himself and her from the division's Assessment Committee because "our focus needs to be on working with people who want to engage in positive assessment." Besides being aware of some of the resistance in student affairs to sharing data, he also commented to Christina that "much of their data seems generated via questionable research methods." If removed from the committee, Christina expresses concern that her students might lose access to vital funding opportunities and she could be competing with student affairs offices for the same grants.

In an effort to make progress on this task before moving on to other pressing matters, Ana contacts Caleb directly and asks for his input on the agenda for the next meeting of the student affairs Assessment Committee. When raising the issue about differing views on the purpose of the committee, he quickly replies that this was a matter that "the VPs would work out." Caleb also said that "both he and Christina felt that there were too many surveys targeted at their students." He thanks Ana for the call and says that he is not certain if he and Christina can attend the committee's next meeting.

Unclear of how to proceed at this time, Ana feels dismissed and somewhat defeated as she hurries to a follow-up meeting with the campus police about an incident of violence that occurred last evening. In glancing over her calendar before leaving her office, she notices that a new event had been added to her calendar titled "Preliminary Assessment Report: Budgetary Priority Session" at the request of her vice president of Student Affairs. She also notices that Bryn Martinez has scheduled an appointment for the next day.

As Ana is waiting for the meeting with campus police to begin, she checks the Twitter hashtag #awstudentorgs and sees that Victor Alvin has tweeted "samuels to the rescue for ames, best coord ever." The positive tone of the message pleases her and she is becoming more at ease with this account, which Greg set up, being connected to Student Involvement.

However, her uneasiness about the uses of technology for connecting with students returns when meeting with Bryn Martinez the next day. Bryn wants to let Ana know that a number of students are feeling left out by Student Involvement. She says that while she likes the enthusiastic way that Greg approaches his work, he seems to think that nearly everyone has ready access to the internet and smartphones. She is concerned that the information Greg sent the vice president of Student Affairs and, then, members of the Assessment Committee was not reflective of a large number of AW students. She indicates that when she spoke with Greg about these issues he did not seem to hear her. Also, because she received training in human subject research ethics during a project she worked on with a psychology professor, Bryn is not sure if students' privacy is protected enough. She does not yet feel comfortable enough in the group setting of the Assessment Committee to raise such concerns.

After Bryn leaves her office, Ana pulls up the draft agenda prepared by Jason and Greg for the next Assessment Committee meeting, which is scheduled to begin in about two hours. As she prepares to finalize the document, she ponders what to include and how she will lead the meeting.

You are Ana. How do you proceed?

Chapter 5

Cases in Admissions

The admissions unit of a college typically operates on its own calendar and in isolation from the remainder of the campus although its actions affect every aspect from basic operation, through budgets to academic quality. Two issues facing many senior admissions officers, perhaps more often than they care to admit, are political influences and economic influences in the admissions process. Nearly every school with even moderately selective admission standards is faced with that borderline student whose success or failure at the institution is difficult to foresee, and often predicated on individual maturity and motivation rather than preparation and past performance.

In Tara Parker and Kathleen Neville's "All Things are Not Equal: College Access and Support for Students of Color," Metropolitan College has implemented new admissions criteria which has students, faculty, and others questioning if the college is meeting the needs of its community. Because of budget cuts, a state flagship four-year institution changes their transfer policies which has major implications for Huron Community College in "Last Minute Admission Changes at Central State University" by Shaila Mulholland and Lynn Ceresino Neault. In "Managing Enrollments or Enrollments Managing? Adjusting Standards to Fill Seats," Bart Grachan describes an admissions representative facing a difficult decision in admitting a transfer student with poor academic performance at his previous institution.

In "The Applicant Everyone Knows (and Hates!)" by William Tobin, a powerful politician attempts to influence the admissions decision for a questionable applicant. A staff member is assigned to create a recruitment plan at an institution that is slipping in the rankings in "Crafting a Diverse Class in Difficult Times" by Paula Steisel Goldfarb. Finally, what happens when an already admitted, but not yet matriculated, student lands in hot water? We find out in "The News No One Wants to Hear (Especially When on Vacation!)" by William Tobin.

Decisions made not just by an admissions director, but also the president and provost have various impacts on the institution as well as the staff. Some results can be positive, others negative; some intended, others unanticipated.

ALL THINGS ARE NOT EQUAL: COLLEGE ACCESS AND SUPPORT FOR STUDENTS OF COLOR

Tara L. Parker and Kathleen M. Neville

Setting

Metropolitan College (MC) is a four-year college with an urban mission to serve the people of the city in which it resides and the surrounding communities. The college enrolls 19,000 students, of which 72% reside within 20 miles of campus. Students are enrolled in liberal arts as well as programs in education, health sciences, and social work. MC is well known for its racial and ethnic diversity as 58% of its students are students of color, including: 18% Black; 21% Latino; 17% Asian/Pacific Islander; and 2% American Indian. Whites make up 42% of the student population. Further, 56% of students are the first in their families to attend college. The diversity of the institution is attributed to protests and activism of African Americans and Latinos in the late 1960s and early 1970s, an outgrowth of activism that was happening within the larger community at the time.

The college has consistently low SAT scores and low graduation rates and as a result has been criticized by local news agencies. Proud of the access they provide to a wide range of students, however, faculty and staff are satisfied with the college's practice of using a non-selective admissions process that traditionally admits more than 59% of its applicants.

Two years ago, however, the Board of Trustees (BOT) argued underprepared students were the cause of low graduation rates. Moreover, developmental education courses were viewed as ineffective and too expensive. During that fall, and into the following spring semester, students at the institution held several demonstrations on campus demanding that the BOT re-examine the need for developmental education and ensure college access for all members of the community. Family members and community activists joined with the students during one particular demonstration to show their support and tell their personal stories about the benefits the college provided them and the larger community. Despite challenges by the students, members of the general public, and the president of the institution, the BOT voted to eliminate developmental education courses and raise SAT score requirements. Shortly after the BOT vote, the president of MC resigned—after 15 years at MC—and accepted a position at a private institution. The new president, Diana King, was on record supporting the BOT decision; arguing that eliminating developmental education courses and raising admissions standards would provide the college with a new opportunity to improve its public image and become a more prestigious institution. The college increased radio advertising and sought to recruit students from further outside of the city in hopes of increasing the SAT scores of incoming freshmen.

Characters

Vice President of Enrollment Management

Diana King, President, Metropolitan College, White female

Sheri Jackson, Dean of Students, Black female

Mike Staley, Professor of English, White male

President of Undergraduate Student Government

President of the Black Student Union

President of Asian American Students Club

President of Latino Students Take Action Club

Members of People of Color Collective

Jonathon Hood, Director of Institutional Research, White male

Case

As Vice President of Enrollment Management, you have been working with the institutional research office to monitor changes in undergraduate enrollment in general and the first year students in particular. While average SAT scores have increased, faculty still complain that students are under-prepared. At a recent meeting to discuss the new admissions policy, one faculty member, Mike Staley, argued, "I don't care what admissions says. My students still have trouble with writing. It's too late for them once they are already in our classes." At the same meeting, Sheri Jackson, the Dean of Students, points out to you that since the BOT decision to change the admissions standards, the racial and ethnic makeup of undergraduate enrollment is changing. Sheri states that over the past two years, there has been a noticeable drop in the proportion of first year students who are students of color.

In fact, the first year after admissions standards were increased and developmental education courses were eliminated, the percentage of Blacks and Latinos in the first year class decreased by slightly more than 24%.

Jonathon Hood, Director of Institutional Research, interrupts to point out that, "Our overall enrollment for first year first-time freshmen is on the rise." The Dean of Students, Sheri, says, "That's because White students are filling in the seats that would otherwise have been filled by students of color."

After the meeting, you talk with your friend and colleague, Sheri. She confides in you to explain, "Some students have told me they were hesitant to even apply to Metropolitan. They heard the news about the changing admissions criteria and were afraid they wouldn't get in. Others said some of their friends went to one of these for-profit schools instead. It's funny. I always thought we were the ones to provide opportunities." Sheri went on to say that she recently had "a conversation with a first year student who was surprised she got in because her high school guidance counselor told her to not even bother applying to Metropolitan. Her high school grades were not that great and her SAT scores barely made the cut-off."

A week later, the college president comes into your office, visibly angry. She said she received a phone call from a prominent newspaper in the area about the decline in student diversity. The journalist wanted to know if the decline signals a shift in priorities at the college; that the institution is no longer interested in serving the community and/or students of color. The newspaper then published an editorial questioning the future of MC:

> Although the administration intends to continue to serve the needs of the greater community, the number of students of color in this year's incoming freshman class has dropped significantly. If indeed the institution wants to maintain its mission and obligations to the community, it is not clear why the institution raised the admissions standards to a level that, by national standards on the SAT entrance exams, systematically reduces the eligibility of students of color. Some institutions have eliminated the SAT as a standard for admission.

It did not take long for the news article to reach the students, most of whom were outraged. The president of the Undergraduate Student Government, the presidents of the Black Student Union, Asian American Students Club, and Latino Students Take Action Club, as well as members of the People of Color Collective demanded a meeting with you. During this meeting, the student leaders questioned the decline in student of color enrollment. The Undergraduate Student Government president threw the newspaper editorial on your desk and said, "We believe your job is to maintain enrollment and ensure the institution is fulfilling its mission to serve the greater community by reflecting the diversity of the community. How did this happen?" The other students further expressed concerns that new admissions standards and recruitment strategies are excluding students of color and other underrepresented groups. The president of the Latino Students Take Action Club, for example, probed, "We know you have supported us in the past but we are concerned about the future. Was it your intention to lower the enrollment of students of color? Is this your plan in order to 'become a more prestigious institution?' What is going on here?"

A member of the People of Color Collective stood up and said, "Do you know that if I was applying to Metropolitan today, I wouldn't get in? I wouldn't be eligible for admission. My high school GPA was like a 2.7. And now, as a student leader on this campus, I have a 3.5 GPA!" The president of the Black Student Union agreed, "So now, we not only have to fight our way out of this school, we still have to fight to get in. Where's the justice in any of that?" The students demanded a formal response from you or the president. They say they will take more drastic action in three weeks if they do not receive an adequate response from either of you.

As the media continues to pay close attention to the happenings at MC, they have picked up on the student unrest. They publish a full news article about the uncertainty at the college. The president is increasingly concerned about the bad press she has worked to avoid. She asks you to put a committee together to develop a plan to increase student diversity while also maintaining admissions academic standards. The president explained, "I am hoping your plan will calm students and regain support from the press and perhaps even the local community. I hope you will keep this as your priority. Show them we are serious about college access, diversity, and student support."

When you ask about the students' demands, the president dismisses your concerns. "They will settle down once we tell them what we are going to do." While you are certain the president is more concerned about the press than making a significant difference, you are still hoping you can also help students. You are hoping to use this committee to improve admissions and develop new academic and social support services for undergraduates.

You now must respond to the students and to the president. Responding to the president, you need to form a committee. Who will you include in this committee? What will the committee recommend to the president? How do you respond to the students? What do you write to them, on behalf of the president?

LAST MINUTE ADMISSION CHANGES AT CENTRAL STATE UNIVERSITY

Shaila Mulholland and Lynn Ceresino Neault

Setting

Huron Community College was founded in 1911 as Huron Junior College. Situated in a multicultural and picturesque city in the Midwest, in 1961 it became part of the state's largest community district, which now has three community colleges, as well as four continuing education campuses and a well-established distance education program to meet industry-specific needs. The district serves about 100,000 students in both credit and non-credit programs. Approximately 10,000 students enroll at Huron Community College each semester. Students choose to attend the college for a variety of reasons: to complete short-term and long-term certificate programs; to study English as a second language; to complete an associate degree program leading to an occupational career; and/or to take an academic program of study for transfer into a four-year university, several of which are located within the same city as Huron Community College.

Central State University is the flagship campus for the state's public four-year university system and is located in close proximity to Huron Community College. It has close to 30,000 undergraduate, graduate, and professional full-time students, and about 5,000 students attend on a part-time basis. In recent years, the university has made significant expansions to its student center and residential buildings on campus. There are also more than 25,000 students enrolled at one of six additional extension campuses located throughout the state—in both rural and urban areas—that are part of the university system. Students may transfer and "reverse-transfer" between the various campuses and there is a large proportion of students enrolled part-time and/or attending school in the evening (approximately 30–40%, depending on the campus).

While Central State University is nationally respected for its research and top-ranking programs, stakeholders expect that as a state university it meets the educational needs of the local community. Central State University has a policy to ensure that local students (both first-time freshmen as well as transfer students) are given priority in admissions over applicants from other parts of the state, as well as preference over out-of-state applicants. The state university system defines local students from within a specified geographical area and nine community colleges are considered local feeders to Central State University. As long as local applicants complete a minimum GPA of 3.0

in high school courses, or the requirements for transfer at a community college, the applicant is guaranteed admission to Central State University. There has been speculation that Central State University would be discontinuing admission preferences for local students due to pressure from the state to increase graduation rates. Students and community members continue to vocalize concerns about the impact the policy changes are having on educational opportunity in the region.

Characters

William Forrest is the Vice President of Student Development and Dean of Student Services at Huron Community College.

Nandi Lee is President of Huron Community College.

Elizabeth Rios is the community college district's Vice Chancellor for Student Services and oversees student services on all three campuses and the four continuing education campuses.

Burton Patterson has been the President of Central State University for a record-long term of 16 years and a strong advocate of raising academic standards at the university.

Edmund Woods is a 23-year-old Huron Community College student.

Stephanie Stephens is a 34-year-old Huron Community College student who began classes one year ago and quickly became involved with the student group, "Students for Transfer."

Kristina Winters is the local state representative and has been critical of the last minute admission changes.

John Finnell is the Vice President for Enrollment Management at Central State University.

Case

As the Vice President of Student Development and Dean of Student Services at Huron Community College, you are responsible for the Transfer Center and Counseling programs. Walking back to your office from the college's Learning and Teaching Resource Center, you are reflecting on the productive two-hour meeting with counselors and administrators from Huron Community College and Central State University. The first of several scheduled for the spring semester, today's meeting discussed a new initiative called Transfer Success that is focused on better coordinating student services at the two institutions. Your hopes are that through this collaboration, both institutions will be able to better identify institutional strategies and student affairs practices to improve and facilitate course credit transfer and student transfer.

For the past two and a half years you have been working with the counselors to try to simplify the transfer process for students at Huron. While you feel the institution has made significant strides in streamlining the process, your counseling team is frustrated with the constant changes in the transfer "rules." Your president is fairly new, having arrived at the college only nine months ago from another state. She does not understand the details of the issues and is still trying to learn the culture of transfer at the college and in the region. She has delegated full responsibility to you.

Gaining admission into any of the state's public institutions has become more difficult for recent high school graduates and transfer students as enrollment spaces have diminished and the demand for enrollment has increased. This past fall, just a few weeks prior to the university's early priority admissions deadline in October, Central State University announced its decision to raise the minimum GPA and SAT requirements for admission. In addition to the changes in requirements, the administration announced that the university's admissions deadline had been moved up earlier by one month. There would be some special consideration offered to programs unable to change the application due date; however, only a few schools and programs pursued exemptions.

While the university contends that the admissions changes were due to the state budget cuts, multiple reasons behind these admissions changes have been suggested. One national educational think-tank criticized Central State University and other flagship universities across the country for inadequately enrolling students from underrepresented minority groups and students from low-income families. The report, called "Quest for Elitism?" stated, "Flagship universities have the important responsibility of producing the future civic, political, and business leaders of their state but the drive to increase institutional prestige and selectivity challenges this vital mission." The report also posited that flagship campuses nationally are investing substantially more dollars to institutional aid based on academic merit, but are significantly reducing institutional aid based on students' financial need. In the defense of the flagship universities, one university president suggested that the problems with K–12 education pose the most challenges for postsecondary institutions that must "deal with" students' inadequate levels of preparation for college.

By the end of the week, the admissions decisions are announced at Central State University. Disappointed when you hear the news, you learn that 3,000 local community college transfer applicants from across the district have been denied admission and another 800 are on a waitlist. More than half of the students denied admission are Huron Community College students who have completed all of the requirements for transfer. In an interview with the local newspaper, the Central State University president explains, "due to budget restrictions, the number of transfer admissions slots was reduced 40%." When asked about whether or not the university would be able to honor the system's local area policy, he answers: "Although it is very unfortunate that we had to turn down so many eligible students from both inside and outside of our local service area, given the historic budget cuts, we are still providing greater educational opportunity for the students of this state and this region. We plan to have approximately 45–50% of the first year class to be from the local service area, which is higher than our historical average of only 40%."

The admissions announcement is quickly broadcast through the local media. Students and community members have continued to vocalize concerns about the impact the policy changes are having on educational opportunity in the region. Several community groups have formed and are organizing meetings in the local community, having discussions on social media sites, and beginning letter-writing campaigns to Central State University, as well as state and city leaders. Public school leaders and local school board members have also spoken up about their concerns.

Students begin calling the counselors and transfer center to find out why they were denied admission. Many want to know what will happen next. Of the students placed on the waiting list, many are still waiting to hear whether or not they will be attending Central State University in the upcoming fall. Students have been instructed to check back in regularly with the Office of Admissions to check the status of their applications. Your counselors report that they do not know the reason for the denial and are angry. The counselors are becoming increasingly vocal with the students and media. The Vice Chancellor of Student Services has spoken to the student services leadership at all campuses about the Chancellor's commitment to a strong working relationship with the university, and advised that the staff not take their frustrations out in the press.

The local state representative, Kristina Winters, is also receiving hundreds of calls to her office. Students and parents are demanding she do something. She announces that she will be holding a town hall meeting to listen to the concerns of the community. A staffer from Winters's office calls and asks for you to speak at the town hall meeting. She also informs you that the president of Central State University will speak. The staffer makes clear that you are expected to speak in protest of the university's recent admissions decisions.

In a packed high school auditorium close to the Huron Community College campus, students speak with great energy about their concerns and frustrations. At the front of the room, there is a table on stage where representatives from various educational groups are seated. Representative Winters is standing at the podium. One of the first students to speak, Edmund Woods, is a 23-year-old Huron Community College student. He shares with the audience and the panel on stage that he was enrolled as a part-time student at Huron for three years before he was able to attend full-time for two semesters to complete the remaining transfer requirements. He further explains that he has had to work full-time while attending community college, which has taken a toll on his studies. His cumulative GPA is 2.3. He applied to Central State University in hopes of completing a bachelor's degree in psychology but recently learned that he has been denied. He concludes his comments by saying, "I know my GPA is not great, but I have worked hard balancing work and school. If I am not admitted into Central State University, I'm not sure where I'll be able to attend since I can't afford to move."

Following on from Edmund's comments, a 34-year-old Huron Community College student named Stephanie Stephens also explains her educational path. Stephanie began classes one year ago. She is a single mother of two children who takes distance education courses due to childcare needs. Her GPA is currently 2.7. Stephanie explains that out of concern about whether or not she would be able to transfer to Huron, she quickly became involved with the student group, "Students for Transfer," which has been vocal in opposing the admissions changes at Central State University.

Representative Winters asks the Central State University Vice President for Enrollment Management whether he would like to respond to the comments. Dr. Finnell begins his comments by assuring students that they are doing everything possible to look out for the interests of local students and the needs of the region. He encourages students to sign up for the waitlist and to "keep an open mind" to the opportunity to attend one of the extension campuses. The town hall meeting concludes with questions from students. One student asks: Is it true that Central State University is considering ending the policy giving admissions priority to local students? Dr. Finnell explains, "The best thing we can do for our community is to hold students to the highest expectations possible. That is what will prepare them to be successful in the workforce." The town hall meeting ends, but dozens of students and community members remain in the auditorium even after all the administrators and staff from Winters's office leave. You have not yet spoken at the town hall meeting. What do you say (if anything) at the event?

The next morning, you receive a frantic call from President Lee's office. The administrative assistant informs you that they just received a fax announcing a planned "sit-in" as protest for the recent thousands of denials to Central State and they are demanding that your college leadership do something since they heard students out of the area with high GPA were admitted over local transfer students. The president is at a meeting at the State Capitol and she cannot be reached. Later that day you learn from one of your counselors "off the record" that many counselors are planning to join the sit-in.

What will you do?

MANAGING ENROLLMENTS OR ENROLLMENTS MANAGING? ADJUSTING STANDARDS TO FILL SEATS

Bart Grachan

Setting

St. Methodius College is a large Carnegie-classified master's institution in the northeast, enrolling roughly 3,600 undergraduates. It is Catholic-affiliated, is considered selective for freshmen applicants, with a near 60% acceptance rate, and has an 85% freshman retention rate, but this is a number which drops off substantially from sophomore to junior year; the six-year graduation rate is 62%, with the four-year rate hovering at 50%. There are a number of factors that contribute to this, not the least of which is housing; students are expected to move off campus after their sophomore year, with no assistance in finding off-campus housing from the college, in an area with either very expensive or very questionable offerings, and little in between.

In this setting, transfer students play a significant, if murky, role in the enrollment management process. There is no hard and fast enrollment number expected for students transferring in, with planning based on setting freshman-enrollment goals for a particular year. Transfers are expected to fill the gaps in retention, transferring in and replacing the 15% of freshmen who left, or over time, the nearly 40% of original freshmen who failed to reach graduation.

The definition of transfer at St. Methodius is malleable; in most years, any student who previously matriculated at another institution is a transfer, but in years where the freshman-enrollment goals are not met, transfers with fewer than 24 credits are reclassified as freshmen for reporting and budget purposes. In these years of reclassification, however, the "transfer" enrollments are expected not to drop, despite this redistribution of numbers, as their primary role is to fill the retention gap. With regard to the offices on campus that are concerned about these issues, there is no contact at all between the Offices of Undergraduate Admissions and Student Retention, and the Office of Institutional Research is primarily focused on external reporting surveys, and is not utilized by either Admissions or Student Retention.

Sixty to seventy percent of students who transfer to the college are from other four-year institutions, with 30–40% from area community colleges and for-profit institutions. In Undergraduate Admissions, there is a single person tasked with recruiting transfer students from the two-year schools and processing all transfer applications. While Undergraduate Admissions receives roughly 5,000 freshmen applications, looking for a class of 900 students, this person handles 300–350 applications and enrolls 200–250 students per year on a rolling basis with no application deadline.

Characters

Max Parker, Assistant Director of Admissions: Max is in his second year in Admissions, never having worked in higher education administration before. He had been a coach at the college for many years in a part-time role, and is very familiar with the college. He is responsible for the transfer applications, and has felt right at home in this role; while not a former transfer himself, he had taken some missteps as an undergraduate early on, and enjoys working with students who are finding their way.

Bill Smithson, Provost of the College: Dr. Smithson has been at the college for over 30 years, as a faculty member, dean of the School of Liberal Arts, and for the last eight years, as the Provost. The Assistant Vice President of College Admissions reports directly to him, including weekly reports on applications, deposits, and enrollments.

Tom Abbott, Assistant Vice President of College Admissions: Tom directs all admissions to the college, including freshmen, transfers, graduate, and the non-traditional returning adult program. Having advanced rapidly at another similar institution, Tom is very young for the position he is in. A factor in his hiring, that the small community of the college is acutely aware of, is that his uncle, athletic director of the college for over 25 years, was on the hiring committee.

Father John Mariani, President of St. Methodius College: Father Mariani has been president of the college for 12 years, and prior to that, was a principal at area Archdiocese primary and secondary schools for 25 years.

Patrick Mulvaney, applicant to the college: Patrick is local, having grown up in the town that the college is in. In fact, Patrick went to the prep school in town that shares a name with the college, where he did reasonably well; well enough, in fact, to have been admitted to the college as a freshman the year prior. He had opted instead to spend his first year at another institution.

Father Jerry Smith, Dean of Students at Iona Preparatory High School: Father Jerry has been Dean of Students at the prep for 20 years, and has sent countless students to the college over the years. He has been friend and colleague to Father Mariani since their days in the seminary. He has always been one to look out for students.

Case

Max had been feeling good about his fall numbers; he had topped the previous two years, and it was the strongest class he'd seen since joining the admissions staff at St. Methodius. He worked hard to that end, in fact, building relationships with a number of community colleges to get students to choose St. Methodius College, strong students who had other options. In the past, the college had been a choice of convenience for many local students, admitting transfers with a 2.0 GPA, and in some cases, even lower. Many students were excellent, however, and through recruiting, Max had targeted these students. The level of students transferring from four-year institutions was harder to influence, as recruiting was not part of the process, so Max had focused his efforts on customer service as a way of getting the best students to commit to the transfer once they had applied. On the other side, he had instituted an essay and an interview requirement (neither being part of the standard application process for transfers) for students whose transcripts indicated some problems. With these efforts, applications, admissions, enrollments, and average GPA were all on the rise, and Max was pleased with his success. Then the emails arrived.

Two weeks ago, Max had received an email stating, "Max, how many of your fall transfers have 24 or fewer credits?" Max responded with, "About 50, roughly a third of his class." He received no follow-up email until today. But the second email wasn't from Assistant Vice President Abbott—it was from the school's Provost, Dr. Smithson. It said, "Max, I just got the numbers— what's going on with transfers this year?" In confusion, Max had stepped into the Operations office to ask for a report and found out that Dr. Smithson was right. His numbers were at 104. One week ago they were at 152. He was stunned. The transfer numbers were down 48 students. He immediately returned to his office, and started going through his spreadsheet, looking up each student individually to find out what had happened. As the pattern emerged, he remembered the email from his boss a few weeks before; all of his so-called "freshmen transfers," students in their first year when they applied to transfer, had been changed to "freshmen" in the system.

He crossed the hall to his boss's office. "Tom, we have a problem," Max said. Abbott looked up and winced. Max continued, "I just got an email from the Provost—he wants to know what happened to my transfer numbers this year, and actually, so do I. What's going on?"

Abbott proceeded to explain that the freshman numbers had been low, and rather than report to the Board that they had missed their mark, the President had asked him where those numbers could be made up. With the shift of some of Max's transfers to the freshman class, the one number the Board actually cared about was made and surpassed, pleasing everyone. Everyone except for the Provost, that is, who was equally concerned about the budget that was maintained by transfer enrollments. He had been bypassed in the numbers-shifting conversation. Max asked Abbott how he was supposed to fill the hole he now had in his numbers, and how he was to explain this to the Provost.

"Well, you still have pending applications, right? And you can admit students right up through the end of add/drop, two weeks into class. You have time to fill the hole. Just tell the Provost that you're reviewing additional applications now."

Now, sitting in his office staring at the two emails, Max was at a loss, but finally decided to do what his boss told him. He emailed the Provost, apologized for the delay, and told him that there were both a number of applications pending and that there were always late summer applications that would help cover the shortfall. What he didn't mention, however, was that the pending applications were mostly terrible. Some were incomplete, but most were students who had done poorly at their previous institutions. He also knew that most applications that came in late in the summer were equally bad, students who had delayed telling their parents that they had failed their courses until the end of the summer.

Two weeks later, Max had received essays and finished interviews with 20 additional students. While they had struggled, all were over a 2.0 in GPA, had reasonable explanations for their performance and their plans to do better, and as such, had been admitted. Unfortunately, that still left him short on numbers, so now he was going through the files of students whose GPA was below a 2.0. Leaning back at his desk, Max read through Patrick's file again.

Patrick had been a solid, if unspectacular student at St. Methodius Prep, the local high school that was no longer affiliated with the college in a formal sense, despite the name, but which certainly maintained ties. He had been utterly terrible at his first college, however. His GPA was a 0.8, over a full year. This was no rogue class blowing up an innocent freshman's GPA—this guy had bombed out. Max scanned the letter again; Father Jerry, local legend and dean at the prep, had written Patrick a glowing recommendation (and cc'd the president of the college, an unusual move), talking about what a good boy he was at heart, and how he deserved a second chance. Max then flipped to Patrick's essay, a rambling missive that blamed the other institution for his struggles and admitted to partying *way* too much, but promised that this would change, because the college had nothing to do and no frats. Max didn't bother with his interview notes; the kid was a nightmare. Arrogant, entitled; these were the least of his problems. Worse was his mention of the daily drinking and self-description as an alcoholic; this was not in itself the concern for Max, rather it was Patrick's insistence that he could handle it, that he wasn't going to get help, and that it was the other school's fault, anyway. Max's recommendation that Patrick establish a solid GPA at the local community college, taking courses at Max's direction to ensure transfer of credits, was met not just with refusal, but open derision.

For Max, there were nothing but red flags attached to this file. This student stood little chance of successful integration into the school and little chance of academic success. Normally, Max would have denied this student long before the interview stage. Patrick's family wasn't wealthy; it would be an investment of loans, but in what? Every indication was that Patrick would fail again, at additional expense to his family and his academic record. Despite this, Max had pressure from the Provost's office for numbers, he had pressure from his boss to help cover the ground left open by freshman shortfalls, and he knew that if he denied this student, the file would probably manage its way back to his desk, via the president's office. Max also knew that it would never come back on him, if he did admit Patrick. Admissions numbers had nothing to do with retention numbers, as the college tracked them, and when Patrick did inevitably fail, it would fall on Office of Student Retention and Patrick, not on Max.

You're Max. What would you do?

THE APPLICANT EVERYONE KNOWS (AND HATES!)

William Tobin

Setting

One of the key issues facing many senior admissions officers, perhaps more often than they care to admit, is the political and economic influences in the admissions process. This issue can impact the morale of the staff and the credibility of the office. A recent example is not only illustrative but no doubt a familiar occurrence. Nearly every school with even moderately selective admissions standards is faced with that borderline student whose success or failure at the institution is difficult to foresee, and often predicated on individual maturity and motivation rather than preparation and past performance.

As in the following example, the decisions made not just by an admissions director, but also the president and provost have various impacts on the institution and the people who work there. Some of these results can be positive, others negative; some intended, others unanticipated.

Janine is the director of admissions at a medium-sized regional public university located in the Midwest. As an indicator of the importance the institution attaches to the role of admissions director, the provost and vice president for Academic Affairs also awarded Janine the concurrent title of assistant vice president for Academic Affairs. Her staff consists of an associate director, five assistant directors, and several admissions counselors, along with support personnel who fulfill vital functions in the office. Shortly after her arrival six years ago, Janine convinced the administration to move toward more selective admissions criteria after a history of virtually open admission for state residents. This caused some controversy among citizens of the state, but was warmly applauded by the faculty, who for years chafed under the popular notion that the university was the state's dumping ground for ill-prepared, underachieving students.

After enjoying a period of relatively robust growth in new student enrollments, the university suffered three straight years of decline, ranging from 4–5% per year. In addition, income from state appropriations remained stagnant during the period (or even declined slightly when adjusted for inflation). Since the university is not a significant player in the research dollars market, any growth in the budget is tied to growth in enrollments, whether by recruitment or retention.

During the course of her tenure at the university, Janine was asked a number of times to give "special consideration" to applicants whose parents were people of substance in the community because of their wealth or political influence. On a number of occasions the athletic department brought pressure on her office to admit students whose records did not meet the published criteria. Janine approached each of these on a case-by-case basis, taking care not to establish a precedent that would give the appearance of favoring the privileged. Nevertheless, she was experienced and shrewd enough to understand that admitting these students can have a positive impact that goes far beyond any problems created. One example was a scholarship awarded to talented but economically disadvantaged students. The scholarship was endowed by the parents of a borderline student. Another instance was the new parking garage on campus which may or may not have resulted from the admission of the son of a friend of the lieutenant governor's. Although no one would want to imply causation, the support of the lieutenant governor during the debate in the legislature on approving the bond issue for the garage came at a critical time.

The president has made it clear to Janine that he does not sell spaces in the freshman class, but neither of them is so naive to believe that an exception to the admissions requirements does not have some kind of quid pro quo attached to it, however unspoken that attachment might be. On the other hand, the most recent case of bending with the winds of political opportunity proved to be particularly explosive.

Case

During the past academic year, the admissions office received an application from the son of a state legislator whose academic record was close to, but in several respects did not meet, the minimum standards for conditional freshman admission to the university. The student's father was a prominent member of the powerful House Ways and Means committee, and thus in a position to exert influence on the manner in which state dollars are appropriated, so the president was especially eager to see that the student received what he called "full consideration."

In most instances, this student's record was close enough to the cut-off point that an exception could have been made, but in addition to poor academic performance in high school, the student was expelled during his junior year for bringing a gun to school, and had a juvenile record for assaulting a teenage girl. Although as a juvenile offender the record should have been sealed, news of the assault was common knowledge in the student's high school, and it came to the attention of the admissions counselor who visits that school on behalf of the university.

Further complicating the issue, the parents of the victim in the assault case wrote letters to the president and vice president for Student Affairs, professing their strong opposition to the student's admission. Although it is not clear how news of this student's application became an open secret among several staff members, the point is moot since the bell had already been rung. Concerns were then raised by senior members of the Student Affairs Division that this student could pose a threat to other students and disrupt the orderly conduct of university business. Of special concern to just about everyone with knowledge of the situation was the student's potential conduct on campus.

Clearly the university could benefit from the political good will generated by admitting this student, but members of the dean of students' staff expressed concerns about the admission of the student. The dean of residential life also expressed strong opinions on the subject since the student would be living on campus during his freshman year. The faculty-dominated admissions committee, which ordinarily serves as an advisory body, asked that they be allowed to review the case. The student's guidance counselor even took the extraordinary step of recommending against admission on the section of the application reserved for such comments.

The president could have easily issued an edict to admit the student if he so chose, but did not want to give the appearance of such a high-handed manipulation of policy for the benefit of such a controversial student. Consequently, this item of business was handed to the admissions director for "appropriate action."

While this situation is somewhat extraordinary in the context, it also presents decision makers with a rather typical dilemma. Namely that in many cases we are seldom presented with a choice between a really good solution and a really bad solution. More likely we are faced with choices in which we are attempting to minimize damage, reduce hurt feelings, or reduce the number of constituents who find the action taken intolerable. This is just such a situation. Regardless of what action the director of admissions takes, there will be some negative fallout with one campus constituency or another, perhaps more than one. Of no less concern to her personally is the effect that any decision would have on her relationship with her superiors, the president and provost, who through the artful but feint political language of the university administration have, to her ears, made their positions clear. And she fully understands the pressures that they are under. Many influential legislators view the university as just another state agency that can and should be manipulated by the legislative body that funds it.

On the other hand, the president and provost are fully cognizant that the university community, especially the faculty, prizes its independence above all other attributes, and often resents the meddling of outsiders in the traditional functions of the academy (i.e., teaching, research, and service), which includes deciding who is taught. The director believes that this is a significant factor in the president's attempting to be above manipulating the process for political capital because there are those on the faculty who believe that he is not one of their own, but an administrator bent on eroding their steadily dwindling perquisites.

The provost asks the admissions director to meet with him next week to discuss the matter.

Assume the role of the director of admissions. What will you present to him and what will your recommendations be? Can you anticipate some of the issues that the provost might raise, and be prepared to address them?

CRAFTING A DIVERSE CLASS IN DIFFICULT TIMES

Paula Steisel Goldfarb

Setting

Ardyn College is a small liberal arts college located in Pennsylvania. The population of the college is 3,000 students, mostly from upper-middle-class backgrounds. The school has continuously been ranked among the top 50 liberal arts colleges in the United States and has some of the leading liberal arts physical science departments in the country. However, in the last two years, the college has dropped in its overall ranking largely due to a reputation for a lack of diversity among students who attend the school. In fact, a recent student situation has highlighted this issue, both on campus and to the broader public, harming the school's reputation.

The college has struggled in recent years to attract and retain students from a wide range of backgrounds—socioeconomic, ethnic/racial, gender, international. Given its location, the college has intense competition from neighboring schools and continues to lose out on attracting students with diverse backgrounds. With increasing pressure from the president, the dean of admissions must develop a strategy for increasing the diversity on campus. The school's reputation is at stake.

Characters

Bruce Matthew – President of the College.

Joan Day – Dean of Admissions.

Laura Carpenter – Board of Trustees member and alumna.

Jake Marks – Professor and author of his course text.

Mike Fellen and **John Lake** – students in Professor Marks's class.

Case

It's a crisp fall morning at Ardyn College. Bruce Matthew, President of the College, is looking out of his window onto campus, remarking how beautiful the campus looks with its historic buildings dotted among the bucolic setting. Leaves on the trees are starting to turn colors. However, he knows today has the potential to be a difficult day on campus. The annual college rankings will be coming out and he will have to field phone calls from all of his constituents—board members, faculty, students, and the media.

Just down the hall, Joan Day, Dean of Admissions, is at her desk, also waiting to hear the news. The media relations department on campus should be hearing about the rankings shortly. She is worried. This determines how difficult her year will be to recruit students to the school. With 20 years of experience in admissions, she knows that students will use these rankings as a key factor in determining where to apply. Between the anticipated rankings and the incident on campus that received national attention, she will have to work even harder to reach her enrollment goals this year.

In the dorms on campus, students are having breakfast together. John Lake, a junior, is eating his cereal and sharing the outcome from last night's meeting of the Diversity and Inclusion Club. The club members could not stop talking about the situation on campus and the administration's poor response. John set up a meeting that day to talk about the school's recruiting practices with the dean of admissions. Based on this year's incoming class, numbers of underrepresented minorities are low. John wants to find out more about what is happening and how he can help. He doesn't want to see the numbers completely dwindle as he is already feeling like one of the few diverse people on campus. And, he is still upset about the incident in his class.

Approximately one month ago during a junior-level English literature course, the students in Professor Jake Marks's class discussed Marks's book that had just been published. Mike Fellen, a junior, mentioned that the book seemed out of date and out of touch with reality. "African American people today have the same privileges and rights as everyone else." John Lake, another student, responded, "That is not true." Remarks passed back and forth between the two students and quickly engaged the whole class. Tensions grew and arguments were heated. Professor Marks's attempts to address the issue were unsuccessful. Rather than let the incident devolve further, he dismissed the class. Students left the class in a state of anger and frustration. News of the incident spread quickly among the students and across the campus.

As a result of the classroom incident, conflict spread throughout campus; students took sides. At a fraternity party the following night, a fight broke out between two students resulting in the police being called and minor injuries reported. Conflict like this was foreign to the tight-knit community, more accustomed to debate and discussion than altercations. The community talked incessantly about the incident while the administration remained silent.

Parents started calling the school after hearing about the incident from their students. They were concerned about campus safety and wondered what kind of school their children were attending. As frustration with the administration grew, a board member, whose grandson happened to be attending, heard about the incident and took it upon himself to contact the president and demand action. The board, in consultation with the college's legal counsel however, advised the president to let the situation go away on its own. Despite President Matthew's pleas that the college address the incident, he was met with resistance and he knew that the situation was going to be divisive on campus. He was certain it would create more issues for the community. He was right. The national media found out about the situation and tried to reach out to students and parents. The college was negatively presented in the press and President Matthew's reputation was on the line, too.

The college asked Professor Marks not to use his own book in class anymore. Professor Marks was outraged at being censored and wrote a letter expressing his views to the college newspaper, which was then picked up by *The Philadelphia Times*. He also included his views on diversity on the college's campus and his disappointment in the college. The faculty senate was also disappointed in the college's response. The faculty began questioning their freedom of speech and the college's treatment of faculty during challenging times. President Matthew received significant criticism for his handling of the incident.

The rankings are reported and President Matthew is once again disappointed. The college dropped several points again this year, making it difficult to recruit students. The media relations office is preparing remarks and a communication that will go out to the community. One member of the Board of Trustees and an alumna of the college, Laura Carpenter, calls and wants to find out what happened. With fundraising dollars dropping this year, already resulting in financial constraints, and the incident on campus, the school is not having a good year.

President Matthew has tried to make the college a more diverse place. He recruited more women faculty and underrepresented minorities, and even supported the Diversity and Inclusion Student Club. Yet his effort appears for naught. Additionally, he can't believe that one incident on campus could have such a large-scale effect on the community and the public. He is still tired from the incident and not sure the college's response was the correct one.

Morale is low among faculty, students, and administrators. President Matthew knows that something needs to be done to address the issue. After hearing from students, parents, and in consultation with the administration, he decides to develop a taskforce to address diversity and recruiting students. While he knows this will not address the incident, he must do something to create a more positive environment and culture on campus. He does not want to see the community continue to be harmed by this incident and he wants to improve the reputation of the school. The first place he looks for help is the admissions office.

You are Dean of Admissions, Joan Day. You and your team notice an almost immediate negative response from potential prospective students, both minority and non-minority students at college fairs and high school visits following the incident. Accustomed to being a highly selective school, your team was not prepared to handle this type of negative reaction from prospective students and their families nor the college counselors, principals, and heads of schools with whom you work. Despite having an experienced and intelligent team of admissions officers, this was not a position the team was comfortable with but they were prepared to meet the challenge that came before them.

As Dean of Admissions, you have been charged by President Matthew to create a school-wide taskforce to increase the recruitment of a diverse student body.

Who will you put on the taskforce? Who will you not put on the taskforce and why? How will you organize the taskforce? What are some of the challenges you will face? What is your plan to recruit more minority students to the college? What will your recommendations look like for year 1, year 2, and year 3? What would *you* like the final outcome to be and why? What are the implications (financial, political, organizational, community, enrollment, media) for your recommendations? Are there any drawbacks to your recommendations?

THE NEWS NO ONE WANTS TO HEAR (ESPECIALLY WHEN ON VACATION!)

William Tobin

Setting

Traditional University has a national reputation for both academics and Division I athletics, and celebrates its Catholic Jesuit heritage of rigorous intellectual inquiry and development. The president, relatively new, has been in office less than two years. The dean of admissions, the vice president for public affairs, and the vice president for student affairs are holdovers from the late administration, but the other senior officers of the university were hired by the current president in a rather breathtaking sweep of the cabinet.

Despite being a wealthy and venerable institution, with stable enrollments and significant research dollars flowing from the federal government, the university suffered during the economic downturn. Its three sources of revenue all took substantial hits. Nearly $100 million of value was shed from the endowment during the market collapse; capital and annual giving have both been off, especially in the past year; and in order to maintain enrollments, more institutional aid was provided to matriculating students, thus depressing net tuition revenue. Consequently, significant cuts to the operational budget were necessary, along with increasing already substantial deferred maintenance. Budget cuts have been particularly painful as positions have gone unfilled (or eliminated completely), pay raises have been minimal, and office budgets have been cut, sometimes drastically; all of this has had a dramatic negative effect on faculty and staff morale. In such a fiscal environment, jealousy and infighting ensue as many mouths try to bite into a much smaller apple.

Traditional's alumni base is extremely loyal and many are what the president euphemistically calls "involved." This devotion is also embodied in the Board of Trustees, which is larger than average for most institutions of this type, and contains members who have served long terms, sometimes for two or more decades. Although scattered about the country, trustees take full advantage of the information age to keep tabs on the institution, making use of the university's website, the school newspaper's online content, and even the school's social networking presence. Traditional's YouTube presence has been a particular hit with the board. However, it's a fine line to walk between keeping trustees informed and enabling their desire to delve into the minutiae of the day-to-day business of the institution, looking over the president's shoulder and second-guessing every operational decision.

Characters

Christopher Barrett – the president, a member of the Jesuit order, has been in office less than two years, after serving a four-year term as provost at another Jesuit university in the West.

Katharine Frances – the provost just completed her first year on campus after serving as dean of a prestigious law school in Virginia. She has been sensitive about making radical changes so early in her tenure since her immediate predecessor was a polarizing figure whom the faculty considered a micro-manager.

Roger Venables – the dean of admissions is a veteran administrator with seven years of service to the university. Well-liked and respected on campus, he has put the university on a stable enrollment footing while increasing net tuition revenue.

William Frederick – the vice president for development and alumni affairs just completed his first year after serving his entire career at a Big Ten school, moving up through the ranks at his previous institution to become an associate vice president of development.

James Carroll – the vice president for finance was brought in by the new president in the wake of a number of revelations of financial mismanagement (though not malfeasance) in previous years, revelations which have exacerbated the university's downward fiscal fortunes in the wake of the crash of 2008. Also brought a hefty reputation as a long-rang planner and has in short order cleaned the university's financial house. Credited by the president with averting disaster.

Alice Tooling – the vice president for public affairs is a long-serving administrator (six years) who was hired from the corporate sector by the previous president. Underrated in part because, as one trustee put it, "With a reputation like ours, her job should be pretty easy."

Michelle Dionne – the vice president for student affairs is the longest serving member of the cabinet, having spent her entire career at the university. An alumna of the school, she returned immediately after graduate school and worked her way up to her current position, and has a strong record of skilled crisis management. She is deeply concerned about the impact the present situation will have on student morale, as well as the ability of the accused student to get a fair shake from students on campus, even if cleared of the accusations.

Case

During those restful few weeks between the May 1 enrollment deposit deadline and when preparations for the next admissions cycle begin, admissions deans often disappear from campus for a week or two and re-charge their batteries. For Roger, the admissions dean at Traditional, his late spring sojourn to the shores of Lake Michigan was anything but restful.

The angst centered on an admitted student-athlete who had been much sought after by several Division I schools around the country. The university's volleyball coach described the student not only as a "difference maker" on the court, but as a "role-model student" with high grades in a rigorous high school curriculum. The coach envisaged the student as a future team captain, and a prominent face of the program.

The shell that exploded in Roger's inbox one beautiful May morning was the revelation in the student's hometown paper (quickly picked up by local and regional TV and radio) that the student and two others were the targets of a recent accusation of hazing on a non-scholastic traveling squad, complete with cell-phone photos, and a grainy video thoughtfully posted on YouTube. Roger learned of the news via a text message from his colleague Alice, the university's vice president for public affairs, who happened to be vacationing in New England at the time. (In the age of the smart phone, no university administrator's vacation is sacred.)

Alice offered to call the other members of the university's cabinet, and the president, who was on a fundraising trip to California. The only senior officers remaining on campus were the provost and the chief financial officer. The provost was busy leading a retreat at a nearby state park for her senior staff, while the CFO was buried in budget modeling for the coming academic year. Formulating a first response for the university will be challenging with the leadership scattered to the four winds. It would also be playing with fire to attempt to reach a conclusion about the student's status while the cabinet is, for the most part, away from the campus.

All this might seem excessive, this attention given to one student by the most expensive employees at the institution. But it is exactly the kind of situation that gets attention from supporters of the school, all of them deeply sensitive of the university's Catholic heritage and values, academic reputation, and athletic standing. As the kindly and avuncular president was fond of saying, "If our problems were easy to solve, somebody would have solved them long before they get to me!"

The more immediate challenge is to craft and deliver the university's initial response without giving the appearance of stonewalling or a rush to judgment. Stories making the rounds on the internet never fail to mention that the student will be enrolling at the university in the fall, thus ensuring that in the minds of the public, the university and the student are inextricably wed.

As the morning wears on it becomes increasingly likely that Roger and Alice will have to cut short their vacations.

Within 48 hours the cabinet assembled in the conference room of the president's suite on campus, with the president phoning in from the West Coast. Given how well-equipped the participants are with the latest communication technology, it should come as no surprise that in the two-day run-up to this meeting, calls, texts, emails, and documents were exchanged between the various cabinet members in a complex web of back channel communications reflecting the still-evolving state of the alliances that seem always to be forming and dissolving within the group.

Chairing the meeting, the provost dispenses with all formality and begins with these questions that she has formulated for discussion:

1. What is the university's stand on this student's status at the moment, bearing in mind that due process is a long way from running its course?
2. Assuming the cabinet reaches a consensus on question 1, what form will the university's official communiqués take on the matter?
3. Will these communiqués be crafted toward all the university's publics:
    (a) Current students,
    (b) Faculty and staff,
    (c) Parents/alumni/friends of the university, and
    (d) Prospective/admitted students and their parents?
4. What specific university values can serve as the foundation for the initial response and deliberations toward an eventual action yet to be determined?
5. What contingencies should the university be prepared to face as the process goes forward?
6. How does the university prepare for the possibility that new revelations of a similar character will come to light during the course of the investigation?

When dealing with issues large and small, it is often interesting to see how the different temperaments and backgrounds of university leaders come into play. Each sees the problem from the perspective of their own operations and the collateral damage that may impact their division in one way, while impacting the concerns of another vice president in quite a different way.

Assume in turn each of the cabinet members' roles. Utilizing the brief biographies supplied, how would you advise the president from each individual's perspective?

Chapter 6

Cases in Advising and Counseling

Advisors and counselors on college campus can be thought of as the "parents" of the university. In their professional roles they must deal with matters as mundane as helping a student decide which general electives to take or as profound as whether or not life is worth living. Everyone who works in student affairs will at some point have served as counselor or advisor to a student, no matter how their official job description is worded.

Mental health issues on a study abroad trip create a dilemma and stress for faculty and staff in Teboho Moja's, "Identity Confusion on Study Abroad in South Africa." Diane Cardenas Elliott, in "Just a Friendly Tutor," describes issues the director of an academic resource center faces when she notices that a tutor takes extra interest in his students. An online class presents challenges for an advisor preparing students for the online class environment while working with faculty new to this form of instruction in Kristen Sosulski and Steven Goss's "Supporting Online Learners at Interurban University." A traditional issue on many campuses is nonexistent or poor faculty involvement in student advising. In "Student and Academic Affairs Collaboration on Advising," Kim O'Halloran and Megan Delaney describe a struggle with this issue at a baccalaureate-granting institution. In Daniel Holub's "Same-Sex Domestic Violence Reporting on Campus" an incident of domestic violence at an acting conservatory presents both political and ethical challenges for the dean of students. Finally, in "Conflict of Community" Samantha Shapses Wertheim describes a student's behavioral concerns that impact the campus environment and bring challenges for the student affairs administration.

In these cases consider contrasts with our textbook ideals. Campuses that should be cooperative, developmental, and other-serving sometimes are not so.

IDENTITY CONFUSION ON STUDY ABROAD IN SOUTH AFRICA

Teboho Moja

Setting

Metropolitan University is a private university in Massachusetts that holds global citizenship central to its mission. Study abroad opportunities are offered on all continents and the university has signed numerous agreements with several institutions all over the world. All students are expected to participate in a semester abroad, an internship, or a short-term program held during the summer session or winter break. Preparatory courses are offered on campus and form part of the graduation requirement. Small scholarships are offered, based on student need, to cover student travel costs.

A popular program among university seniors is a four-week program offered in South Africa where students study the political activism that led to the collapse of the former oppressive and discriminatory government system. They visit prisons where political prisoners were held, meet some of the country leaders who were active in dismantling that system, meet security force members who enforced the oppressive system, and listen to presentations by local scholars. They visit schools to learn about how the history of this new country is being re-written and taught in new ways so that there is continued healing and forgiveness. The program is emotionally taxing, given the country's history of past injustices, but it is also uplifting to observe people moving forward together to rebuild their country.

Characters

Henry Kosovo – the director for the study abroad program. He has helped establish many faculty-led programs that take place during the summer and winter breaks each year.

Jane Clarke – the assistant director, assigned responsibility for programs set in Africa. She is responsible for the logistics and financial accounting of those programs.

Professor Thelez – the faculty member leading the summer study abroad program to South Africa. The program has been running for ten years.

Steven Scott and **Robert Tisch** – students on the study abroad program to South Africa.

Aletta Tingo – a security officer at the hotel where students were housed during the study abroad program.

Case

There was general excitement as students gathered in front of the university building, waiting for the bus to take them to the airport. Friends were there to bid them farewell and wish them well on their four-week trip to South Africa. Steven arrived, wearing his summer shorts, an oversized T-shirt, and shoes with laces loosely tied. In one hand he held one piece of luggage, a canvas laundry bag, and in the other, a stack of books to read on the long flight. The books, recommended additional readings, consisted mainly of biographies of some of the country's great leaders. Steven had prepared for the class and trip, working overtime to raise additional funds needed to sponsor the trip. As part of his preparation, he often asked to meet with Professor Thelez to ensure he was on track. He seemed most interested in one black consciousness leader and read almost everything written about him. The books he held were all about that leader who had started a black consciousness movement as a student and was later killed in prison by security forces.

With all on board, the bus travelled to the airport for their flight. During the 15-hour non-stop flight Steven stayed up reading biographies and was too excited to fall asleep, given this was his first trip outside the United States. He was more quiet than usual and was a bit distant from the other students in the group. Upon arrival at the international airport in Johannesburg, the group transferred to a domestic two-hour flight to Cape Town, their final destination. Disembarking after a long journey, all were happy to finally get room assignments and roommates. Steven and Robert were assigned to share a room.

Steven was interested in learning more about the lives of people in South Africa through informal conversations. In class, the professors had discussed and encouraged such conversations as one mode of getting a variety of perspectives on social issues within the country. That evening Steven spent time chatting with Aletta, the woman night security officer at the gate until the early morning hours.

In the morning Robert asked to meet with Professor Thelez. He expressed discomfort with Steven's behavior, and mentioned that Steven brought Aletta, the security lady, to their room and shared his bed that night. He found the behavior disrespectful because Steven had not even asked him for his permission to bring a guest to their room.

The next day the students were given time to recover from the long flight, but were asked to reconvene for an official welcome dinner in the evening.

The dinner was set in a typical African restaurant where communal meals are shared. The students enjoyed the local cuisine meal, but Steven sat at the table quietly and did not partake in the celebration. Later he told Professor Thelez that he had spent the free afternoon in the local village with Aletta, at her home. In sympathy to her family's circumstances, he gave them most of his money to buy groceries and toys for the children.

Professor Thelez felt unprepared for this behavior, and feared that Steven was losing touch with reality and becoming emotionally imbalanced. Faculty on study abroad programs are not trained to diagnose mental illness nor are they oriented on what to do under such circumstances. As such, Professor Thelez called Ms. Clarke in Massachusetts to discuss Steven's behavior. Thelez suggested that it might be better to send Steven back to the United States at this early stage of the program, suspecting that this might be a mental health issue. Ms. Clarke informed Professor Thelez that the same rules that apply on campus in the United States apply overseas during study abroad programs. On campus students are allowed to have guests in their rooms, therefore, students are allowed guests in their rooms on programs overseas as well. The next day Professor Thelez spoke to Steven and made clear to him that out of respect for his roommate he had to consult with him before bringing in overnight guests.

The program continued as planned but other students started feeling uneasy about Steven's behavior. His occasional questions in class became monologues meant to showcase his knowledge and the extra readings he had done about African leaders. It became clearer and clearer that Steven was struggling with an identity issue. In Professor Thelez's experience, it was not uncommon for students during study abroad courses to question their identity as they learn more about themselves. In the South African context, Whites had been perpetrators of the suffering of the Black people in the country, and students often have mixed reactions to this past. Some of the White students visiting the country feel ashamed and worry that the general public does not know that they are visitors and therefore might be mistaken for White South Africans. Black students on the other hand often feel angry about the past injustices and the trip is a visit back home. However, Steven's case seemed extreme, and Professor Thelez suspected that Steven was uncomfortable as a White male and might have a deep wish to be a Black male.

As the trip continued, Steven remained aloof from other students and did not socialize with them. Students raised concerns with Professor Thelez in informal settings about Steven, and Robert reported that Steven's behavior continued to be odd but agreed to continue to share the room with him. Given the other students' reactions, Professor Thelez requested a tele-conference between herself, Ms. Clarke, and Mr. Kosovo. Taking into consideration the sacrifice Steven had made to raise funds to participate in the program, as well as the fact that the program was halfway completed, together they decided to let Steven continue in the program.

In the third week of the program, Steven started to spend more time alone and in the evenings he left the hotel on his own, despite the warnings that for safety reasons students should not go out alone at night. The daily journal entries he wrote for class were becoming increasingly disturbing, written from the perspective of a Black male and reflecting on shady places he had recently visited. Professor Thelez had another meeting with Steven to remind him that he was not supposed to go out at night alone.

Soon after the warning, Thelez received a call from the police reporting that Steven had been mugged, stabbed in his shoulder, and was in hospital. Fortunately the wounds were not deep and he was released that evening. Steven had no money to pay for his treatment so Professor Thelez paid his bill. The following day Thelez reported the incident to the study abroad office and was again told to let him continue with the program. The program ended without any other incidents and the group returned to Massachusetts.

Soon thereafter, Steven was diagnosed with a mental illness that had not been diagnosed prior to his trip. He was provided with psychiatric treatment, and his parents filed a claim against the university for his injury while on the study abroad program. Steven's parents argued that he was not sufficiently protected during the program, and they also argued that his mental illness should have been detected during the trip and that he should have been sent back home before the program was over.

Discussion

1. What should Ms. Clarke have done after receiving the first report from Professor Thelez that Steven's behavior was a bit odd?
2. Should Steven have been sent back after the second call to the university? Or after the teleconference about his disturbing behavior?
3. As Mr. Kosovo, how would you present the university's case in defense against the accusation of negligence?

JUST A FRIENDLY TUTOR

Diane Cardenas Elliott

Setting

Union College (UC) is a regional, state-funded, four-year college located in Unionville, an urban city 20 minutes outside a major metropolitan area. Unionville is a racially diverse working-class neighborhood comprised mostly of recent immigrants from the Caribbean, Central America, and Eastern Europe. Most high school seniors in Unionville go directly into vocational training programs. However, over the past ten years, UC has worked diligently with local community organizations and schools to establish the culture among local parents that college attendance is valued. Consequently, in the past decade enrollment has steadily increased.

UC was originally established as a small teacher's college with a mission of serving the local community. Today UC offers bachelor's degrees in a variety of academic fields including Business, Arts and Sciences, Engineering, Visual and Performing Arts, and Education. It is a moderately selective college that recruits mostly from Unionville's public schools. In fact, the vast majority of UC's 3,000 students are from Unionville.

Many UC students are first-generation students who rely heavily on financial aid and institutional support, particularly in the form of on-campus jobs, to pay their college expenses. As a result, on-campus employment and financial aid are central components of UC's recruitment efforts. However, UC offers no campus housing for students. Most of the students are traditionally aged commuters who continue to reside at home while pursuing studies at UC. As a result, UC has a high transfer rate for upper-class students. A recent institutional research report showed nearly 50% of UC's sophomore class did not return to UC for their junior year. Many students view UC as a good option for completing the first two years of college. Accordingly, the vast majority of course offerings at UC consist of general education requirements and introductory courses with few upper level courses offered. In addition, many UC freshmen struggle with their first year of classes, and about 30% of incoming freshmen are placed into remedial classes.

Characters

Debra Wain is the manager of the Academic Resource Center (ARC). She has worked at UC for eight years and initially began as a part-time employee before being offered a full-time position as the ARC manager.

Paula Concord is a tenured Chemistry faculty member who has worked at UC for over 20 years.

Melanie Gage is the Vice President for Academic Affairs, a position she was appointed to five years ago.

Russell Whipple is a former UC student who majored in Chemistry. He transferred to another local institution, but continues to be an active member of the UC community.

Emily Lan is a freshman student at UC who is majoring in Engineering.

Christie Chong is a sophomore at UC who is majoring in Chemistry.

Mitchell Simpson and **Abby Keyes** are sophomore students majoring in Biology at UC.

Case

The Academic Resource Center (ARC) is a support center where students needing academic assistance can go and receive tutoring. When the ARC was first created, the college hired you (Debra Wain) as a part-time employee, to oversee the center. Since funds were limited, services were offered haphazardly in a single room in the basement of the student union. As a result, academic departments established their own informal tutoring services using advanced students. For the ARC and UC this was problematic because limited funds were scattered across various departments with duplication of services. In addition, UC's high transfer rate resulted in a shortage of advanced students capable of providing tutoring services. Consequently, student tutors were often recruited by both departments and the ARC causing competition over the most qualified tutors.

When Vice President Gage was appointed, she made it a top priority to ensure students received the academic support they needed to be successful. To achieve this goal, she merged all tutoring services into the ARC. Although many academic departments and faculty were not pleased, she assured them they would continue to play a role in the provision of tutoring services. Vice President Gage secured funds to hire you as a full-time manager of the ARC. In addition, the ARC was relocated into a fully renovated space with updated computers, tutoring software, and a tracking system that enabled the ARC to measure student usage.

Together you and Vice President Gage worked to expand services to include all academic fields. To garner faculty support and decrease tension between the ARC and academic departments, you worked hard to ensure that faculty were involved in the selection of student tutors. You actively sought out student tutor recommendations from faculty and altered the tutor application to require at least one letter of recommendation from a faculty member. Further, you overhauled tutor training to include a discipline-specific component during which faculty would meet with new and continuing tutors to discuss content areas students struggled with and tips for helping students be successful.

Last year you received a recommendation for Russell, a Chemistry tutor, from Paula Concord. Russell was a former student who had worked as a tutor in the Chemistry department when he was a student at UC. He had transferred to another institution, but he is an older student who still lives in the area and was interested in working as a tutor at UC. According to Paula, Russell had a solid grasp of the concepts taught in the basic and advanced chemistry courses. In addition, Paula knew Russell had helped many students struggling with Chemistry 101 successfully complete the course. On the basis of Paula's recommendation, you hired Russell in the ARC. Paula was so pleased she gave the ARC access to her chemistry PowerPoint slides, books, and volunteered to help train science tutors.

Although Russell seems very popular with students, over time you have become uncomfortable with some of his behavior around students. In particular, outside of the ARC you have observed him often having lunch and flirting with some of his female tutees. In the ARC, you have noticed he dedicates more time to the female students (even in group settings) and in your opinion sits too close to the female tutees.

Several weeks ago, Emily Lan came to the tutoring center seeking help in Chemistry. When you mentioned that Russell was available for help, Emily indicated that she would prefer to work with someone else. Since no other chemistry tutors were available, Emily left. Last week, Christie Chong came to your office. You know Christie well because she had been a frequent user of the ARC last year. As a freshman, Christie had struggled with Chemistry 101, but had managed to earn a B in the course with Russell's help. Christie mentioned that she was interested in getting tutoring in Chemistry again, but did not want to work with Russell. When you pressed Christie as to why, you learned that Russell had asked Christie out on several occasions. In addition, Christie mentioned Russell had offered her additional free tutoring help at his home. This made Christie very uncomfortable and consequently she did not want to have Russell as a tutor. Unsure what to do, you decided to gather additional information from Russell's other tutees and seek out Emily. Emily indicated Russell had not only asked her out on several occasions, but also frequently put his arm around her and put his hand on her knee. Emily felt very uncomfortable by his behavior and felt it was inappropriate for a tutor.

Based on these accounts, yesterday you called Russell into your office and fired him. Russell was livid and indicated he had never acted inappropriately. He was so enraged that you had to call security to have him escorted out of the ARC. After his dismissal Russell went around the campus talking to students and letting them know he was unjustly terminated. As a result, Mitchell Simpson, along with several other students and former tutees of Russell stormed into your office demanding to know why Russell was let go and advocating for his return. They threatened to stop using the ARC. Today you learned that Abby Keyes has gone to the Office of the President in hopes of meeting with him over Russell's dismissal. In addition, you found out that Mitchell is circulating a petition demanding that Russell be rehired. Throughout the day several students have stopped you in the hallway to let you know what a good tutor Russell is and how he personally helped them be successful students. You also just received an email from Paula Concord asking to meet with you, presumably to discuss Russell's dismissal.

What do you do?

SUPPORTING ONLINE LEARNERS AT INTERURBAN UNIVERSITY

Kristen Sosulski and Steven Goss

Setting

The Adult Learning Division (ALD) at Interurban University (IU) is dedicated to providing an IU education to busy adults who have not had a chance to earn their bachelor's degree. It was apparent that the convenience of online courses would be a good fit for ALD students. Lee Stoppard, Divisional Dean of ALD wanted to ensure that the programs they developed were of the same caliber as the on-site classes. He partnered with the university's Office of Online Education (OOE), to craft a strategy to bring ALD online. By the fall 2011 semester, ALD launched two undergraduate completion programs online: the Bachelor of Arts in Social Sciences and the Bachelor of Science in Leadership and Management. To date, ALD offers close to 50 courses online and a growing set of student services.

Characters

Vang Deng has been the Educational Technologist of the Office of Online Education for two years. He reports to the Director of Online Education.

Kelly Vanna has been the Student Advisor for the Adult Learning Division for over ten years. She reports to the Director of Student Advising.

May Berra is a member of the writing faculty at the Adult Learning Division and she has taught various writing courses for more than 30 years.

Janis Higgins is a 26-year-old undergraduate student in the creative writing major in the Adult Learning Division. She is in her junior year.

Robbie Alvarez has been the full-time help desk technician for the Online Continuing Education Program for five years. He reports to the Associate Director of Online Education.

Lee Stoppard is the Dean of the Adult Learning Division.

Case

Long-time faculty member, May Berra will be teaching an online course in the spring semester entitled "Storytelling and Memoirs." Her course begins in one week. This is the third time in two years Dr. Berra has taught the course in an online format and her confidence in teaching online has grown rapidly. To help her students become acquainted with the online course format and the learning management system used to deliver the course content, she creates a pre-course online activity. May's objective is to develop a sense of class community. May introduces students to the pre-course activity through an email message that she sends all students enrolled in the course. In the email she asks students to introduce themselves to her and the other students in the online course discussion forum.

From: May Berra

Subject: Introduce Yourself

Date: 1/11/2011 6:46:59 PM

There is one thing I would like you to accomplish inside the online learning environment before our first meeting. Please introduce yourselves to each other and to me in the Introduce Yourself forum. Instead of posting a typical "who am I?" introduction, write your post as if you were being asked to write a brief introduction to your memoirs. Your posting should be no more than 200 words and may include any personal information as long as it is appropriate. Also include a small photograph of yourself—a picture that could be appropriate for the dust jacket of your memoirs. All introductions should be completed before our first meeting on Thursday, January 20.

Yours,

Professor Berra

This assignment is always popular among the students and this semester is no different. Professor Berra is pleased to find that all of the students completed their introduction with more than enough time for her to read what everyone has written. In response to the student's postings, Professor Berra sends everyone a personal message, giving feedback and sharing some information about herself. Professor Berra feels this helps to connect her to her students, most of whom are off-campus and at a distance.

She may also ask the students to correct simple mistakes, such as grammar or formatting. This semester, the students appear to be strong writers and, to her relief, technologically savvy. Aside from one student, Janice Higgins, she does not have to send any messages out requiring students to do additional work on their introductions. Janice is an above-average student in her junior year of studies at IU. This is her first course online and she freely admits that she does not spend too much time online, except to answer email.

Janice did not post a photo of herself to the forum. Professor Berra knows uploading images can be challenging for some students, but feels it's an important aspect of the assignment. To make sure students know how to post a photo, she requires that all students attend the asynchronous Online Student Orientation offered by the Office of Online Education at IU. Professor Berra has not heard anything from Janice since her initial posting. In her feedback, Professor Berra reminds Janice to post a photo and directs her to the online student orientation. The orientation course provides clear demonstrations on how to use the learning management system, including how to upload photos.

From: May Berra

Subject: Reflection on your memoirs

Date: 1/19/2011 9:45:40 AM

Hi Janice,

What a great introduction to your memoirs! I'm curious to find out more about this novel you mentioned. Is this something you've been writing for a while and how far along are you? I wanted to mention that you still need to add a picture of yourself to your posting. Do you have one?

Best,

Prof. Berra

PS: You may add an image using the Add Image button. You will also find this information in the student orientation, which I require all students to attend. This is clearly outlined in the course syllabus. If you're having difficulties, you should email Robbie Alvarez, at ralvarez@UNCY.edu or extension 54588. He will help you with your pictures.

Janice sends a reply to Professor Berra, within the same day.

From: Janice Higgins

Subject: RE: Reflection on your memoirs

Date: 1/19/2011 12:34:42 PM

How do I get one into my computer? I tried to upload my image and my computer froze. And I can't run it on my tablet – iPad ARGGGH!

Two days later Dr. Berra responds to the student.

From: May Berra

Subject: RE: RE: Reflection on your memoirs

Date: 1/21/2011 09:38:16 AM

Hi Janice,

Did you figure out how to upload your photo? Remember, the deadline for the student introductions has passed. Also, make sure you review the assigned module for this work week.

Yours,

Prof. Berra

Over the next few days, Professor Berra's course continues on as scheduled. Aside from the absence of Janice's participation in the course, she finds her students to be an active bunch, responding to forum discussions and engaging deeply with the course assignments. She finds herself almost as busy as she was when she first started teaching online. However, she now spends more time interacting with the students than working hard to keep one step ahead of them. At the end of the first week, Professor Berra receives another email from Janice. In the message, Janice explains that she is dropping the course.

From: Janice Higgins

Subject: RE: RE: RE: Reflection on your memoirs

Date: 1/28/2011 01:11:19 AM

Prof. Berra,

Unfortunately, I think I will need to drop your class. Neither my computer or tablet runs the IU online system properly. I must say I'm upset. I really wanted to take this course!

Professor Berra is unsure what else she can do for Janice. She decides that since the student is asking to drop the course she should notify the student's advisor, Kelly Vanna. She sends Kelly a note, along with the student's message that she is thinking of dropping her course.

From: May Berra

Subject: FWD: RE: RE: RE: Reflection on your memoirs

Date: 1/28/2011 04:35:59 PM

Hi Kelly,

See forwarded message from Janice Higgins. Has she tried to contact you? She's thinking about dropping my course. Please let me know what should be done.

Best,

May

Kelly has not heard from Janice since she advised her for the spring semester. She reads her email and wonders why Janice hasn't contacted her.

She also does not understand why she is saying that she is unable to get access to the IU learning management system, since she was able to post her introduction to the course forum. She decides to contact the Educational Technologist, Vang Deng, who manages the student orientation and works closely with the Help Desk, to find out if he knows about the student and what support she received.

From: Kelly Vanna

Subject: Online Student Janice Higgins

Date: 1/29/2011 09:22:12 AM

Hi Vang,

Have you heard from this student? If not, could you contact her and let her know that the Help Desk is able to assist her with the technical issues she's experiencing? It seems strange to me that she is unable to get the IU system to work. Please keep me updated on this.

Thanks,

Kelly

Vang has not heard from Janice. He sends her a message letting her know that her advisor has contacted him and that he and Robbie Alvarez are there to troubleshoot her computer problems and any issues she may be experiencing with the IU Learning Environment.

From: Vang Deng

CC: Kelly Vanna

Subject: Support for your online course, Storytelling and Memoirs

Date: 1/29/2011 012:21:34 PM

Hi Janice,

You should be able to upload a photo using your computer or tablet, but you won't be able to edit the photo on your tablet. The Help Desk Manager, Robbie Alvarez (ralvarez@IU.edu) should be able to help you troubleshoot this issue, just send him an email and let him know when you're free to talk. FYI: older versions of Safari and Internet Explorer are not compatible with the IU Learning Environment.

Vang

Kelly waits for a response from Janice or an update from Vang. She is aware that the longer it takes to get the issue resolved, the more of an impact it will have on the student being able to drop the course and obtain a full refund. By the end of the week she sends Vang an email asking him whether he has heard anything more from Janice. Vang sends a quick response.

From: Vang Deng

Subject: RE: Janice Higgins???

Date: 2/6/2011 09:46:04 AM

Hi Kelly,

I sent several emails to the student, trying to help, but there was no reply.

Vang

The following week, Janice drops the course. She sends a message to the Office of the Dean at IU Continuing Education saying she finds it unfair that she does not get a full refund, because of the technical troubles she experienced. During the review of the case, Dean Stoppard becomes aware of the communication Kelly Vanna and Vang Deng had with the student. He asks that Kelly and Vang get together to figure out what the problem was to begin with and to find a solution for more effective communications in the future. He adds, that he would like their summary before the end of the week.

What would you do if you were Kelly and Vang?

STUDENT AND ACADEMIC AFFAIRS COLLABORATION ON ADVISING

Kim C. O'Halloran and Megan E. Delaney

Setting

Brook State College (BSC), located less than 15 miles from a major city, is one of ten state institutions that serve a suburban metropolitan area. Since it was founded over a hundred years ago as a Normal School to educate teachers, many of its students continue to come to BSC to pursue a teaching career. While the college has several applied doctoral and master's degree programs, the primary enrollment of the institution is baccalaureate programs.

As a result of the rapid increase in the college-going population in the state, undergraduate enrollment has increased by 15% in the last eight years and the college now enrolls 15,000 undergraduate students, 8,000 of whom live on campus. This growing student population and doubling of the number of students who live on campus has presented the entire campus with new challenges. The student body has also become increasingly diverse, and the majority of undergraduates are first-generation college students.

Characters

Susan Mayberry, Ed.D., the Vice President for Student Affairs, recently joined BSC. She was previously Dean of Students at one of the other state institutions and has had a long career as a student services administrator.

John Clinton, Ph.D., is the new Dean of Students, having previously served as a tenured history professor at the college for 15 years. He was hired by the president as the first Dean of Students with a faculty background in hopes that he would help to build partnerships between the faculty and Student Affairs.

Leslie King is the Director of Academic Advising and **Sheila Jimenez** is the Director of Career Services, both of whom report to the Dean of Students.

Christina Kowalski, Ph.D., is an untenured faculty member who teaches in the higher education leadership master's program.

John Anthony, Ph.D., is a tenured biology professor who is also chair of the Faculty Senate and very active in the faculty union.

Case

As Susan Mayberry, you are responsible for oversight of the division of student affairs. When you were hired last year, the president asked that one of your first priorities be to increase the number of partnerships with faculty and the division of academic affairs and specifically, ways to improve academic advising of students.

In a recent meeting with John Clinton, you discussed several issues related to academic advising. A recent report issued by the office of institutional research describes a growing problem with student retention and graduation rates. The college's first to second year retention rate has declined by 20% over the last eight years, which is also the time span where the college has experienced significant enrollment growth. In addition, more students, including an alarming number of first-generation students, are taking close to six years to complete baccalaureate degrees. The office conducted a recent survey of students and concluded that students felt that the academic advising system was cumbersome and did not provide students with the accurate information needed to plan their academic careers. The survey results indicated that professionals in the Academic Advising Office and faculty major advisors were not always as responsive as they could be to students, did not appear to communicate with one another, and often gave students conflicting information. Students were not sure to whom they should go for what type of advising.

John Clinton met with Leslie King regarding the results of the survey. Leslie King, who has been the director of the office for ten years, has struggled with efforts to work with faculty to improve the current advising system. She has indicated that she is frustrated and not sure what can be done realistically to address the student concerns and outcomes.

John Clinton has also brought to you a proposal authored by Sheila Jimenez, Director of Career Services, regarding a potential merger of Academic Advising and Career Services. In her proposal she indicates that she and her staff often engage in academic advising as part of their roles in Career Services. With the economy in a state of downturn, the Career Services Coordinators have seen more students earlier in their academic careers seeking advising regarding what major will help to ensure that they find a job once they graduate. In addition, they have seen an increase in the number of first-generation college students who are experiencing stress in selecting a major that will ensure that they can begin to pay back their student loans after graduation. Sheila proposes that uniting the two offices will allow for a more comprehensive advising approach for students and will reinvigorate the advising function. She states that this is a model that she used with success at her previous institution. John feels that there must be a way to build on Sheila's experience and enthusiasm, especially in light of

Leslie's frustration, but is wary of making such a recommendation without involving faculty.

Last week, you received an email from Christina Kowalski, who would like to start a research project to examine academic advising related to student retention and persistence. Christina had approached Leslie King regarding the project but received no response. She would like to apply for a grant to support this research project but recognizes that she needs support from someone like Leslie in the division of student affairs to be successful.

John Anthony called this morning as he heard the results of the Institutional Research survey at last night's Faculty Senate meeting and is concerned that the faculty voice needs to be included in the discussion about advising. He is especially concerned that any additional responsibilities for faculty in this area will be unrealistic, given expectations for publishing and teaching.

You have a responsibility to develop the plan to address the academic advising issue going forward, and to do so in partnership with the faculty. What do you do?

SAME-SEX DOMESTIC VIOLENCE REPORTING ON CAMPUS

Daniel Holub

Setting

Premiere Conservatory, an acting school located in a metropolitan and artistic hub in the United States, is a magnet to students seeking a practitioner-based curriculum which will present opportunities to work within their field of study. This aggressively paced program allows its students to complete their coursework in three years and receive credit for performance work during their final year. Created 50 years ago as a non-profit institution, Premiere's original founder retains her position as president and sits on the board of trustees with its 11 other members. Enrollment has grown from 150 to 2,000 students under the leadership of its current (and only) president. Premiere has earned its reputation through a faculty of world-renowned stage and screen performers who provide a colorful, albeit non-traditional, pedagogy when training their students in areas ranging from stagecraft to Shakespeare. Premiere's team of student affairs and student services administrators is a small, yet committed group of professionals who have a background in both performance and education.

Given the nature of the field of study and its cohort, Premiere has a large population of gay, lesbian, bisexual, and transgendered students. This GLBT student population gives Premiere high marks for inclusiveness and routinely cites its diversity as a reason for attending the program. Concerned with funding and institutional liability, Premiere's president recently eliminated its sexual/social wellness seminar from their first year student program.

Characters

Roger Marin has been Premiere's Dean of Student Affairs for six years and manages all the counseling needs of its student population. He has a Ph.D. in Higher Education and reports directly to the president.

Greg Baxter is the Director of Public Safety and former Chief of Police in a small community approximately 75 miles outside of Premiere's urban campus. He has been in his current position for 17 years.

Marcus Christie is the Vice President of Student Services.

Stella Proscenium has been the President of Premiere for its entire history and began her career as an actress. She attended a prestigious two-year, visual arts conservatory on the West Coast in her youth. She has no formal training or credentialing in higher education.

Derrick Starr is an acting student who is repeating his second year at Premiere after being expelled for violating the code of student conduct.

Skylar Magen is a senior honors student who has been accepted into a respected master's program in performing arts. He is currently the head of student government.

Case

It is the fifth week of the fall term and Roger Marin has called in Derrick Starr for absentee concerns that have reached the level of academic probation and possible dismissal. During the course of their meeting, Derrick Starr confides in Dean Marin that he has been struggling since his return to the program after being expelled due to personal problems he is having in his residence hall.

After initial query, Dean Marin ascertains that Derrick Starr is making accusations of domestic abuse on the part of his roommate and one-time boyfriend, Skylar Magen. Dean Marin collects information pertaining to this situation in a similar manner to domestic abuse reports that have occurred amongst opposite-sex partners. Their interview lasts for 45 minutes and Derrick Starr shares three separate accounts of abuse; two verbal and one physical event that required a trip to the emergency room. Skylar Magen escorted Derrick Starr on the trip to the emergency room for minor facial lacerations, but no formal charges of abuse were reported.

At this point, Dean Marin contacts Skylar Magen for an initial interview to collect information pertaining to the case. During the course of their meeting, they discuss Skylar's involvement in an upcoming focus group coordinated by the president that deals with the relationship between students and faculty. Dean Marin broaches the subject of Skylar's roommate and the tone of their conversation subtly changes, with Skylar appearing to agitate. As he questions him about the nature of his relationship, he first denies that they were linked socially, but then later he admits that they had had an intimate relationship lasting for over a month. When pressed for details that might lead to information substantiating Derrick Starr's claims, he indicates that they had a very physical relationship, but that all actions were consensual. Skylar asks if anyone other than Derrick made this claim and what proof was presented to substantiate the accusation.

Given the sensitivity of the situation, Dean Marin contacts the Vice President of Student Services, Marcus Christie, and explains that he is dealing with a roommate conflict that warrants an administrative move. Without going into details, he indicates that the roommates are having irreconcilable differences and that it is in the interest of both parties to relocate one or both students. Within 24 hours, both individuals have been moved to single rooms across campus from one another. Following the administrative housing move there are no reports of inappropriate behavior as reported by either student or the residential housing staff.

Confident that any imminent physical threat has been controlled, Dean Marin consults with the school's Director of Public Safety who suggests that the matter be brought to the attention of the school's president. Stella Proscenium is contacted directly by Dean Marin and is given a summary of his conversations with both students. President Proscenium instructs Dean Marin to take no further action until she can consult with her administrative team.

Two weeks have passed and Derrick Starr appears to be doing better academically. However, Derrick is now curious as to the status of the case he reported weeks earlier. Dean Marin assures Derrick that the matter is under investigation and requests a meeting with the President to follow up on the status of her deliberations. President Proscenium acknowledges that she made initial inquiries with her administrative team, but there did not appear to be sufficient evidence to move forward with a formal investigation. The president also alludes to the academic status of the individuals involved in the case and how "out of character" this behavior would be for Mr. Magen.

Later that day Dean Marin runs into his colleagues Marcus Christie and Greg Baxter, Director of Public Safety, both of whom are on the president's administrative team. The three have a brief conversation about data collection for monitoring campus crime statistics. Vice President Christie is not aware that the administrative roommate switch that was done earlier in the month was connected and asks if any further information had been obtained regarding the same-sex domestic abuse case mentioned earlier by the president? Caught off guard, the Dean shares his conversation with President Proscenium who stated that the team did not give the case a complete vetting, given the "nature" of the interactions, indicating, "this may be nothing more than a roommate conflict that got out of hand."

Also unaware of the situation being discussed, Greg Baxter asks for a full report of the alleged incident and states that any reports of violence, domestic or otherwise, have to be part of campus crime statistics, even if the participants remain anonymous. Baxter also points out that as a matter of safety and security of all students, this information should have been reported to campus police immediately so the office can follow trends and respond when appropriate.

Skylar Magen has begun to share the details of his conversation with Dean Marin both on social networking sites and directly with his peers in student government. Although an official inquiry was not made, he is critical of the conservatory for *slandering* him. He is threatening to resign from his student government post and has alluded to getting his parents involved to address any legal matters that may arise.

It is nearly a month after the initial report of same-sex domestic abuse was reported on campus. Derrick Starr is doing well academically and is currently visiting with his counselor on a weekly basis to process recent events related to his roommate. He is also meeting regularly with an academic success support group to better manage his academic life. Derrick has not shared this incident of the conservatory's involvement with his parents, and he is questioning whether he should withdraw his complaint.

Dean Marin contacts the president's office to be placed on the agenda of next week's meeting with the president's administrative team.

Prepare what you would report to the administrative team regarding this case, if you were Dean Marin.

CONFLICT OF COMMUNITY

Samantha Shapses Wertheim

Setting

Lloyd University is a private mid-sized university with an enrollment of 7,000 undergraduate students and a population of 2,000 graduate students. Composed of six academic colleges and four graduate schools, Lloyd University is considered an elite school, attracting students within the top 10% of their class. Due to Lloyd's prestigious reputation it attracts a relatively diverse population of students that come from different locations and life experiences. While Lloyd University traditionally had a larger male to female population, in recent years the university has experienced a surge of female applications and now the student body consists of 43% men and 57% women. Lloyd University sits upon a traditional college campus on the outskirts of a mid-sized metropolitan city.

　　While academics are at the forefront of concern for most students at Lloyd University, the administration seeks to provide a robust social life and is focused on the needs of students both in and outside of the classroom. While the Office of Student Activities serves as a focal point for student engagement and leadership, much of Lloyd's undergraduate campus life for first year students is built upon a residential college system. The residential colleges serve to support community building among students, integrate academics into students' residential lives through a faculty affiliate program, promote interactions between students outside of the classroom, and foster rituals central to the Lloyd University experience. The first year residential colleges have a college director, faculty affiliate and two residential assistants per floor. Approximately 40 students live on each floor, and each building consists of four floors.

Characters

Opal Berger is the College Director of Maple Residential College.

Dash Adams and **Sara Sanchez** serve as residential assistants on the 2nd floor of Maple College.

T.R. Al-Sultan serves as a residential assistant on the 1st floor of Maple College.

Michael Levine is a first year 2nd-floor resident.

Phil Jacobs is the Dean of Residential Life.

Dr. Cathy Ramirez is a psychologist who works at the university health center to provide counseling for students in distress.

Case

While the beginning of the year is always a challenging time for Opal Berger, it is also one of the times that she cherishes working with college students. There is something about the fresh cohort of open-eyed inquisitive students that reminds her why she entered this field in the first place, and motivates her to create a residential college that is open and welcoming for students from all walks of life. Since having completed her master's in Higher Education three years ago, Opal has been interested in how residential colleges serve as support for first year student adjustment to college, particularly for students' mental health concerns. In her past three years as the college director, Opal has noticed that there have been a significant number of students who struggle with mental health within her residential college, and she is considering pursuing her doctoral work on this topic in the future.

While the first week of school is exciting, it is also exhausting. In addition to assisting 160 first year students moving into Maple College, Opal spent the two weeks prior facilitating an intense training for her residential assistants (RAs) as part of Lloyd University's Residential Assistant Training Program. In this two-week period, the RAs have been engaged in workshops on both the logistical aspects of the job, as well as the more complex topics such as student alcoholism, suicide prevention, and emotional intelligence. Needless to say, Opal hopes that there will be no major bumps during the first couple of days of school.

On day 2 of orientation, Opal receives a knock on her office from two very panicky students, Dash Adams and Sara Sanchez who are the RAs on the 2nd floor of Maple College. It seems that during a routine ice-breaker, one of their residents, Michael Levine, revealed to the entire floor that he has "suicidal tendencies." Not knowing exactly how to handle it, Dash and Sara proceeded with the exercise and later informed Michael that they would like to speak with him later. They have come to Opal for advice on how to handle this matter. Opal explains that although this is unsettling, students who are seriously considering suicide usually do not announce their intentions. She suggests that she herself meet with Michael Levine and directs Sara and Dash to send him to her office. Later that night, Michael is sent to see Opal. Michael assures Opal that he is not suicidal and that it was a "joke." When she asks him why he would joke about something like that, he doesn't have an answer. Opal suggests to Michael that maybe he would like to utilize the university counselor, Dr. Cathy Ramirez, but Michael says that he isn't interested in talking to a "shrink." Opal is satisfied that Michael is not suicidal and since Opal cannot force him to attend counseling she writes up her notes from the meeting and makes a mental note to check in with Dash and Sara.

Several weeks go by and nothing with Michael develops further. Sara and Dash tell Opal that he is not a very sociable student, and he has numerous heavy metal posters on his walls. Michael has started to attend their Sunday night floor dinners, and they think that his overall attitude is improving. Since there is no obvious threat, Opal decides to let him adjust to college life on his own. Besides, Opal is left busy with a number of other student issues including a sexual harassment complaint on the 4th floor, and abuses of alcohol throughout the building. She is also currently managing a relationship between two of her RAs who are partners, but do not get along.

One day T.R. Al-Sultan, an RA on the 1st floor, comes to her office with something he says is urgent. T.R. tells Opal that several of his female students have felt that someone has been sneaking into the 1st floor bathroom while they are showering. Although no one has been caught, at least three of his students claim that they turn around and see someone running out the door. The students have no proof that this is occurring. Opal is concerned by this but is at a standstill until they have true confirmation of a sighting. She confers with the Dean of Residence Life, Phil Jacobs, and he assures that her desire to "wait and see" is correct. This continues to go on for two weeks at which point she receives a call from T.R. in a hushed voice claiming that he is standing in front of the bathroom door, and the student voyeur is inside. Opal rushes to the 1st floor, opens the door to the bathroom and discovers that the voyeur is Michael Levine from the 2nd floor.

After several conversations with Michael and Phil Jacobs, Michael discloses that this intrusion is something that he has been practicing for several years and cannot control. He readily admits that he needs help to manage what he considers to be a horrible secret, and that he is willing to get help and desperately wants to stay at school. In a session with Dr. Ramirez, Michael discloses that he was abused as a child until the age of 14.

Meanwhile on the floor, the residents are very upset. The students are unsettled and the community that they have worked hard to build has been threatened. While Dash is sympathetic to Michael, Sara feels violated as a woman on the floor and says that she would like Michael kicked off. Opal is also struggling with her own feelings, as she feels somewhat violated since she lives in an apartment in Maple College as well.

Before Michael goes before the Judicial Committee, which will determine what happens to him, Phil Jacobs asks Opal to write a letter of recommendation for the committee as to how Michael's situation should be handled.

In light of Opal's commitment to supporting students with mental health concerns, her personal feelings of violation, and her responsibility to bring unity to Maple College, what should Opal's letter say? Is there anything that she could have done leading up to the discovery of Michael as a voyeur? Are there any resources or people Opal can consult prior to writing this letter? What should her next steps be in terms of reconciling the community and restoring safety at Maple College?

Chapter 7

Cases on Academic Issues

At first thought, academic issues may seem to fall outside the purview of student affairs. Nevertheless, in many instances student affairs staff must work in partnership with their academic colleagues for the resolution of academic issues. The academic issues presented in this chapter affect a wide range of student affairs professionals.

A plan to go online with remedial mathematics courses raises concerns in "Remediation at Downtown Community College" by Katherine Conway. Conflict arises in Erich Dietrich's "Critical Observation or Voyeurism in Study Abroad?" when study abroad students disagree about a curriculum that allows them not only to study poverty but to see it as well. In "Racial Dynamics in the College Classroom" by Tara Parker and Kathleen Neville, a Dean of Students at a four-year public institution must handle a difficult conflict involving race in a college classroom. Valerie Lundy-Wagner's "Promoting Young Scientists" describes controversy over whether programs to promote learning in science curriculum trump concerns about cost.

Lakshmi Clark-McClendon describes a four-year institution that confronts challenges as it must meet the needs of students with disabilities at study abroad sites in "Accommodating Students with Disabilities in Study Abroad Programs." "Culture Clash: International Student Incident" by Julie Nelson, Florence Hamrick, and Marissa Amos describes students' aggressive behavior toward their teaching assistant as symptomatic of greater campus issues and a young professional gets caught in a web of miscommunication. Finally, in "Transfer Problems at Southeastern Community College," Katherine Conway describes administrators' attempts to deal with difficulties that arise when courses students take do not match future curricula.

In these cases student affairs staff at all levels of practice must consider academic issues in their day-to-day practice.

REMEDIATION AT DOWNTOWN COMMUNITY COLLEGE

Katherine M. Conway

Setting

Downtown Community College is located in a large urban metropolis in the western United States. Founded in the mid-1970s, Downtown's student population has grown exponentially in the last three decades, mirroring the growth of the city in which it is located. It is one of 98 community colleges that operate as part of the Western State university system, which also includes state colleges and university campuses. Community colleges in Western State, like Downtown, are open admission to any state resident, 18 years of age or older, with a high school diploma or a general equivalency diploma (GED). The state colleges are more restrictive, and base their admission on a combination of high school grades and test scores. In addition, students are required to submit scores from the statewide proficiency exams in Math and English, which are taken in the 11th grade. The university campuses in Western State are even more competitive, rivaling Ivy League colleges in their degree of selectivity. The result is that the community colleges admit students who are the least prepared for college.

Downtown enrolls slightly more than 20,000 students, most attending part-time. Downtown is one of the most diverse colleges in the country with a student population that self-identifies as 41% Hispanic, 24% Asian/Pacific Islander, 19% White, 12% Black, and 4% other. Slightly more than half the student body speaks English as a second language. Almost two-thirds of the students are female and the average age is 29. Students enroll at Downtown with a variety of goals: one-third hope to transfer to a state college or university, one-third enroll in a vocational program, and the remainder seek basic skills or are unsure of their future plans. Fewer than 5% of students arrive at Downtown with college-level Math skills and fewer than 10% arrive with college-level English skills. Last semester, developmental courses (remedial with no credit) accounted for 28% of all sections offered in the college.

Characters

Joanne Arredondo, Director of the Developmental Skills Department, faculty member for 21 years.

Roberto Montoya, student, age 19, born in Western State; his parents are Mexican immigrants. He was raised in the city's Los Perro district, which is predominately Spanish speaking.

Claire Hachey, Associate Professor of Math, faculty member for five years (currently tenure is granted after seven years).

Richard Eggers, Chair of the Math Department, faculty member for 27 years.

Rifat Palit, Assistant Professor of Developmental Skills, faculty member for one year. Professor Palit worked as an adjunct in the department while finishing up her doctorate, and also taught in a high school while earning her master's; both degrees are in Teaching English as a Second Language (ESL).

Howon Kim Yuh, student, age 22. Received high school diploma in Korea and began taking college classes there before emigrating to the United States last year. Howon is enrolled full-time at Uptown Community, another community college in the Western State system.

Case

As Joanne Arredondo, Director of Developmental Skills, you work hard to help students achieve college readiness. Downtown, like other open admissions institutions, has successfully provided access to higher education for thousands of students who might not otherwise have had the opportunity to attend college. You have to advocate often and loudly that the college's mission to provide access requires the availability of developmental course work. Unfortunately however, Downtown, like many of its peers, is under criticism because so few students graduate, a problem many correlate with the low level of English and math skills of entering students.

Given the diversity of the local population and Downtown's mission to provide access, the college offers a range of remedial or developmental classes, from basic skills to pre-college. In Math there are four levels, in English there are three levels and in ESL there are six levels of developmental courses. More than half of Downtown's students enter the college needing developmental courses at the most basic level. A student, entering with the lowest skill set in all three areas, could hypothetically enroll full-time for three semesters before successfully completing all remedial course work. However, financial aid requirements mandate that students make progress in a combination of developmental and college-level (credit-bearing) courses, earning at least six credits a semester. As a result, students remain in developmental level courses for four, five, or even six semesters.

Roberto Montoya is a typical Downtown student, who graduated, barely, from Central High, and upon admittance to Downtown Community College was placed in developmental courses in Math, Reading, English and ESL. Roberto balked at being placed into ESL classes but his scores were so poor on the proficiency exam, there was no alternative. Even though he was born in the United States, his high school work was sub-standard and because Spanish was primarily spoken at home, his English, both spoken and written, is fraught with grammatical mistakes. In his second semester at Downtown, Roberto is still taking developmental courses, but for financial aid purposes enrolled in six credits of "real" or college-level work. Unfortunately there were no courses for which he satisfied the necessary prerequisites in his major, Business Administration. He ended up taking an art class (in addition to the one he took in his first semester), plus a course in typing and health education, in order to achieve the necessary six credit hours. Roberto is discouraged that after a year in college he will only have earned two "real credits" toward his degree. He is unaware that he is also spending his financial aid on a lot of developmental coursework which may make him ineligible for additional aid in the future, if and when he transfers to a baccalaureate program. Spending financial aid dollars on developmental coursework is a difficult problem to measure, since so few developmental students make it to the baccalaureate level. Because so few developmental students persist into the second semester for college, re-enrolling in the spring makes Roberto unusual, though the odds of his completing a degree at Downtown are not good.

For the last five years, fall-to-spring persistence at Downtown has hovered around 55%. Persistence varies greatly depending on the student's background. Students who received a high school diploma outside the United States are most likely to enroll in their second semester, followed by U.S. high school graduates and then GED holders. Students who already have a college degree are least likely to re-enroll. You suspect that the latter group enrolls in courses for a very specific reason, such as improvement of English language skills, or to gain an understanding of business terminology. Once the short-term goal is accomplished, these students don't re-enroll. Six-year graduation and transfer rates hover in the high teens.

Since your department does not offer a degree, you think little about graduation, and only since becoming chair of Developmental Skills three years ago did you even start attending the graduation ceremony. Your department offers courses in ESL as well as Critical Reading. Developmental courses are also offered in the English and Math departments. Twenty years ago, prior to completing your doctorate (an Ed.D. in Teaching English as a Second Language), and joining the faculty at Downtown, you taught high school English. A background in high school teaching is not uncommon among the members of your department. The Developmental Skills faculty members teach only developmental or non-credit bearing classes, though there is resentment that ESL courses are sometimes referred to as remedial.

You try to educate faculty outside the department that learning English as a Second Language is analogous to U.S. students studying French in college but to no avail. By comparison, the English and Math department faculty are more likely to hold a Ph.D. in their discipline and to have joined Downtown directly from graduate school. Most English and Math faculty dislike teaching developmental-level courses and prefer to teach electives related to their graduate studies and current research. Not surprisingly, a greater proportion of the developmental classes in the Math and English departments are taught by adjunct faculty.

At a recent college-wide Personnel and Budget meeting it was announced that the Math department would be piloting a new program to teach some developmental Math classes online. The project, which is partly grant-funded, will be managed by Professor Hachey, a highly regarded young faculty member, who oversees the Math department's remedial courses. You are not a fan of online learning, and didn't think Richard Eggers, chair of the Math department, was a supporter either. This announcement has caught you off guard, and you wonder what the implications are for your department. After the meeting you pull Professor Eggers aside and ask about the program. He is non-committal, saying that the administration wants to reduce the expenditures associated with offering developmental classes, and that Professor Hachey was willing to pursue the grant so he basically plans to "stay out of the way." He also mentions that he is a few short years away from retirement, and that he never would have believed how the college's academic standards have slipped since he started at Downtown. "When I first got to Downtown we only offered one pre-college course, now developmental courses dominate our offerings. If I wanted to teach arithmetic, I'd be in a high school!" You bristle a bit at his comments about high school teaching, but you say nothing and walk away.

On Wednesday at your departmental meeting, Professor Palit asks about the Step Up program. You are unfamiliar with Step Up, but another faculty member states that it is a program recently started by the college to offer developmental coursework in a concentrated time frame to students at a lower cost than the college's tuition rate. Students might enroll in Level 1 ESL for 5 hours a day, 5 days a week for 3 weeks or 75 hours, at a cost of $250. By comparison, Level 1 ESL is offered by your department as a 0-credit, 6-hour course over a 14-week semester, for a total of 84 hours, and an equivalent cost of approximately $700. What follows is a very animated discussion among your colleagues who suggest that the college is trying to take ESL out of the curriculum, and that their department and thus their jobs might be at risk. Professor Palit is particularly concerned and meets with you afterwards. "Joanne, as you know I chose Downtown instead of one of several high schools that offered me a position. I am happy with my choice but worry that the future of ESL in community colleges is in jeopardy and that without tenure

I am at risk. I could still move to a high school, but would prefer to stay here. I don't however want to make that transition five years from now. If we are headed in that direction, I might as well start on the high school tenure track as soon as possible." You tell Professor Palit that you plan to find out more about Step Up and that when you do, you will let her know.

You call a colleague at Uptown Community College and ask her if she has heard anything about Step Up. In fact, she knows all about it, because the program was piloted at her college and the results have been pretty good. Students who completed Step Up enrolled in credit-bearing courses the following semester and 87% of them finished the semester successfully. The bad news is that Step Up is taught by adjunct faculty in the Continuing Education department. The results sound impressive, but as you note the sample size is very small, and the students have to be willing to commit to attending full-time, a real problem for many of your working students. On the Uptown Community College website you find more information about Step Up, including a profile of a successful "grad," Howon Kim Yuh.

You have to get back to your faculty with an update on Step Up and you have to write your department's annual report which includes future goals. You need to know that the readers of the report include your faculty members, as well as members of the Presidents' Cabinet, who include the Vice President for Academic Affairs and the Vice President for Planning and Administration, as well as the Dean of Continuing Education.

What will you write in your report?

CRITICAL OBSERVATION OR VOYEURISM IN STUDY ABROAD?

Erich Dietrich

Characters

Vincent Carter – Director of the Office of International Programs (OIP) at Braxton University. Vincent began working as OIP assistant director five years ago and was recently promoted into his position.

Andrew Blake – OIP assistant director, began working at OIP one year ago after earning his master's degree.

Professor Sandra Emory – faculty director of the study abroad trip to Brazil. Emory is a respected sociologist whose expertise is on poverty and urban development, although up to now her research has focused on the United States.

Wendy Stone, Ronaldo Garcia, and **Sandra Knowles** – Braxton student participants in the study abroad course.

James Banry – Dean of Students, has been dean at Braxton for seven years.

Case

Braxton University is located in an urban setting in the Northeast United States. As part of a commitment to internationalization, it has developed several short-term (two- to three-week) study abroad programs serving undergraduate students. To encourage participation and underscore the university's commitment to the endeavor, many students receive partial scholarships, paid from the university's budget, to subsidize their participation. You are Vincent, the Director of the Office of International Programs.

Various faculty members propose the courses and then teach them abroad during the university's January session ("J-Term"). OIP provides logistical, financial, and student services support for these courses. This year, one of the faculty-led programs will take place in Rio de Janeiro, Brazil, examining issues of poverty in urban settings. Professor Emory is excited to incorporate a comparative international perspective in her teaching and research, which is another goal of the university's internationalization plan.

Students from several different majors, ranging from history and chemistry to African American studies and ecology registered for the course, and represent a diverse cross-section of the city's urban population. During the fall semester, the class meets four times to prepare for the course by completing background readings and developing group research projects.

It is November, and the final itineraries for all J-Term Abroad courses are due to your office for final budget approval and other checks—for health and safety, insurance, and ensuring that the course design is in line with student learning outcomes. Andrew Blake is assigned to support the Brazil course, and he will be traveling with the group as a program assistant for the professor. He comes to your office early on a Wednesday morning to tell you he thinks there is a problem with the course.

Last Monday, Professor Emory and Andrew sat down to review the final itinerary for the course. Activities on every day of the two-week course are carefully planned (including weekends because safety is a concern for this group of undergraduate students). Most days are devoted to site visits: at universities for guest faculty lectures, to nongovernmental organizations doing community organizing and education work, to government ministries overseeing policy, or to cultural events as co-curricular activities. But one day is wide open because a guest speaker just cancelled. Professor Emory thinks it is too late to line up a new speaker with expertise on the topic, and she thinks it would be a good idea, anyway, to try to mix up the formula a bit and find something more exciting than another lecture. A Brazilian colleague of hers, who is also a professor of Latin American studies, suggested a "favela" tour. The students have been reading about the favelas, Rio's infamously large (and sometimes dangerous) slums, where a huge number of the city's poor people live in homes they constructed themselves, often one makeshift brick structure right on top of another. Professor Emory admits she doesn't really know anything about the favelas or what the tour would be like, but since the course is focused on poverty and urban development, she thinks this is a good activity to include on the open day.

Professor Emory asked Andrew to discuss this idea at the next group session the following day. She couldn't make it herself because of a faculty meeting, but Andrew welcomed the opportunity to lead the class session alone, excited that Professor Emory showed confidence in his ability to guide discussion.

The next day, Andrew went to class eager to see the students, and the class session commenced with its usual upbeat mood in talking about studying in sunny, warm Brazil in January! After about half an hour, Andrew brought up the topic of the favela tour as the class talked through the daily itinerary. Wendy Stone, a junior political science major, raised her hand. "I read about the favelas in a Latin American studies class," she said, "and we learned that the whole travel in Brazil industry exploits them just to make money. I for one don't want to walk into people's neighborhoods and gawk at their poverty. Why don't we just drive over to East Baltimore and start staring at people?!"

Ronaldo Garcia, a sophomore history major, jumped in and said, "My parents are from Argentina, and they traveled a lot in Brazil. They've told me that the favelas are super-dangerous. But I want to see them. What's the use of going to Brazil and studying poverty if we're just going to stay in rich areas and avoid poor people?"

At this point the students started talking excitedly with each other, and Andrew felt like he was losing control. He called the students to order and began to say that he would bring the issue up with Professor Emory, but he was interrupted by Sandra Knowles, a senior chemistry major and president of the Students for Social Justice Association: "I would like to ask you something, Mr. Blake. How do you feel, as a Black man, taking a group of students to a predominantly black favela to exploit their misery for our learning? And how do you think that might be different for Professor Emory, as a white woman?" As Andrew paused to formulate his answer, another student chimed in, "That's an unfair question! Maybe we should think about how we can help the residents of the favelas rather than just thinking only about ourselves and our feelings. How selfish!" A fifth student yelled out, "Why is the university spending money on a tour company that is profiting off of poor people?" The class fell back into chaos.

Later that evening, Andrew and Professor Emory opened three different emails addressed to both of them. One was from Professor Emory's colleague who had suggested the tour, providing contact information on the tour company and an article he wrote on the Brazilian government's recent attempts to reduce poverty and crime in the favelas. He is glad, he says, that the group will be able to see the favelas first-hand because that's really the only way to understand the situation fully. The second was from student Wendy Stone, who had organized a group of students objecting to the favela tour and threatening to drop out of the study abroad course. The third was from the dean of students, forwarding two emails from parents worried about the safety of their children.

While Andrew sits in your office, your boss Michelle Dean, the Vice President for Academic Affairs telephones. She got wind of the controversy, and wants to know whether you're going to approve the favela tour, and what you're going to tell the students and parents.

RACIAL DYNAMICS IN THE COLLEGE CLASSROOM

Tara L. Parker and Kathleen M. Neville

Setting

Remington State University (RSU) is located within an urban environment in the Northeast. Founded as a Normal School in 1868, RSU serves as the educational and cultural center for the greater community and region. Campus grounds are located within an affluent and politically influential neighborhood and, like many communities in the Northeast, the city itself is residentially segregated and racially isolated.

RSU is a predominantly White institution. Approximately 7,000 undergraduates and 3,000 graduate students are enrolled at the institution. Of the undergraduate students, 18% self-identify as students of color and 6% of the graduate students do the same. According to the department of Human Resources, of the 356 full-time faculty members and 327 part-time instructors, only 29 (4.2%) identify as individuals of color. These faculty members comprise: 16 Asian American/Pacific Islanders, 7 African Americans, 5 Hispanics, and 1 Native American. In addition, there are 12 international faculty members who represent various nationalities.

In an effort to prepare for the changing demographics of students attending college and universities, campus leaders have engaged in conversations regarding increasing the enrollment, retention, and success of students of color during the next five to ten years. Conversations regarding increasing the recruitment and retention of faculty of color have also been at the forefront of these conversations. Both of these goals are prominent in the first draft of a new strategic plan for the university.

Characters

Dean of Students

Marabel Conroy – 22-year-old student, junior, White.

Janelle Taylor, Ph.D. – Assistant Professor of History, tenure-track, African American.

Timothy Anderson, Ph.D. – Dean of Arts and Sciences, White.

Jo Jo Jamison – full professor, tenured, African American. Also serves as chair of Multicultural Affairs and Diversity Committee.

Case

Assistant Professor Janelle Taylor is in her third year at RSU, teaching undergraduate students in the history department. Her research interests include the influence of slavery during the revolutionary war, constitutional government, and civil rights. As a tenure-track faculty member, she is teaching four (3-credit) courses and recently submitted her dossier for her third year faculty review. She is currently working on two new articles for publication, serving on the university's Multicultural Affairs and Diversity Committee, and advising the African American Student Association. This semester, Dr. Taylor is teaching a new elective entitled, "The influence of the Civil Rights movement in the United States."

You are the Dean of Students and on a Tuesday in mid-October Dr. Timothy Anderson, Dean of Arts and Sciences, called you to report that Dr. Taylor filed a complaint against a student and he needs your advice on how to proceed. According to the Dean, Dr. Taylor was concerned about disrespectful and disruptive behavior by some of the students in her class, particularly Marabel Conroy. He explained further, "I do not get many complaints about students so I was surprised by Janelle's complaint. She said it had been going on for a while." While you were on the phone with Dean Anderson, you could tell he was quite upset by this complaint. He went on to say that he knew the student, because she was a "wonderful work-study student" in his office, and he had planned to talk with her to get her side of the story. He said he would call you back so the two of you could strategize on what to do next.

The next day, Dean Anderson called you again. He was quite expressive as he told you that he had talked with the student, Marabel Conroy. Ms. Conroy informed him that she feels alienated in Professor Taylor's classroom. "According to Ms. Conroy," Dean Anderson lowered his voice, "Dr. Taylor favors the colored students in the classroom. She also said that during class discussions she feels that all white people are being called racist so she is not comfortable expressing her views and opinions in class." Dean Anderson also stated the student complained about a "very disturbing and condescending email" that Dr. Taylor sent to the class regarding classroom behavior. Dean Anderson said the student was very upset that Dr. Taylor would send an email to the class "scolding them" and "addressing them as if they are children." Dean Anderson tells you that he is concerned this student is feeling uncomfortable in the classroom and he does not know how to proceed, as there are no policies or standard procedures within Academic Affairs for how to handle this type of issue. Further, the student code of conduct does not include policies for what has been reported to date. You therefore offer to meet with Dr. Taylor and inquire about her (and the student's) concerns.

You meet with Dr. Taylor on Thursday of the same week. Reportedly, the student was often late for class and she was constantly texting and talking to those sitting nearby her. The student's behavior had also become increasingly disruptive. During your meeting with Dr. Taylor she said, "Lately Marabel has been getting up out of her seat, nearly every class, to leave for a few minutes or throw things into the trashcan during lectures." Dr. Taylor also stated that during the previous week she distributed a pop quiz in class and "Ms. Conroy shouted out, 'This is not fair!'" Dr. Taylor also stated she observed Ms. Conroy leaning over to her friend and rolling her eyes as she whispered, "What a bitch." Per your request, Dr. Taylor also brought a copy of the email she had sent to the class. The email stated:

> Dear Class,
>
> I am writing to formally address the inappropriate behavior many of you have exhibited in the classroom. I find the constant texting, talking, and note passing to be disruptive and disrespectful. In the future I expect you will turn off your phone prior to class and you will refrain from small talk. If I feel your behavior continues to be disruptive, I will ask you to leave the classroom.
>
> Sincerely,
>
> Janelle

Dr. Taylor also pointed out that she reviewed her cell phone policy on the first day of class. As of late, however, the texting and talking was "getting out of hand." According to Dr. Taylor, since this email was sent, Marabel was now blatantly texting on her phone during class. Dr. Taylor indicated that she originally had no intention of bringing this student's behavior to Dr. Anderson's attention because, although this type of behavior is frustrating, it is also "quite common." Marabel's behavior, however, seemed to be escalating so Dr. Taylor turned to her dean for support. She is unclear as to why you called her into your office; "I reported this to my dean. I haven't heard from him so I am surprised that you asked to meet with me. Have you already spoken to Marabel? What are you planning to do?"

That afternoon, your friend and colleague, Jo Jo Jamison, Chair of the Multicultural Affairs and Diversity Committee stops by your office. "I hope you are going to do something about these students who seem to have no respect for Black female faculty in the classroom." You explain to Dr. Jamison that you are investigating the situation but that it is more complicated than what she understands. You explain to her that the student is also complaining about Dr. Taylor. "Apparently, the student is saying that Janelle does not treat White students fairly!" Jo Jo tells you that it is your duty to address this student's behavior "as faculty of color must often teach to a class that is predominantly White. And some of these kids can't handle that. They are not used to seeing a person of color in authority. Just think about how many stereotypes they probably conjure up in their heads! There are very few faculty of color on this campus so I'm sure they think we are unqualified and have no business teaching them." Since there have been no policies in place to address such issues prior to this, Jo Jo is hoping that you will help to give faculty of color a voice by taking Dr. Taylor's complaint seriously.

On Friday, you call Dean Anderson to tell him about your conversation with Dr. Taylor. You explain to him that she said she was having ongoing issues with Ms. Conroy in the classroom and that the situation seemed to be getting worse. In a frustrated tone the Dean says to you, "I just don't know what to do here. This is a classic she-said/she-said situation. Personally I don't understand why Janelle would send out such an email to her class and not talk to them directly about their behavior. I am very concerned she is not clearly articulating her expectations of students in the classroom." He adds that the student "has always shown herself to be a lovely young woman" and he previously had her in class and "never had a problem with her behavior." Upon further conversation with Dean Anderson it becomes quite apparent that he is more concerned with the actions of Dr. Taylor than he is with the behavior of the student. Meanwhile, Dr. Taylor is waiting to know how her initial complaint against the student will be handled.

What do you do? Who else do you involve in this case?

PROMOTING YOUNG SCIENTISTS

Valerie Lundy-Wagner

Setting

Budding Scientists University (BSU) is one of the oldest private technical schools in the country. It primarily serves students in the surrounding large metropolitan area, with most students coming from the within two hours of campus. BSU offers only a bachelor's and master's of science or engineering, and has a few doctoral degree programs in related fields. Approximately 12,000 students are enrolled, 85% undergraduates in traditional (90%) and continuing education (10%) in Bachelor of Science or Engineering degree programs. The four largest fields of study among undergraduates are: Computer Science, Electrical Engineering, Biology, and Biomedical Engineering. Given the institution's location in an urban center, part of the curriculum includes summer internships and/or co-op opportunities that provide students with practical experiences to complement their academic coursework. This exposure to work experience as an undergraduate is often touted as a major factor for BSU's high employment rates for graduates.

Given the nature of BSU's degree-program emphasis on science, technology, engineering, and mathematics (STEM) fields, numerous strategies have been employed to expand STEM access from the application process through matriculation, for women, historically underrepresented minority students, and low-income students. While there are still large differences in representation at BSU by gender (70% of undergraduates are male), ethnicity/race (White and Asian students comprise 70% of undergraduates), and the proportion of low-income undergraduates receiving Pell grants is up to 13% (from 6% ten years ago), the primary administrative focus is on improving graduation rates. For all full-time undergraduates, the five-year graduation rate is approximately 70%; however, this rate ranges from a low of 40% for African American and Native American/Alaskan Natives, 40% for Latina/os, 70% for White, and 80% for Asian students.

Characters

Cindy Chen is the Associate Dean of Academic Affairs, spending most time of her time focused on curriculum and accreditation issues.

Carmen Gutierrez, Ed.D., has been the Associate Dean of Student Services for the past two years. She reports to the Dean of Student Services and Activities.

Dr. Arunja Singh is the BSU president and has held this position for 12 years. Prior to this, Dr. Singh held a distinguished chair and faculty position in the Electrical Engineering department at a large public research university.

James Pierce is a senior policy analyst in the Institutional Research office and has worked in that department for seven years, focusing on retention-related interventions.

Jermaine McDonald is a 19-year-old sophomore undergraduate student, majoring in Computer Science; he is from the neighboring community and leads a tutoring program at his alma mater.

Renisha Flores is a 25-year-old undergraduate with junior standing, majoring in Biomedical Engineering; she is also the Vice President of the Engineering Honor Society, Tau Beta Pi.

Donna Bradshaw is the manager in the Registrar's Office.

Case

As Carmen Gutierrez, you are responsible for the suite of services available to students that will promote social and academic engagement and involvement. Among that milieu you include diversity-related initiatives to promote persistence to degree completion for all students, although most of your attention is on undergraduates. Services to historically underrepresented groups are open to all students (i.e., supplemental tutoring, advising, and mentoring), but you have directed your staff to recruit students that qualify based on past academic performance, socio-demographic characteristics, and high school quality. You work closely with the Academic Affairs staff for accreditation-related inquiries or grant proposal applications.

During your first few years at BSU, Dr. Singh sent directives to all departments to improve their attention to STEM access. In response, you focused on working with admissions to recruit historically underrepresented students, with the registrar to enroll Center for Academic Excellence students with shared schedules, and with financial aid to advocate for more need-based scholarship and grant opportunities. These particular initiatives have been helpful in improving the proportion of African American, Native American and Latina/o students at BSU. Annual student surveys for the past five years show high levels of satisfaction in terms of the support services available, making you well-known on campus as an effective advocate and manager.

However, during the establishment of these programs, Dr. Singh added to the directive attention to graduation rates. Coming directly from the BSU Trustees, improved graduation rates for students considered "at risk" has been considered a goal for all programs and departments. The Faculty Senate is also supportive of this initiative, although their perspective often pits diversity and quality of incoming students against one another. That is, in their view, students with better standardized test scores, high school GPAs, and exposure to college-level courses (e.g., Advanced Placement) are more likely to persist in STEM degree programs and complete their bachelor's degrees within a timely manner (i.e., six years). The Faculty Senate does include dissenters, primarily the tenured faculty of color and older faculty members who have worked at BSU for more than 30 years.

Despite the contemporary perception that STEM access and success is reserved for only the most academically privileged students, the more seasoned faculty at BSU have a different sentiment. In fact, up until the mid-to-late twentieth century, students entering many STEM fields were largely lower-income students with decent grades and few resources (e.g., human and social capital). These primarily male students were often first-generation college students who understood the job security that came with fields like engineering. Although many current faculty members do not believe this scenario from a time when student quality was relatively non-competitive, James Pierce has been able to collect and analyze institutional data over the past few years to address this issue. Contrary to the current beliefs, Mr. Pierce was able to decipher that indeed, many of the students entering BSU between the 1940s and mid-1970s had relatively low high school grade point averages and composite standardized test scores, and little exposure to higher level math and science courses.

In recent years, active students like Jermaine McDonald, a second year Computer Science major, have forced BSU to re-evaluate and re-assess the typical tension between diversity initiatives and promoting student success. Besides staging sit-ins, rallies, and other protests at Dr. Gutierrez's office, Jermaine has been in discussions with staff in student services, faculty allies, the registrar, Donna Bradshaw, and the Institutional Research office to better understand where students fail to persist.

Given the challenges with obtaining institutional data, Jermaine has used anecdotal evidence and information from informal conversations, concluding independently that persistence rates were higher in the 1980s when undergraduates were allowed two "free summer courses." Not technically free summer courses, Jermaine surmised that BSU charged students full tuition for their first and second year. Those students who earned math (e.g., pre-Calculus/Calculus) or science (e.g., Biology, Chemistry, or Physics) grades below a "B," and were otherwise in good standing with the registrar were allowed to re-take one course. Though typically on the side of quality over diversity, Renisha Flores, the Vice President of the Engineering Honor Society recently teamed up with Jermaine based on her uncle's enrollment experience at BSU in the mid-1980s. In fact, he recalls having taken Physics 2 for "free" after his second year at BSU, an opportunity he suggests allowed him to firmly establish himself in preparation for more challenging Civil Engineering courses. With the coalition between all students – those for diversity and those for increased graduation rates – rumors have spread throughout BSU's student body, faculty, and Trustees about these "free summer courses."

The increased attention to the so-called "free summer courses" instigated a meeting between President Singh, Dr. Gutierrez, Cindy Chen, the Associate Dean of Academic Affairs, and James Pierce, as well as the Provost and a few other senior level administrators. The meeting is planned for next Thursday, and all parties are hoping to obtain data from James and Donna to learn more about this so-called "free summer course" policy, and how to proceed. The Trustees are especially sensitive to the outcomes of this meeting, given that it is recruitment season for the upcoming fall class. In addition, BSU launched a moderately sized development campaign two months ago primarily to support student achievement and faculty through facilities upgrades. Student unrest about the issue has infiltrated the local newspapers and national higher education outlets (in print and online), posing only a small nuisance at this point.

As you prepare for the meeting on Thursday morning, Dr. Gutierrez calls you frantically about an op-ed in the *New York Times* where BSU is highlighted. During the conversation, she mentions that it's related to the so-called "free summer course" policy, and essentially claims that BSU is the type of institutions that is "overly concerned with exclusion and elitism" that is contrary to expanding the STEM pipeline. The author also mentions BSU (and other institutions) as "repulsed by anything that smells like remediation," even if it would promote access to and success in STEM fields. Local businesses chime in to local news media suggesting that "schools like BSU" are not playing their role in promoting STEM success, forcing the recruitment of graduates from outside the metropolitan area and state. Dr. Gutierrez wants a full report from you at Thursday's meeting.

Given the increasingly poor preparation high school students are receiving in math and science, the stagnant graduation rates between students from higher- and lower-income and ethnic/racial groups, and the apparent reality of this "free summer course" policy that quietly ended 15 years ago, what do you do, as Cindy Chen? How do you determine whether or not this free summer course policy can be reinstituted? What kind of data would be helpful? How, if at all, will the controversy affect admissions recruitment from local and regional high schools? What will either decision mean for publicity?

If you reinstitute the policy, how will it affect the curriculum and accreditation? Does reinstituting the policy adversely affect BSU's ranking? Should your office collaborate with Carmen's office, why or why not? And how?

ACCOMMODATING STUDENTS WITH DISABILITIES IN STUDY ABROAD PROGRAMS

Lakshmi Clark-McClendon

Setting

Spence University (SU) is a large, private institution located in a densely populated, metropolitan city on the West Coast of the United States. While the central campus area is located in a residential and business area known for its vibrant student life, arts, and cultural activities, the university has campus buildings throughout the city. It has a mid-sized population, having enrolled a combined total of 16,812 students during the fall 2010 semester.

In addition to the central campus, the university has six study abroad sites. The university also has partnership and exchange programs with several international institutions.

Characters

Nellie Mann is the Director of Global Academic Services and Supports.

Sal Hammond is the Assistant Director of the Disability Resource Center.

Heather Murphy is the Assistant Director of Academic Programs, Faculty of Arts and Sciences.

Brett Claremont is the Senior Campus Counselor at SU Sydney.

Bruce Drummond is the Director at SU Sydney.

Marco Brunelli is the Assistant Director for Academic Support at SU Milan.

Candace Rutger is the Director of Student Life at SU Milan.

Margo Turner is the Programming Coordinator at SU Milan.

Margaret Cloud is a SU Milan student.

James Pierce is a Law student at SU Tokyo College.

Caroline Radcliff is the Administrative Manager at SU Tokyo College.

Case

You, Nellie Mann, are the Director of Global Academic Services and Supports. In this position, you manage the academic programming of SU's ten academic centers and determine exchange policies and practices of visiting students and SU students who study abroad at host universities. You are also on SU's Expansion Initiate Taskforce, a committee charged with carrying out SU's global plans, a top priority of the university president. SU currently ranks fifth highest in the percentage of students studying abroad. The president hopes that at least 50% of the student population will study abroad during their academic career and would also like to increase the university's ranking. He has charged you and other staff with promoting study abroad to the student population. Your role requires that you also look to develop new study abroad programs, within SU and in partnership with international universities.

You have been in your current position for two years. In that short amount of time, you recognize that the study abroad demographic is shifting slightly. Although the majority are undergraduate students, and primarily Caucasian and female, a more diverse population has studied abroad or sought information about studying abroad in the past two years. Your research shows that more students of color are applying to SU's programs, and short-term programs have become popular with graduate students. Another population of students who attend at higher rates is the population of students with disabilities. This particular population requires attention to academic accommodations, mental health services, the campus's physical accessibility, the host cities' accessibility, and cultural norms regarding disability.

All accommodations requests are made through SU's Disability Resource Center (DRC). The DRC's primary role is to determine qualifying disability status for students requesting accommodations. Students with learning disabilities, attention deficit disorders, psychiatric conditions, mobility impairments, chronic health impairments, and students who are deaf or hearing-impaired may register with the DRC. All accommodations are considering on a case-by-case basis and may vary depending on program requirements and standards. Accommodations may include but are not limited to: extended time on tests and exams; supplemental class notes; use of a computer for exams; sign language interpreters; smaller proctored testing environment; alternate format texts; or use of adaptive technology. The DRC is also responsible for assisting with campus housing accommodations.

Currently, all SU and visiting students needing accommodation and attending any site abroad are required to register with the DRC to request accommodations. Each global site has an assigned liaison responsible for assisting with the provision of accommodations. The site liaisons are campus administrators whose primary job responsibilities are not disability-related. At SU Milan, for example, Marco Brunelli, Assistant Director for Academic Support, coordinates testing and exam arrangements; at SU Sydney, Brett Claremont, Senior Campus Counselor, assists with accommodations. Since the site staff are not all disability specialists, Sal Hammond, Assistant Director of the DRC, has been available to provide guidance and advice about implementing accommodations.

During a lunch meeting with Sal, he shares with you information about trends in his office. Not only is the number of students registering with disability offices increasing, but the complexity and severity of disabilities is as well. More students with severe psychiatric conditions and chronic medical conditions are attending and requesting accommodations. The DRC staff have noticed the increase, and have also noted the increase in students requiring complex accommodations who study abroad. While several policies and procedures have been revised, recent cases are evidence of the complex interactions required of support staff, academic staff, and global staff.

At lunch, you and Sal recall Margaret Cloud, the first student in a wheelchair to study at SU Milan during Summer 2006. Margaret is a student with a degenerative muscular condition who uses a motorized wheelchair. She applied and was accepted to the SU Sydney summer session. She only disclosed her disability status after registering for classes. She registered with the DRC and requested a personal aid, and a modified living residence, and an in-class note-taker. The site, while having accommodated students with a variety of disabilities had not hosted a student in a wheelchair. After a conversation with Brett Claremont, senior campus counselor at SU Sydney and Bruce Drummond, the director, it is determined that the site is not wheelchair accessible. Given building codes and requirements, alterations to the two townhouses which make up SU Sydney could not be made. The townhouses are not elevator-equipped, the doorways are narrow, and the entrance to the building is not accessible. You, Sal, and Heather Murphy, Assistant Director of Academic Programs, Faculty of Arts and Sciences at SU determined that it may be appropriate to offer Margaret an alternate site. You and the staff proceeded to contact other SU sites to determine the accessibility of each.

It was found that some sites were partially accessible, but most did not have the level of accessibility required for Margaret. Margaret was at first reluctant to consider an alternative site; she has had dreams of living in Sydney, but agreed to consider another location. In this case, Marco Brunelli and Candace Rutger, Director of Student Life at SU Milan, agreed that it was reasonable to make modifications to some buildings in order to accommodate Margaret. Since all of the buildings at the SU Milan site are historic, permanent modifications could not be made; however temporary ramps were built to allow access to the academic and administrative buildings. Margo

Turner, the programming coordinator at SU Milan, and the facilities staff researched and rented an all-terrain wheelchair from a local company. The all-terrain wheelchair allowed Margaret to navigate the steep slopes between the two sides of the campus. Margaret was also given permission to bring a personal aid with her, in this case, a friend of hers who would help with daily living activities. Heather Murphy agreed that her department would absorb costs related to transportation for school-sponsored excursions or site visits. The site staff ensured that all excursions and visits to historic sites were wheelchair accessible. They rented accessible buses, and in fact, cancelled a group trip to a local attraction because it was not accessible to Margaret. All of the arrangements were made in approximately three weeks.

While Margaret was able to participate in all of the academic and co-curricular programming, she reported feeling confused about all of the attention given to her. Sal conducted a site visit to SU Milan during her stay there to ensure things went smoothly, and the site staff checked on her daily. Margaret said she felt singled out and wanted to feel that her stay there was not anything out of the ordinary. Overall, however, she loved SU Milan and hopes to return to the city.

During a wrap-up meeting, you and the staff wondered whether enough time was spent discussing how other sites could perhaps be modified to accommodate a student in a wheelchair, rather than dismissing potential sites due to a short time frame. SU Milan, at first glance, is not entirely accessible, yet relatively inexpensive modifications were made in a short amount of time. Moving forward, the DRC and Office of Global Programs is considering ways to accommodate students with a spectrum of disabilities within an increasingly global and complex campus.

James Pierce, a student with cerebral palsy, a visual impairment, and a major depressive disorder was admitted to a law degree program at Spence Law at Tokyo College (SU) for fall 2011. James requires extended time on exams, alternate format texts, and an in-class note-taker. He lives in Washington State and will not be studying at the central campus area at all during his time at SU. In order to register with the DRC, staff agree to hold the registration appointment and documentation review online and by phone.

The Tokyo campus itself is partly urban, but has a number of hilly and grassy areas. James plans to bring his cousin with him two weeks before the start of the semester in order to help him acclimate. He did not request a personal aid, and reported that he will be able to manage on his own after she leaves. James worked with the DRC to secure books in large print for the first semester, and Caroline Radcliff, the Administrative Manager at Tokyo College agreed to assist with any additional texts for his next three semesters.

Unlike Margaret, James is studying at a non-SU global campus, and is considered a student of both SU and Tokyo College. Students with any medical conditions are required to be cleared at University Health Center at Tokyo College but there is no designated office for arranging accommodations. Caroline Radcliff was assigned the task upon James's arrival and has not had experience working with a student with a disability. Caroline has only one assistant and the two of them are charged with managing the academic and registration needs of all incoming students. When Peter arrives, Caroline sends you an email expressing some concerns:

> I am writing you concerning James Pierce. I did not realize how much assistance he would need. In fact, my assistant gave him a tour of the campus and he fell once and had a difficult time managing the stairs. We changed his residence hall to one with fewer stairs, which seems to be working better for him, but we are still concerned with him managing day to day. Also, he is asking us to enlarge, print, and copy all of his books, which would total more than 10,000 pages if enlarged and would be a financial burden for us. I understand he is reluctant to use any adaptive technology which would save on the time and money spent printing. He is generally pleasant but at times seems a bit down. He has fallen asleep a couple of times during group orientation sessions. The facilitators brought the sleeping to his attention, but he assured them he was fine. We want his experience here in Tokyo to be successful so I am writing to you for any advice.

What do you do?

"CULTURE CLASH: INTERNATIONAL STUDENT INCIDENT"

Julie R. Nelson, Florence A. Hamrick, and Marissa E. Amos

Setting

Middle Valley University (MVU), situated in a southern state, attracts students from across the nation and around the world, although state residents comprise the majority of the 36,000 student population. MVU is a land-grant, research-intensive university and is known for its outstanding programs in engineering, technology, agriculture, computer science, and natural sciences. Roughly 8–10% of undergraduates and 22% of graduate students in these areas are international students, many of whom serve as teaching assistants (TAs). The percentage of international students on campus has increased 5% during the last two years.

The growing number of international undergraduate and graduate students reflects two of the top priorities in MVU's strategic plan: to increase the number of graduate students in targeted programs and to build MVU's international reputation and reach. Strengthening undergraduate education is a third top priority cited in the strategic plan.

Characters

Carolyn Higgins is Assistant Director of International Student Affairs. She reports to the Director of the office, who in turn reports to the Associate Vice President for Academic Affairs. She has been Assistant Director for five years. Her responsibilities are ensuring international students' compliance with visa provisions, programming, budgeting, and advocating for international programs and priorities.

Maggie Johnson is the Zoology and Genetics Department Chair and a Faculty Senator.

Hae-Jung Kim is a second year Zoology doctoral student from South Korea who teaches the required introductory Zoology course for prospective majors. Zoology faculty regard her as one of the strongest doctoral students in the program.

Steve Ward and **Carl Bennett** are first semester first year students.

Burton Ward is Steve Ward's father.

Greg Thomas is a Sergeant in MVU's Public Safety department.

Timothy Morton is Dean of Students.

Case

As Carolyn Higgins, you are used to hearing stories from international graduate student TAs about domestic undergraduate students who express concerns about understanding their TAs' heavily accented English. TAs frequently say that once they share with undergraduate students their own difficulties understanding the local accent and then suggest patience on all sides, students' frustrations usually ease and the classroom environment improves. All international TAs at MVU are screened on the basis of TOEFL scores and are encouraged to attend a series of workshops offered by the Center for Teaching Excellence. You have concluded that the levels and types of complaints by undergraduate students are probably typical for a university of MVU's size.

Your supervisor, the Director of International Student Affairs, left yesterday for a two-week trip to Asia with MVU's president, two admissions staff members, alumni representatives, and the dean and three department chairs from the Engineering college. Just before you leave for a lunch meeting on Monday, Professor Maggie Johnson calls to speak with your supervisor, so a support staff member forwards the call to you instead. Maggie is a former member of your office's campus advisory board, so you feel like you know her well.

After exchanging greetings, Maggie says, "I need to make you aware of a situation that I just became aware of this morning—It's infuriating! I wouldn't have believed it, but one of our TAs, Hae-Jung Kim, showed me the Facebook page and videos herself. It seems that, for the last three weeks, two students in Hae-Jung's introductory course have used their cell phones to secretly make short videos of her during her lectures, and then they've posted the videos along with mocking, disrespectful comments about her accent on a Facebook page called 'Your Tuition Dollars at Work—Not!' In the past week, it looks like students from other universities have started to post similar videos and mocking comments. Talk about brash—the videos show the instructors' faces clearly, the comments include the instructors' names, and at least in the case of these two students, they've used their real names and photos. I called Public Safety because of this troubling situation. The officer—I believe his name was Greg Thomas—told me there was probably nothing he could do because MVU has no policies regarding students' use of Facebook and similar sites, but I insisted that he contact the two students. And I want to give their names to you, too: Carl Bennett and Steve Ward. Will you check into this, too?

Our TAs shouldn't be subjected to this kind of treatment from students, and I think the violation of Hae-Jung's privacy is a grave concern."

You thank Maggie for calling, and when you consult the online student directory, you see that both Carl and Steve are first year students who have declared Zoology (pre-Medicine) majors. You decide to call Timothy to let him know about the situation, and Timothy encourages you to investigate further and talk to the students. He concludes, "Let me know what you find out, and then we'll decide what should happen next." You ask your assistant to contact Hae-Jung, Carl Bennett, and Steve Ward to make separate appointments with each of them as soon as possible, and then you leave for your meeting.

When you return, you see a note from your assistant that confirms a 1:30 p.m. meeting today with Hae-Jung and a 2:30 p.m. meeting with Carl. You also have a meeting with Steve scheduled for 3:00 p.m. on Thursday.

At 1:30, Hae-Jung comes into your office. She sits in the chair you offer, and she calmly tells you the following: "This is my second time as the TA for this particular course. English is not my first language. I tell my students the first day if they have trouble understanding my accent, please tell me. I have trouble understanding sometimes what they say, too. Also, most students use laptops, cell phones or other devices during class. They do not always listen and pay attention. I think it would be easier for them to understand me if they pay attention. On Sunday, I talked with a friend, who is also a graduate student and Korean. She showed me the Facebook page with the videos and comments left by students. I saw that two students in my section created the group. I have seen them with phones in my class, but students always have phones in their hands. It makes me upset because they make fun of me. I am also upset because they never told me that they could not understand my lectures. But they do well in the class—they both made As on the last quiz. My friend, she printed out a copy of the comments from the page." Hae-Jung gives the pages to you. You thank her and look over the pages briefly. You ask Hae-Jung whether you can keep the copies and if she has anything else to share. She nods and replies, "Yes, keep the pages. I have other copies. Mostly, I do not want to make such a big fuss. I just do not want to be bothered in class or made fun of. That is not right. They should respect their teachers." You tell Hae-Jung you will follow-up with her and ask her to contact you if she has questions or concerns.

As you wait for your 2:30 p.m. meeting with Carl, you use the copy of the Facebook page Hae-Jung has given you to search online for the page but are unable to find it, so you are thankful to have the copy from Hae-Jung. You are not aware of Facebook's account and privacy settings in great detail, so you make a mental note to seek this information.

Your phone rings at 2:20 p.m., and you take the call: "Greg Thomas here. I just spoke with Professor Johnson, and she asked me to call you, too.

Professor Johnson said that you're aware of the situation. I was only able to talk to one of the students—Steve Ward. Based on what I've learned, there aren't grounds for Public Safety to take any further action. The student wasn't happy answering my questions, and he was fairly arrogant about the whole thing, but I'm betting they'll take down the Facebook page before you know it, so that will take care of the problem for you."

When you greet Carl at 2:30 p.m., you ask him to explain the events that have taken place in class and on Facebook. He says, "Well, a friend and I, we are taking an introductory Zoology course, that's a prerequisite for the major. I mean—I am doing well in the class and so is Steve—but it's hard to understand what the instructor—what she's saying. When I enrolled in the class, I knew I was getting a Chinese teacher and I checked her out on this website, ratemyprofessor.com but I didn't know her accent would be as bad as it is. I mean we're doing well, but other students who end up in a class with her won't be so lucky. Steve thought we should show how she talks in class so that other students could be prepared. Steve used his phone and uploaded videos to Facebook—umm, but they aren't there anymore—and then students started to comment on the videos and the page. Students were saying some mean things, about Chinese and Asian people, but we can't control what other people say. The reason the videos aren't there any more is because we saw for ourselves that things were getting out of hand, so we deleted the page and Facebook group."

Your assistant knocks on the door to ask if you would please take a call from a parent who is extremely angry and upset. She says, "I'm sorry for the interruption, but it sounds like he's been getting the runaround this afternoon." You ask Carl to wait in the outer office, and he agrees. As Carl leaves, you take a deep breath and answer the phone. The caller snapped, "This is Burton Ward. Who am I talking to now? I've been transferred so many times, ma'am, and frankly I'm tired of it!" You explain who you are and he continues. "Well listen here, I do not appreciate this university badgering my son! Why did a police officer track him down for questioning? He didn't do anything! I pay top-dollar for Steve to attend this university and I would expect him to be treated just as well as you seem to treat the foreign students! Steve is a good student! I've seen his test grades and so far he is doing well! If he wants to blow off a little steam about the teaching assistants by commenting on this other boy's Facebook group—well as long as he's not hurting anyone, leave him alone! Here's a better idea: Maybe you should hire more teachers who speak English and then these kids wouldn't have to work even harder to try to learn from people with those accents!" Mr. Ward abruptly hangs up the phone.

You call Carl back into your office and ask if there is anything else he would like to share. He says, "Yeah, I do. Well I don't think it's fair that we're the ones being singled out. Aren't we allowed to express our opinion publicly, just like Samantha Tilly? She's a senior here now, but she has an entire website called 'Don't Speak Louder, Speak English!' that she started three years ago. And she just got accepted to medical school! Her website has dozens of videos and hundreds of comments about TAs and even Professors that don't speak English, but she never got into any trouble! I don't dislike foreign professors—it's just that it's so hard to understand them."

You thank Carl for coming and tell him that you'll be in touch soon. Carl leaves the office and you pick up the phone, do a quick time zone calculation, and call your supervisor's cell phone. When he answers, you provide a quick description of the situation and ask his advice. He replies, "I know you want to be the director of an office like this at some point soon in your career, and this will be a good way for you to spread your wings. It doesn't sound as if anyone is at risk of being deported or arrested or injured, but even if that weren't the case, I'm comfortable with your handling this situation. Be sure to keep the appropriate people informed. You're the acting director in my absence, and you have my full support."

What do you do?

TRANSFER PROBLEMS AT SOUTHEASTERN COMMUNITY COLLEGE

Katherine M. Conway

Setting

Southeastern Community College is located in a coastal community on the southeastern seaboard of the United States. Originally founded as an outpost of the state university's main campus in the capital city, the college initially provided opportunities for programs in marine mechanics and repair and agricultural research that weren't feasible in the urban environment of the main campus. Over time the college expanded, and 20 years ago was established as a separate institution within the university system, granting two-year degrees. Today the 12,000+ student body is comprised largely of liberal arts and business majors who plan to transfer to a baccalaureate program within the university. The most recent enrollment shows a student body that is 53% female, with 46% of students enrolled in liberal arts and 22% in business. Because of its location and history, Southeastern offers several programs that are not typical of community colleges elsewhere. The college offers an Associate of Applied Science (A.A.S.) degree program in Maritime Technology which enrolls approximately 600 students. The college also offers two agriculture programs, each enrolling approximately 500 students annually. The agriculture programs are also A.A.S. degrees with specializations available in Golf Course management and Equine Business Management.

Not unlike other community colleges nationally, Southeastern is focusing on improving graduation and transfer rates. The college keeps detailed records on students who graduate or who transfer to the state university prior to graduation. In the last five years the combined six-year graduation and transfer rates have averaged 23%.

Characters

Mary Boothe, Dean of Academic Advisement and Transfer. Dean Boothe joined the college last year from Metropolitan College, a large northeastern community college where she served as Assistant Dean for a number of years.

John Furman, a tenured professor and chair in the Maritime Technology department. Professor Furman has been on the faculty for almost 30 years.

Louis Emory, a tenured professor and chair of the Agricultural Sciences department. Like Professor Furman, he has been at Southeastern for more than two dozen years.

Mark Hopkins, President of Southeastern Community College.

Angela Lynn, student, age 20, majoring in Business Administration.

John Lydon, student, age 27, majoring in Maritime Technology.

Case

As Mary Boothe, you and several of your colleagues on the Ad Hoc Committee for Student Success are tasked with trying to improve Southeastern's graduation and transfer rates. The task force includes faculty members and staff from institutional research and admissions. In your role as dean your staff includes six full-time advisors, who work closely with students on setting goals and taking the right coursework to successfully transfer to the state university. You spend most of your time working on articulation agreements with your counterparts at various campuses of the state university, as well as a handful of private local colleges. Your office hosts several transfer fairs each year, where representatives from four-year programs set up booths and speak to students about admissions. Your department also administers the university "Excelerate" program, a scholarship for students who succeed in graduating within two years of enrollment.

During the past year you have made an effort to meet the department chairs of the various academic disciplines within the college and to make individual department presentations to faculty about transfer requirements. Faculty are an important part of the transfer and advisement process; students outnumber counselors by approximately 2000:1, so much of the information students receive is from a faculty member.

Many of the faculty and staff members at Southeastern are natives to the area; while you are a recent and obvious northeast transplant. Your accent, your clothing and your "get it done now" attitude all seem to distinguish you from the laid-back approach of your new colleagues. More than a few faculty members have become indignant at what they perceive as "the new girl giving them orders."

You have reviewed the college's most recent Factbook and see that only a small number of students in the Maritime Technology program graduate or transfer. The state university no longer offers a Maritime Technology program. In speaking with Professor Furman, it became apparent that he did not think there was a problem, as many of his former students had "lucrative jobs in the local boatbuilding industry." The Maritime Technology department occupies a sizeable portion of the college's square footage due to course requirements that include fiberglass repair, welding, and introduction to diesel engines. The Maritime Technology department offers a 60-credit A.A.S. degree but many if not all of the students take only the ten courses in the major and then leave to seek employment. The local boatbuilding industry is stagnant and has been that way for a number of years. Students work locally initially but often leave the area for their subsequent career move. Currently, only two boat builders remain in the area, as a number of others sold their waterfront property to condo developers.

Southeastern's campus is fully built out and buying or leasing additional space in the area is not realistic. Even in the current economic downturn, property in Southeastern's immediate vicinity is much in demand, as state residents have discovered the town as a scenic vacation home destination. The charming harbor, quaint inns, galleries and restaurants all attract an influx of weekenders and day-trippers from the larger metropolitan area 2.5 hours away. There is little in the way of industry to mar the bucolic setting.

The Agriculture program also utilizes significant space on campus, primarily a series of greenhouses, a stable and a paddock, on the southern end of the property. The stables and paddock are currently leased to a local horseback-riding instructor who offers private lessons. Your meeting with Professor Emory, chair of Agricultural Sciences was not quite as off-putting as the meeting with Professor Furman, but daunting nonetheless. Students in golf course management tend to be older and already working at a local golf course. For many students this is a second career, and they view their classes at Southeastern as a means of acquiring knowledge, not necessarily gaining employment. They want to graduate but don't feel pressured to do so, and don't seem interested in attaining a bachelor's degree in the future. Students in the equine business management program are younger on average and more transfer oriented. The state university doesn't offer a transfer program, but two small local colleges, within a 100-mile radius of Southeastern offer a bachelor's degree and have been wooing Southeastern students. These two private colleges are happy to accept Southeastern transfer students, with or without a degree.

While mulling over your most recent meeting with Professor Furman, you are interrupted by Maria Rivera, reminding you that it is time for your weekly staff meeting. The advisors are encouraged to share stories of student successes as well as challenges. As you go around the room, soliciting feedback, a recurring theme becomes apparent. Students are questioning the courses they are required to take, saying that many of the courses will not transfer to the state university. This isn't news to you. Shortly after arriving at Southeastern you were confronted by an angry student who found out that 15 of the 60 credits in his program will only fill elective requirements at the state university. Upon investigation you found that the student was correct.

At this morning's meeting Maria relates the story of Angela Lynn, who will be graduating this year with 82 credits, only 68 of which will transfer. When asked why she had so many credits, Angela replied that she "learned mid-way through her degree that several courses would not transfer and that there were other courses she would need to enter the state university's business program at the flagship campus." Angela was irate at both the time and expense she felt she wasted and stormed out of Maria's office.

The business major at Southeastern requires that students take general education courses, liberal arts electives, and courses in the major. If students want to gain admission directly to the state university's flagship business program upon graduating from Southeastern then they need to take very specific liberal arts electives, including calculus, advanced statistics, micro-economics, and world literature. If students choose other electives they will be admitted to the state university in the College of Liberal Studies, until they can complete the requirements for the business program. Students at Southeastern have the ability to take the required courses while still at the community college but only if they are aware of the transfer requirements and take the proper prerequisites in a timely fashion. The degree requirements at Southeastern don't specify the state university requirements, because the faculty and administration at Southeastern believe that students may not necessarily attend the flagship program because it requires a competitive grade point average. Additionally Southeastern faculty and staff don't want to create a program that is a reaction to decisions made at the state university. Faculty cite the state university's recent change in its Introductory Accounting class as an example. The state university curriculum change resulted in Southeastern's Introductory Accounting class no longer fulfilling the accounting requirement, and transferring as a general elective. When you asked Bob Brewster, a faculty member in the accounting department about the impact on Southeastern students, he shrugged and replied that "They would simply have to take accounting again, as the department had no imme-diate plans to revise its course to reflect the state university's curriculum."

Two days later, things go from bad to worse. An article in *The Egret*, the campus paper, states that large numbers of students are taking credits they don't need and that won't transfer. You have barely finished reading the article when you receive a call from the local cable channel because they want to run a story on the futility of taking college courses at Southeastern. Angela Lynn will be a guest on *Morning Talk* later in the week. You refer the cable producer to the college's director of public relations, but realize that this is an issue that won't go away soon.

Later in the afternoon you meet with John Lydon, a student in the Excelerate program who you are mentoring. John is majoring in Maritime Technology, after serving in the Navy. He is one of the success stories in the Maritime Technology department in that he hopes to pursue a bachelor's degree in Maritime Studies. Financial aid will be the determining factor as to whether John chooses a public or private college out of state to continue his studies. John has been very happy at Southeastern, especially since he was accepted into Excelerate. The scholarship has enabled him to attend full-time, and he plans on meeting the two-year graduation requirement. Unfortunately, today John isn't happy. He just came back from registration for next semester and found out that two of the maritime courses he is required to take will not be offered next term. Because of the department's low enrollment, courses are not offered every semester. Students need to pick and choose strategically if they want to graduate on time. Limited course availability is not widely discussed with students, because faculty in the department believes that it is a chicken and egg situation. As Professor Furman commented "If we tell the students that low enrollment may limit course offerings, then they reconsider selecting the major, which results in lower enrollment and even fewer course offerings."

As you head home, you realize that in less than a week the Ad Hoc Committee on Student Success needs to present its recommendations to President Hopkins. Probably before then, he will be calling you about *The Egret* article and the cable program. President Hopkins made it clear that he wants the committee to be bold in its recommendations and to think about the long term. The president is under fire from the university's chancellor to increase revenue and improve graduation rates in the coming decade. Revenue is a direct function of enrollment demand, which is expected to continue to increase as the college offers a low-cost open admissions alternative to the state university's four-year programs.

What should you recommend to the president?

———

Chapter 8

Cases Regarding Identity

In the past decade issues regarding student identity have become more visible and more diverse. Such cases can be among the most difficult for the student affairs professional and often require helping students to see that granting other students' rights does not diminish their own.

In "Student Media and the 'Satirization' of Native American Life" Michael Dumas and Sandi Wemigwase describe a campus administration that seems ready to forgive a student publication's racist article as satire. A staff member deliberates about the advice she will give to her superior. A private liberal arts college faces changes to its student services and facilities in response to the increase in the Muslim student population in "The Growing Presence of Muslim Students at St. Francis Xavier University" by Mark Hummell. Jealousy between two club members results in "Cyberbullying on Campus" by Sara Klein. In "Whose Rights are Right in the Union?" Florence Hamrick, Houston Dougharty, and Paul DeStefano describe problems when there is a mismatch between student visitors' and their academic hosts' values. Kim O'Halloran and Megan Delaney discuss the painful ramifications of a roommate conflict between religious beliefs and identity in "A First Year Student's Struggle with Identity."

The identity problems described in this chapter remind us to continually work toward greater knowledge and understanding as we work with college students.

STUDENT MEDIA AND THE "SATIRIZATION" OF NATIVE AMERICAN LIFE

Michael J. Dumas and Sandi M. Wemigwase

Setting

Mallory College is a small, private liberal arts college located in Pacific Falls, a small city in the Pacific Northwest. Primarily known for its rigorous curriculum and commitment to environmental scholarship and activism, Mallory is regarded as one of the most prestigious institutions in the nation. Members of the Mallory community—faculty, students, and staff—take pride in the intellectual milieu of the college, and see themselves as engaged in the pursuit of knowledge for its own sake. Fully 92% of Mallory's undergraduates pursue some form of graduate school or advanced training.

As one of the most expensive colleges in the country, and one with very few faculty of color, Mallory struggles to recruit a racially and economically diverse student body. Currently, 81% of the 1,100 students at Mallory are White, 11% are Asian American, 2% are African American, and less than 1% each identify as Latino or Native American.

Mallory places a high value on student participation in college governance, and until very recently, most student life activities were coordinated by students and recent alumni, who stayed on after graduation to serve as residence life staff and advisors to student organizations. The rationale for hiring recent graduates was that only members of the Mallory community—or "Mallards"—could truly understand and respect the school's unique campus culture and student experience. Although the dean of students, hired just four years ago, has introduced professionally trained student affairs staff in key entry-level positions previously held by alumni, students—particularly upper-class students—still view professional staff with suspicion. The dean advises his new staff to view their roles primarily as advisors to students, rather than directors; students and student organizations, rather than staff, are empowered to oversee decisions about programming, allocation of student funds, and most student life judicial matters.

Characters

Randall Edwards is a resident director and coordinator for student diversity programs, which includes overseeing the new Diversity Center and advising diversity-related student organizations. He is in his second year in this entry-level position, and reports to both the director of residence life and to the associate dean of students. Randall is African American.

Laura Finnegan is associate dean of students, and oversees student retention programs, career services, and the health center, in addition to diversity initiatives. Dr. Finnegan is White.

Marlene LeBlanc is president of the Mallory Native American Student Union (MaNASU), and a junior from northern Michigan. Marlene is a member of the Ojibwe tribe.

Joe Shinos is an active member of MaNASU, and a freshman who grew up in San Francisco. Joe, like many Native people from California, identifies as a "California Indian." He is beginning to learn more about his ancestry and culture.

Marc Drake is a staff writer at the *MalContent*, a self-described "irreverent quarterly student journal on culture, politics and assorted minutia." He is in his senior year, and is from Seattle. Marc is White.

Richard Wainwright is the faculty advisor for the *MalContent*, and holds an endowed professorship in comparative literature. Dr. Wainwright is White.

Bob Turley is vice president and dean of students. Dr. Turley is White.

Case

Marlene LeBlanc happened to be walking past just as someone dropped off a huge stack of the latest hot-off-the-copy-machine edition of the *MalContent* at the welcome desk in the student union building. At first she didn't notice the headline, but immediately recognized the photo, which depicted a group of young people on stage at the annual Pow Wow held in downtown Pacific Falls a couple weeks ago. She and others in the Mallory Native American Student Union (MaNASU) had taken the bus down to participate, and to staff a recruitment table for the college.

But then her eyes focused on the headline: "CIRCLE THE WAGONS! Indians gather to hawk their wares, peddle heart-clogging snacks, and beat some drums." Stunned, she kept reading as she walked slowly up the stairs to the MaNASU office. The author of the piece, Marc Drake, whom Marlene knew only in passing, explained that he had been downtown sitting at his favorite coffee shop, plowing through readings for his existential philosophy seminar, when he had been distracted by some incessant banging from down the street. Annoyed, and no longer able to concentrate, he went to check out what the commotion was all about, or as he wrote: "I wanted to see who was fucking up my day."

Drake's piece went on to describe the "packs of Indians in gaudy, over-the-top costumes," the "cheesy flea-market atmosphere," and the "monotonous chanting which he couldn't understand." And what, he wondered, was cooking in all that grease? "The sign said, 'frybread,'" he wrote, "but all I could think was, deathbread, dude! These people are trying to kill me! Call it 'reverse genocide!'"

Marlene made it to the office just in time to wince once more as she finished the article: "OK, kemosabes, for the record, I made it safely back to campus without being scalped! But next year, will someone tell me when this gawd-awful event is happening so I can be far, far away. Like, at the other end of the Oregon Trail." Marlene sank into her office chair, absolutely numb.

It is at this moment that you—Randall Edwards—pass by the MaNASU office. Marlene thrusts the *MalContent* into your hands. "Have you seen this, Randall?! I am more pissed than . . . than, I don't know." Alarmed, you quickly scan the cover, noting the headline and taking in the general gist and tone of Marc Drake's piece, which you assess as offensive and racist on several counts. You recall that Marc is also a resident assistant, although not in your building.

"We've got to do something," Marlene insists. "A sit-in. A protest. Something. This is the last straw!" Marlene reminds you that MaNASU had led the unsuccessful fight to get tenure for Mallory's only Native American professor, and had been active in pushing a resistant campus administration to increase recruitment activities in nearby Native communities. And now this. "It's like we're invisible," Marlene states. "And that's just no longer acceptable." You offer to investigate further, so that MaNASU can more effectively strategize their response, and promise that you will get back to her by the end of the day. Marlene agrees, and thanks you for your commitment to students of color. "Before you came, there was no one to stand up for us. The White folks just looked at us like we were crazy."

As you walk to the main administration building, you reflect on your time at Mallory since you arrived about one-and-a-half years ago, just two months after completing your master's degree at a nationally recognized student affairs graduate program on the East Coast. Given your experience in working with academic support services and retention programs for students of color, you had assumed that your first position would be at a more accessible, and likely, larger public institution. However, Laura Finnegan, the associate dean at Mallory, and a Ph.D. graduate from the same student affairs program you attended, pursued you at the national conference, and insisted that she wanted to push Mallory forward on issues of diversity and access, and urged you to consider the benefits of gaining the experience of working at a small, selective college, in an entry-level position in residence life and multicultural affairs. Convinced, and excited about stretching beyond your comfort zone, you had come to Mallory. Your primary appointment is in residence life, for which you report to the director of residence life, who is also an assistant dean. Your "quarter-time appointment" is a new position, as coordinator for student diversity programs. In this role, for which you report to Dr. Finnegan, you function more as a counselor than an administrator. Still, you enjoy your work, and have developed some popular initiatives on campus that have sparked dialogue among students and staff on issues of equity, identity, and privilege. A few of the younger faculty members have been supportive, and have been active in these discussions, but for the most part, faculty have been ambivalent, at best, about your efforts. Even so, your residence life responsibilities take the majority of your time, and you do not want to be perceived as neglecting your work there—much of which is done as a team, with the other two resident directors—in favor of your assignment in diversity programs.

When you get to Laura Finnegan's office, you notice she already has a marked-up copy of the *MalContent* on her desk. She looks up at you and sighs. "What are your thoughts about how we should respond to this?" she asks. "I know Marlene must be heartbroken." You concede that Marlene is indeed angry about the article and that you imagine other MaNASU students will be as well. Other student-of-color groups are also likely to join MaNASU in protesting not only the article, but the *MalContent* editorial staff, and anyone else they deem responsible for allowing the piece to be published. For these students, this isn't just about this one incident, you explain, but about a pattern of racism, of which this article is but the latest evidence.

Dr. Finnegan shares that she has already spoken to Richard Wainwright, the *MalContent* faculty advisor. Dr. Wainwright offered that the *MalContent* "follows its own conscience and whim," and it would not be appropriate for him to interfere with the editorial policies of an independent student publication. Dr. Finnegan appears ready to concede Wainwright's point, reminding you the *MalContent* is funded entirely by student funds, and the unpaid editor is chosen by a publications committee in student government, which is advised by Dean Turley, but only informally and somewhat infrequently. You point out that the *MalContent* is also published electronically, on the official college website, under a "mallory.edu" URL, and as such, it is difficult for the college to simply deny any responsibility for the inflammatory article. Dr. Finnegan nods, suggests there should be some kind of campus response, and says that she will talk to Dean Turley and get back to you in a few hours.

On the way back to the student union, you cross paths with a deflated Joe Shinos, the usually animated first year who has quickly become a student leader on campus, both with MaNASU and the Environmental Club. "I am so not feeling Mallory today," he says sadly. "If I could just pack my bags today, I would. Why should I put myself in debt to subject myself to this modern colonialism?" You ask Joe if he has spoken to Marlene today. "Yeah, she wants to mobilize a big protest, maybe bring in some students from other campuses, or try to shut down the *MalContent*. Something like that. It's all good; I mean,

I'm down for whatever. But right now, I just don't know if I have the energy for it. I'm just going back to my room, 'cause if I have to see another White person today, I'm gonna lose it." Shoulders hunched, his cap slung low over his brow, Joe shuffles toward a residence hall on the other side of campus, promising to be in a different state of mind tomorrow.

At lunch in the dining commons, you are surprised to bump into Marc Drake. It turns out that he had sought you out. Marc has never attended any student diversity programs, but he knows that you are the one "responsible for race stuff" on campus. He had received word from some friends that Marlene had been overheard in the library lobby talking about how racist his "Circle the Wagons" article is. "Apparently," Marc tells you dryly, "Ms. LeBlanc doesn't understand satire." He explains that the entire piece is meant to be taken tongue-in-cheek. "I mean, of course I didn't literally think I would be scalped at their event. I have actually been surrounded by Native Americans before, in high school, when we took a trip to a reservation. Any rational thinker would have to conclude that I was taking creative license, offering a nod to popular conceptualizations—reductive, to be sure—of Native Americans. If anything, I was pointing out the absurdity of racist representations, not contributing to them. But now Marlene wants to play the proverbial race card, which I think is beneath her, and beneath the Mallard ethos of free thought, unapologetic expression and creative criticism." You are not sure how to respond to Marc, and unsure if this is even the time or place. However, you do suggest to him that he might want to speak directly to Marlene, since he has only heard her perspective second-hand, and that he should consider the possibility that others may not interpret his piece as merely satirical. You tell him you would like to talk with him more about this tomorrow.

Later that afternoon, you receive an email directly from Bob Turley, which is unusual, since you do not report to him. He asks you to review the text of a message he is drafting to the entire campus community:

> The Mallory campus is renowned throughout the world as a haven for ideas, tolerance and free expression. However, a recently published satirical article on the Pacific Falls Pow Wow seems to have caused concern both on and off campus, with regard to the racial climate at Mallory. To the extent that anyone may have been offended by this article, we offer our sincerest regrets. We understand how the article might be viewed by some as ill-advised, at best. The content of the *MalContent* is determined by students who volunteer their time to be active in its production, and does not reflect the values or opinions of the Mallory community as a whole. Although we would never seek to censor student media, or quash student protest of that media, we urge all of our students to exercise reasoned judgment, and to not engage in racial generalizations about any group. Go, Mallards, go!

"Please advise," Dr. Turley writes.

What should you do next, and in the days immediately ahead?

THE GROWING PRESENCE OF MUSLIM STUDENTS AT ST. FRANCIS XAVIER UNIVERSITY

Mark Hummell

Setting

St. Francis Xavier is a mid-sized university in the Westchester County region of New York State. It began as a Catholic institution, and still has a large number of Catholics associated with the student body and the university's board. Since its founding in 1874, St. Francis Xavier has had a predominately White student body, and although it has accepted students from all faith traditions since 1968, Christians remain the majority of the religious population. Although the university maintains a strong alliance with the Jesuits, a Roman Catholic religious order, the board consists of secular lay-persons from various faith traditions. The university president, however, is always a Jesuit priest, elected by board members, and approved by the Provincial of the order. Although the president does have the right to veto decisions made by the board, this has never occurred in the history of the university. Since 2002, the university has had a mandate from the board and the president to increase their diversity.

The university has 12,000 students, 8,500 undergraduate and 3,500 graduate students, with approximately 80% of undergraduates and 20% of graduate students living on campus. The grounds of the campus have a distinct Catholic character, with a large gothic church in the center of the campus, as well as a smaller spiritual life center down the street from the church.

Characters

Maria Rodriquez is the Associate Dean of Students.

Phillip Sopke is the Dean of Students.

Father Anthony Swain serves as the primary university chaplain.

Imam Ali Abdullah is a consultant in architecture and design for college campuses. He specializes in working with institutions that want to make their environment more accessible to Muslim students, faculty, and staff.

Fatma Ahmed is a student in her junior year.

Mariam Amin and **Ibrahim Faraj** are second year students.

Abbas Mohamed is a first year student.

Patrick O'Brien is president of the student government.

Case

As Maria Rodriquez, you are the Associate Dean of Students. Your primary responsibilities include serving as an administrative resource to the student government. You also assist with the development of campus clubs and activities. In addition, your role is to develop and maintain leadership and education in the university's mission and goals.

Growing up as a Catholic yourself, you can identify with the rich religious identity in the university. You also want to make the environment more open to students from other faith traditions, and have actually worked with the students and the university chaplain, Father Anthony Swain, to speak with students about possible interfaith dialogues, faith-based service projects, and bringing guest lecturers to the university to provide lectures on faith traditions in addition to Catholicism.

You have been in your role of associate dean for three years now. Prior to that, you were an assistant to the dean of students in a similar-sized secular college in the Midwest. You are aware that an increasing number of Muslims have been moving into the region, and have begun to attend St. Francis Xavier. About five years ago, the university decided to develop a focused effort to increase religious diversity, and in the past two years, the number of Muslim students attending St. Francis Xavier has increased from 47 to 82.

As the university contemplated increasing their diversity among inter-cultural and interfaith lines, they hired a consultant to perform a needs assessment for a variety of populations. Imam Ali Abdullah was contracted to assess the needs of Muslim students, faculty, and staff on campus. Imam Abdullah recommended that the university build special prayer rooms for the various prayer times of the Muslim students. A devout Muslim prays five times a day. He also informed administration of the need for Muslims to perform ablutions, special washing of the feet, etc. prior to the prayers, and he recommended the creation of special ablution stations near the prayer rooms. Also, Imam Abdullah wrote in his report about the need for the kitchen staff to be mindful of the halal dietary needs of Muslim students.

After five years have passed, the university administration has offered a multi-use Spiritual Life Center for Muslims and any non-Roman Catholic students. Although the university states that this Spiritual Life Center accommodates various faith traditions, it does not include many of the recommendations made by Imam Ali Abdullah. A number of students stated that performing their ablutions in the nearby campus restrooms is an embarrassment to them. Mariam Amin met with you, in order to share her concerns about lifting her feet to the sink in order to perform the ablutions, and the embarrassment it causes her in front of the other students.

Mariam and a number of the female students also pointed out the fact that as women, they sometimes avoid the Spiritual Life Center for prayers, and try to perform them on their own in their rooms. She mentioned that the Center lacks the appropriate level of privacy, as several postures that are taken during prayers are awkward, and are distracting if male students enter the Center where the door is located, behind them. During the Muslim prayers, several physical stances are taken. She expressed special concerns with the ruku (bowing down) position and the sujud (kneeling prostrate with knees on the ground, simultaneously while the forehead is touching the ground) position. She also noted how cleanliness of the room itself is a concern, as Muslims are instructed to take their shoes off, and many of the non-Muslim students who use the center do not remember to do this, thereby making the space seem unsuitable for prayers. It should be noted that five years ago, Imam Ali Abdullah recommended that the university provide at least a half a dozen prayer rooms segregated by male only and female only throughout the campus for this very reason. According to your supervisor, Phillip Sopke, the Dean of Students, the university decided not to build the prayer rooms at that time due to budgetary constraints.

Some of the male Muslim students have also encountered difficulties of another sort. You were once called by staff leaders of a community service learning project on route to Haiti, over the last Spring break, as a second year student, Ibrahim Faraj, was detained by Homeland Security at JFK Airport for four hours. Ibrahim missed the flight with the other students, and he feels that other students now view him suspiciously. One student even jokingly calls him a terrorist, and although Ibrahim laughs it off, he expressed to you that this event has changed his relationship with the other students. He vows never to do another project again, or to put himself in the humiliating position of traveling through any airports with a group of students.

At times, the students have made general suggestions to the university about their concern over the cafeteria staff's lack of awareness over serving halal (permissible for Muslims to eat) food. In particular, the concern is over pork products served in close proximity to other foods. Also, the students mentioned that they have seen bacon fried on the same griddle as eggs and pancakes in the morning.

One of the reasons that many of these Muslim students decided to attend St. Francis Xavier is because the nature of a Catholic university informs and supports someone who is devoutly religious. Of course, many of the parents encourage their students' decision for this very reason. The segregation between male and female dorms, the attentiveness to religious holidays, the acknowledgment of breaks in the day for prayers, and some of the religious garb that Catholic priests and nuns wear, afford Muslim students a sense of comfort and familiarity with their own faith tradition. Catholic students seem unfazed by seeing a woman wearing an abayah (long black dress) and shelya (a scarf that covers a woman's hair) and a man wearing a kandorrah (a white wrap that covers the body) and gahfeyah (white cap). But, the students expressed a need for more Muslim character to integrate into a predominately Catholic university without completely assimilating and losing a sense of their Muslim core.

Fatma Ahmed, a student who is in her junior year, expressed concern to you, that although Father Swain provides general information about Islam and informs students of the two nearby mosques in Westchester County, she finds it difficult to establish a rapport with the Imams and the members of the mosques, as they are mostly families with young children, with no focus on the development of college-aged students. Although she likes Father Swain, she asked if the university could provide a part-time Imam for the growing number of Muslim students.

In addition to the concern about Muslim identity through a pastoral presence of an Imam, some students have expressed an interest in forming a club for Muslim students. Abbas Mohamed, a first year student, has completed paperwork in order to form the first branch of the Muslim Students' Association (MSA) at St. Francis Xavier. According to the MSA's National Board goals, they strive to assist Muslim students on college campuses to form Islamic programs and projects. They also mobilize and coordinate the human and material resources of Muslim student organizations. Finally, they educate, mobilize, and empower students.

The procedure of formally creating a student club at St. Francis Xavier is to submit an application through the Student Activities Office, which is under the auspices of the Associate Dean of Students. This includes a Club Proposal Form, a formal Constitution, elected officers for the club (a President, Vice President, Secretary, and Treasurer), a proposed schedule of events for the first six months of the club, a budget, departmental approval for any university departments involved with the club, and approval of the student government.

So far, Abbas has followed through with all aspects of club formation, but he is meeting resistance with gaining approval from the student government. The president of the student government, Patrick O'Brien, informs you and Abbas, that the student government performed some basic internet research on the history of the MSA, and has some concerns over allowing it to obtain club status. Patrick said that members of the Muslim Brotherhood formed the MSA in 1963 at the University of Illinois, Urbana-Champaign. The goal of the organization was, and remains, to spread Islam to students in North America. Patrick conveyed to you that the concern of the student government centers itself in allowing the MSA to host lectures and other events on campus that may garner support to advocate for extremist Islamic causes, and recruit members for possible subservice activities that are sometimes identified with the Muslim Brotherhood.

Finally, Patrick said that, given the fact that all groups who reach club status receive $1,000 in university activities funds per year, are given free space throughout campus to hold events, and have presence on the web, which identifies them as an official St. Francis Xavier University club, this may ally the university too closely with a radical Islamic ideology.

Abbas contends that the ties between the MSA and the Muslim Brotherhood were historic in nature only. He mentions that the main purpose of bringing the MSA to club status at St. Francis Xavier is because it will provide Muslim students with a club to gather and celebrate their heritage. The MSA can help with providing conferences to students on campus, as well as some events to raise money for charity and community service, and finally, to provide an awareness of Islam in a productive and non-threatening way. Abbas mentioned that the MSA might be viewed as Newman Centers are viewed in the Catholic world.

Given your role as the Associate Dean of Students, how would you respond to:

1. The concerns expressed by students over the physical space and the needs of Muslim students?

2. The need for Muslim students to express themselves socially and spiritually on campus, in particular, forming a chapter of the MSA as a club?

3. The possible existence of Islamophobia on campus?

CYBERBULLYING ON CAMPUS

Sara Klein

Setting

Panorama College is a small liberal arts college enrolling an estimated 2,500 undergraduate students. Students are attracted to the small, friendly institutional size, as well as the charming campus with panoramic views of the ocean. Ninety percent of the students live on campus.

With such a large percentage of students residing on campus, nearly all of the students, staff, and faculty know one another personally. The students who attend Panorama College tend to be involved in the co-curricular life of the campus, each student often participating in and serving in a leadership capacity in more than one student organization.

The college has a racially diverse student population as compared to other liberal arts colleges of this size; 22% of the student population identifies as Black or African American, and an additional 14% identify as non-White and, 64% of the students identify as White.

Characters

Matt Millman, Director of Residential Education.

Sharon Rodriguez, Resident Director.

Charlotte Patterson, Director of Student Activities.

Madelyn Caruso, Dean of Students.

Brian Bennington, Campus Psychologist.

Paul Lee, Director of Information Technology.

Ariana Jackson, Black Student Association President. She is a student leader in many capacities on campus, including her position as a Resident Assistant. Ariana identifies as African American.

Kathy Shapiro, Black Student Association Treasurer. She has a history of minor student conduct concerns, and she sees the campus psychologist weekly. Her position as Treasurer of the Black Student Association is her only leadership position at the institution. Kathy identifies as White.

Case

You, Matt Millman, the Director of Residential Education, arrive at work on a Monday morning to find an unusually high volume of emails in your inbox. It appears that there has been quite a bit of activity over the weekend. You begin to skim through the Incident Reports and notice that one of the Resident Assistants, Ariana Jackson, is named on a report. You are shocked by this, as it is rare for any Resident Assistant to be involved in an incident. However, Ariana's involvement in particular is surprising to you. She is a stellar Resident Assistant and has always been a strong role model for her peers in Residential Education. From what you know of Ariana's personality and background, it is very much out of character for her to have threatened another student as the report alleges.

The incident report states that student Kathy Shapiro has reported to her Resident Director, Sharon Rodriguez, that Ariana Jackson is harassing her. According to the report, Kathy alleges that Ariana cursed at her and threatened to start a physical fight as they were leaving a Black Student Association (BSA) meeting the previous afternoon. The students are both on the executive board of this organization. Sharon also happens to be Ariana's direct supervisor for the Resident Assistant position.

You stop in to Sharon's office and ask her about the incident. Sharon gives you some background on the relationship between Ariana and Kathy. Based on what Kathy has shared with Sharon, you learn that Ariana and Kathy have exchanged verbal insults on multiple occasions, but have never before brought any concerns to the attention of administrators. Both students feel that the other student is the instigator. Sharon also tells you that, not five minutes ago, a student came by to tell her about an inappropriate Facebook profile that is quickly circulating around campus. Apparently, this profile was created to look like Kathy herself had created her own profile, showing Kathy intoxicated and wearing hardly any clothing. The creator of this profile is "friending" a majority of the Panorama student population, exposing these pictures of Kathy to the entire campus.

Sharon, like you, seems shocked by these allegations against Ariana. Although she understands why Kathy feels that Ariana might have created this profile as a result of the tension between them, she cannot imagine the Ariana that she supervises harassing another student. Additionally, Sharon feels that Ariana would have come to her earlier for guidance if there were concerns brewing between her and Kathy.

You leave and return to your office to think further about the situation and to plan your response. First, you view the profile. The user has nearly 900 friends already, which is almost half of the total student population. There are a series of somewhat scandalous photos of Kathy, as well as some information that the user has filled out, pretending to be Kathy. The profile states that her employer is a "pimp" and that she works as a "whore."

You then inform the Dean of Students as well as the Director of Student Activities about the situation, since the two involved students are on the executive board of a student organization. You are the hearing officer for the case, but you feel that it is appropriate for you to inform your supervisor (the Dean of Students) and your colleague in Student Activities. Charlotte, the Director of Student Activities, commits to informally meeting with and counseling both students, as you will serve in the capacity of hearing officer.

Before you have a moment to contact Kathy and Ariana to invite them to meet with you and discuss the incident, Kathy knocks on your office door, her face filled with tears. She slumps into a chair next to your desk and begins to cry uncontrollably. She asks if she can show you something on your computer, and proceeds to pull up the degrading profile. She explains her tumultuous history with Ariana and also brings up the incident from the weekend. She explains that after the public disagreement following the Black Student Association meeting, she approached Ariana privately to have a conversation about what had occurred. Kathy said that the discussion very quickly became heated and many insulting words were exchanged, at which point both Kathy and Ariana left the situation to avoid heightening the tension.

Based on these incidents, Kathy is convinced that Ariana created the profile. She tells you that the pictures were taken during an evening out when the two women were friendly, and that Ariana is now using them to embarrass her in front of the whole school. You attempt to calm Kathy, ask a few more questions about the incidents, and assure Kathy that you are investigating the situation and will contact her later in the day with next steps. Kathy shares an additional concern with you about her personal safety on campus. She feels that since Ariana is a Resident Assistant and has access to the master keys for the residence halls, Ariana could enter her room in retaliation. You assure her that you will speak to Ariana and hold her accountable to her expectations as a Resident Assistant. Kathy leaves your office, still visibly upset.

Charlotte, the Director of Student Activities, then calls to inform you that three students have come to her office separately since you last spoke with one another, each concerned about the situation between Kathy and Ariana. These students, members of the BSA, strongly support Kathy and feel that Ariana is responsible for the Facebook profile. These students are demanding that Ariana be suspended from Panorama based on her behavior. In addition, these students aired the concern that Ariana might receive special treatment due to her role as a Resident Assistant.

You then contact Ariana, who schedules a meeting with you for the afternoon. You also leave a message for Brian, the campus psychologist, with whom you work closely. You want to alert him about the situation and specifically discuss Kathy's emotional state, a student who you know sees Brian on a weekly basis. Finally, you leave a message for the Information Technology staff to see if they can determine who created the profile.

Upon her arrival to your office later that afternoon, Ariana is calm and professional. She takes you through her detailed version of the argument with Kathy from the weekend, and also provides insight regarding the hostility that had been brewing between the pair over the past few weeks. Ariana feels that Kathy and some of the other members of the BSA had been ganging up on her because she documented a party that they attended a few weeks prior in the residence halls. This sub-section of the BSA had been rude to her ever since that night and there is now a clear divide within the organization's membership. Some of the members of the BSA support Ariana, while others stand behind Kathy. This division in the BSA is, for the most part, causing a rift within the Black community at Panorama College. Once a united and tight-knit community, the Black community is now divided.

You specifically ask Ariana about the Facebook profile and she adamantly denies any involvement. You are unsure of whether or not to believe her. You also mention to her your concern that a Resident Assistant, a student who is serving in the capacity of a role model and student leader for her peers, would be involved in any harassing or disruptive behavior such as this. You let Ariana know that a formal hearing will be scheduled within 48 hours, after you complete your initial investigation. Additionally, Ariana is temporarily suspended from her duties as a Resident Assistant until the decision is made about the incident. If she is found responsible, she will be terminated from her position. She informs you that she will be involving both her parents and a lawyer, and leaves your office in a hurry.

While you were meeting with Ariana, you missed a call from the Director of Information Technology, Paul. You call him back, and he informs you that he has viewed the activity linked to Ariana's IP address. Ariana, like many other Panorama students, was definitely on the Facebook website during the time when the profile was created. However, Paul cannot determine what exactly she was doing on Facebook at that time. Since it is typical for many students to spend significant amounts of time on Facebook, this information does not assist with the investigation. Paul recommends contacting Facebook to take down the profile, which you do immediately after speaking with him.

The phone rings again, and the caller is Kathy's mother. She demands information about the situation and wants to know what you're going to do to resolve it. You give her basic information about the student conduct process, the timeline, and where you are at in your investigation. You inform her that both Kathy and Ariana will be going through the student conduct process, as both students were allegedly involved in violations of college policy. Kathy's mother shouts at you, "This is absolutely unacceptable. My daughter is being harassed and now she is the one in trouble? She will not go through your student conduct process. Expect to hear from our lawyer." She then hangs up the phone.

Your supervisor, Madelyn, sends you an email asking you to meet with her first thing the next morning to discuss how you will proceed with the situation. She also adds that she has had calls from Ariana's lawyer, as well as from the Panorama College President, who is concerned about the situation because Ariana's parents are important donors to the college. Her parents have contacted him to express their frustrations with the allegations and with her temporary suspension from the Resident Assistant position.

What is your plan of action? How will you respond to this case?

WHOSE RIGHTS ARE RIGHT IN THE UNION?

Florence A. Hamrick, W. Houston Dougharty, and Paul S. DeStefano

Setting

Prairie State University (PSU) is a large public midwestern university enrolling almost 25,000 students, most of whom are state residents. Summer school enrollment is approximately 20% of PSU's academic year enrollment. In part because of its pastoral campus setting and close proximity to a large urban area, PSU has established a busy and profitable summer conference and housing operation.

One PSU student organization that has made tremendous strides recently is the PSU Pride Alliance, known generally as "the Alliance," which sponsors educational programs and support groups for LGBTQQIA (lesbian, gay, bisexual, transgender, queer, questioning, intersex, and ally) students at PSU. Last fall, Alliance members were asked to serve on a campus advisory board to discuss possible gender-neutral housing options at PSU.

Characters

John Hemmings is the Director of Student Activities and reports to the Dean of Students.

Lynda Anderson is John Hemmings's administrative assistant.

Susan Adams is the Director of the Summer Conferences Bureau and reports to the Vice President for Business Affairs.

Catherine Carlisle is Dean of Students. She is currently on a week-long wilderness hiking trip.

Bob Cassle is an assistant professor in the Computer Science department and became the Alliance's faculty advisor last year.

Timothy Frisch has been Vice President for Student Affairs for 17 years.

Joyce Smith is a rising senior and current president of the Alliance.

Scott Miller is advisor to a national youth group holding its annual conference at PSU this year.

Rasheed Martin is Facilities Coordinator of PSU's Student Union and reports to the Director of the Student Union, who in turn reports jointly to the Vice President for Student Affairs and the Vice President for Business Affairs.

Grant Thomas is a rising sophomore and a new Alliance executive board (e-board) member-at-large.

Howard Williams is the senior staff assistant to PSU's President.

Case

As John Hemmings, you are responsible for monitoring student organizations, training faculty and staff advisors, coordinating student leadership development, advising PSU's student government, and establishing and enforcing policies relating to student activities and organizations. You also serve as the primary liaison to the Student Union staff. Over your six years at PSU, you have cultivated effective working relationships with other campus units, and you are credited with developing strong student leaders.

In late spring this year, the Alliance received extensive, positive media attention when they peacefully protested a speech by a regionally well-known anti-LGBT evangelical minster by visiting the site of his address the following day with brooms and mops to "sweep up the hate." According to the organization's constitution, the Alliance is committed to "support, educate, and work toward social change." Looking back over the past academic year, you are proud of the Alliance's accomplishments and conclude that the extra time you spent with Bob Cassle, who is a new faculty member at PSU and a first-time student organization advisor, has really paid off.

On this Monday morning in early August, you continue revising the agenda for the Fall Student Leadership Retreat; you relish the large blocks of time available during summer to think and plan. Your colleagues on the Student Union staff, however, are still in full swing with their busy summer conference operation that involves staffing a minimum of three large residence halls to house conference guests, using virtually all of the Union's meeting rooms, and working closely with dining services on catering arrangements for each visiting group. When you walked in this morning, you saw a lot of young people—around high school age—milling about in the Union and some signs that read "Welcome—Living Legacy Association." You aren't familiar with this group, but you recall that Susan had personally worked very hard to attract them and their four-day conference to PSU. Revenue projections from the conference are very high. Additionally, the conference gives the 3,500+ delegates an opportunity to see the PSU campus and perhaps consider seeking admission to PSU.

Just before 10 a.m., Joyce knocks on your open door and steps in, visibly shaken and angry. She says, "Someone broke into our display case and stole everything—the posters, the pictures, everything! They even stole the wedding bands we had on display. They were loaned to us from one of the first gay couples to be married in Massachusetts after it was legalized. I called campus police and reported it. I told them it had to have been the 'no-brains' from Living Legacy. The Alliance reserved the main display case in the Student Union this week for the express purposes of documenting marriage equality rights and protesting their bullying tactics! Now they broke the lock and stole from us. They aren't going to get away with this, are they?"

Joyce then asks you to go upstairs with her to examine the display case. You first phone Susan and ask her to meet you there. When you and Joyce get to the display case, six adults in business casual attire—all appearing to be between 40 and 50 years old—are standing nearby talking quietly. Each is holding a clipboard.

Joyce shows you the case and the broken lock, and one of the adults hands his clipboard to another in the group, walks over, and extends his hand to you: "Hello, are you on the staff here? I'm Scott Miller, and I'm affiliated with the national organization 'Defenders of American Values.' The Living Legacy Association is our division for high school students, but you may have heard our students refer to themselves as 'right-brains'—that's their nickname. Anyway, you will want to know about the terribly insulting display that was in this case earlier. I couldn't find a staff member with a key early this morning, but I just had to take down the display since it was so disrespectful. The few right-brains who saw this were really upset and angry—justifiably so." Scott nods toward the group of five adults nearby and continues, "We'll pay for the damage to the lock and return the display items, but we will not abide the display's being put back up while the conference is going on."

You see that Joyce is getting visibly upset, and you ask her to wait for you in your office. As Joyce leaves, Susan arrives accompanied by Rasheed. You introduce them to Scott, who continues, "You know, we didn't pay all this money to PSU to pass by this offensiveness every time we go to or from a meeting in this building. We've called our national headquarters and notified our attorneys. But in the meantime, I know that our delegates who saw the display this morning have already posted pictures of the display on Facebook and have been tweeting and texting the other delegates. I'm guessing that there is a lot of anger among the delegates already, and I just can't assure the safety or well-being of anyone who may try to put the display back up while the group is here. I'm just trying to be honest with you."

Susan and Rasheed continue a conversation with Scott while you return to your office where Joyce is waiting. She is very angry. "Can you believe that man?! He admitted to breaking into the display and stealing. And some of the display pieces were one-of-a-kind and valuable—like the wedding bands. He's so matter-of-fact, like there was nothing wrong with it. He's more concerned with them being comfortable than with doing what's right and working toward equality for everybody. He's clueless. I didn't tell you this before, but when we were putting up the display early this morning, two of the high school kids from Living Legacy came over to us and told us how grateful they were to see the display since they were gay and not out. I feel sorry for them, but it confirms that we've got to stand up— for ourselves and for young people like them and others in similar situations. Isn't that what the Alliance is here for? I'm going to call Bob and text the rest of our e-board now. We'll decide what to do." Joyce leaves your office.

A moment later, Susan knocks and ducks her head into your office. "Now, you know me, John. I'm all for students expressing their opinions, and Rasheed confirmed that the Alliance had gone through appropriate channels to reserve the display case. But this is our biggest conference this year, and we have a lot riding on their having a positive experience. Haven't the Alliance students made their point already? Can't they let it be? This group will only be on campus for a few days. I need your help on this, John, but now Rasheed and I have to put our heads together about all this."

The office phone rings, and shortly afterward Lynda calls out: "Howard Williams on Line 1 for you, John."

You answer the phone and Howard says, "John, what's going on over there? The advisors of the group that's meeting on campus just brought by a petition signed by 2,000 of the members and all of the officers objecting to—what did they call it—the 'slanderous display and the disrespectful treatment' they've received at PSU and 'the malicious hacking' of their website, which apparently now redirects visitors to another website—yes, here it is—the 'Marriage Equality Consortium.' They claim that some of our students are responsible. What's happened? For heaven's sake, didn't this group arrive just yesterday?" You interrupt Howard because your cell phone is ringing, and you see that the call is from Timothy. You tell Howard that you will look into it further and call him back.

You greet Timothy, who says, "John, what's happened? My assistant tells me that the Alliance just sent out an email blast calling for students to protest the Union. Apparently their Facebook page and Twitter are also asking people to meet outside the Union at 2:00 this afternoon. It won't be long before the press gets wind of this, and they'll hear of it well before 2:00. The last time students protested, they at least waited until the speaker had left town. Do you really think it's wise to allow this to happen with the conference still in session this afternoon at the Union? I need for you to figure out what's going on and come up with a strategy. Call me back."

As you hang up the phone, Bob Cassle steps into your office. "Sorry for interrupting you, but Joyce told me about the display case and the hacked website. She and the other Alliance officers are also very angry that they're being blamed for the website, and they all insist that they're not responsible. I can tell you that I attended the e-board meeting last night. The officers finalized their plans for filling the display case at the Union, and that was the only action item they discussed. But now that I think about it, I wonder about another student—Grant Thomas—who joined the e-board this spring as a member-at-large. He was a student in my internet security seminar this spring, even though he was only a first year student. As you'd guess, we discussed numerous types of security breaches and how to remedy and prevent them. He wrote his final seminar paper on internet disruption as a political protest strategy. A very good paper, but now I'm wondering if he might possibly have done this. At e-board meetings, it's clear from his comments that he thinks the Alliance has been too passive and reactionary—not radical and confrontational enough in its actions. I'm busy all afternoon teaching my summer class, but I'm back in my office around 4:15 if you need to contact me."

Lynda says, "A Mr. Scott Miller left this while you and Dr. Cassle were visiting," and hands you a stack of frayed papers, several large photographs, and two silver rings—the contents of the Alliance display case—as well as a photocopy of the signed petition addressed to PSU's President.

What do you do?

A FIRST YEAR STUDENT'S STRUGGLE WITH IDENTITY

Kim C. O'Halloran and Megan E. Delaney

Setting

Myers College is a small, liberal arts institution located in an affluent suburb. It is primarily a residential institution, as the majority of its 3,000 students live on campus. Majors include the humanities and social sciences, and the college is proud of its success in sending many of its students on to graduate and professional school for advanced degrees.

The college has a very loyal alumni base who demonstrate their loyalty through donations that allow the institution to provide scholarships to offset high tuition rates. Following a successful capital campaign, the college has been able to establish a number of scholarship programs that have consequently attracted a more diverse student body, including a number of first-generation college students for whom the college would otherwise be out of reach financially.

Characters

Kevin Dean is the Director of Residence Life.

Sharon Burns is a senior Resident Assistant.

Fiona Brennan, Ph.D., is the Director of the Student Counseling Service.

Joseph Takeem is the Executive Director of Institutional Advancement.

Susan Hernandez is a first year student. She is an undeclared major and a first-generation college student.

Jenna Maggiano is a sophomore transfer student majoring in Religious Studies. She is a member of the Executive Board of the Catholic Students' Association.

Jack O'Brian is the College President.

Case

As Kevin Dean, you are responsible for oversight of residential life programs and services and have ultimate responsibility as supervisor for all residence assistants. Last week, Sharon Burns, the resident assistant for Benton Hall, came to you for advice on how to deal with a roommate issue. Susan Hernandez and Jenna Maggiano are roommates in her hall. Sharon has been checking in periodically with all first year residents to see how they are handling their college transition. During her first semester check-ins with Susan, she indicated that she wasn't sure she had made the right decision in coming to Myers and generally reported that she was feeling down much of the time. Sharon encouraged her to vising Student Counseling Services, which Susan agreed to do. During Sharon's check-in with Susan during the second semester, Susan shared that she was struggling with her feelings about a classmate. She was attracted to another woman she met in class. She is beginning to think about and explore her sexual orientation. While she had experienced feelings for other women while she was in high school, this was her first experience where she was thinking about acting on her feelings. She confided in her roommate, Jenna, whom she thought she could trust.

Jenna told Susan that she believes that homosexuality is a sin and that even thinking such thoughts was wrong, especially since Susan is Catholic. Since Susan confided in her, Jenna has been making negative remarks about those whom she believes are lesbians on campus, which makes Susan feel uncomfortable. She has begun to spend all of her free time alone in the library to avoid seeing Jenna in the room.

Once Jenna began to make the homophobic comments, Susan also decided to confide in her mother and tried to convince her mother to allow her to leave school. Susan's mother responded by calling Jack O'Brian and accusing the college of encouraging its students to embrace a gay lifestyle, stating that she chose Myers because it was a small college in a conservative town and that she expected more. Joseph Takeem has called you to ask that you deal with this student issue so that it does not escalate further and become a public news item.

Upon hearing from both Sharon Burns and Joseph Takeem, you decided to call Fiona Brennan to discuss the situation, as Susan had agreed to visit the Student Counseling Service. Fiona explains that she cannot discuss what Susan shared with her counselor as it would violate confidentiality rules.

What do you do?

Chapter 9

Cases in Campus Life

The heartbeat of the campus might be felt in the residences and student organizations. Here we find some of the stickiest areas of student affairs. These areas "belong" to the students and teem with activity 24 hours a day—classes are offered, lectures delivered, movies shown, and art exhibited. Yet, students do not always have the information nor the experience to wield their responsibility wisely. Unfortunately these areas can also showcase some of the negative aspects of campus life—personalities, cultures, and customs clash when people from many areas of the country and the world attempt to create a "home away from home." Somehow, administrators and advisors must find a way to guide and educate students while allowing them freedom to make their own decisions.

In "They Won't Fire the Whole Staff" by Kim Yousey-Elsener, a hall director faces a difficult decision when confronted with a resident assistant who did not follow the college's alcohol policies. A fraternal organization at Oceanside University hosts a Culture Night event that brings charges of racism, however the university has few options to pursue disciplinary actions in "Campus Climate at Oceanside University" by Benjamin Gillig and Shaila Mulholland. Diane Cardenas Elliott and Audrey Loera describe what happens when a student member of a search committee places demands on the process in "Hiring in the Valley." Fine shades of difference in what constitutes fighting words create a dilemma in John Downey's "Fighting Words at Carpe Diem."

In "Intercollegiate Athletics at Clayton College" Ginelle John describes how an attempt to create gender equity in athletics brings an alumni's threat to withdraw a promised donation. An urban institution has designated a new space for a religious group on a college campus which brings questions about fairness and expression of religion in "A Case of Religious Intolerance at

Greenwich University" by Shadia Sachedina. Finally, Rachel Wagner and Tracy Davis describe what happens when a Greek letter organization and its members face suspension after abhorrent, misogynistic material is found in a residence hall room in "It's Not Just the Weather: A Chilly Climate for Women at Carlford College."

These cases demonstrate the range of issues faced by the student life professionals as students become more sophisticated about their rights to manage certain resources. Hopefully they will help you expand your repertoire of administrative responses to similar campus problems.

THEY WON'T FIRE THE WHOLE STAFF

Kim Yousey-Elsener

Setting

Hometown Technical College is home to around 14,000 undergraduates. A public technical college, this institution's most popular majors are in the fields of engineering, computing and information sciences, business, and applied science and technology. Located near a mid-sized city, students spend the majority of time living, working, socializing, and studying on campus.

Approximately 50% of the college's students live on campus. Campus housing consist of a choice between traditional residence halls and apartment-style living. While first year students must live in the residence halls, upper-class students choose their living situation depending on their personal preferences and lifestyles. The residence halls also serve as home to seven special-interest housing options based on themes as well as six fraternity and sorority chapters.

Characters

Amy Rhodes – Assistant Director of Residence Life and supervisor for an area of six residence halls, including those that house the fraternity and sorority chapters.

Jennifer Feder – Hall Director responsible for three residence halls which house the fraternity and sorority chapters.

Alyssa Palmer – member of the facilities crew in the buildings that Jennifer Feder supervises.

Officer Cave – campus safety officer.

Josh Hampton – Resident Assistant (RA) for the Alpha Beta floor and member of the organization.

Other RAs – RAs who work in the buildings that Jennifer Feder supervises.

Matt Schoffler – Director of Judicial Affairs.

Case

Jennifer Feder is in her office very early the morning of opening day. While she is tired from a busy two weeks of RA training, the excitement of meeting new residents, greeting returning students, and the overall energy of opening day has given her a renewed sense of energy. As she is preparing for the day, her phone rings. She picks it up to hear a frustrated Alyssa Palmer on the line. Alyssa was walking through the buildings doing final checks of the rooms to make sure they were ready for everyone to move in and found a large mess in Alpha Beta's chapter room. The mess included several cases of empty beer bottles, opened and used hard liquor bottles, and a case of open and mostly finished wine bottles, as well as garbage, food left open, and unwashed dishes. She immediately called Officer Cave who came and took a report, but felt she also needed to call Jennifer so that she could properly follow up with Alpha Beta after opening day was finished. Alyssa reported to Jennifer that in addition to the room being "trashed" the night before, there were several cases of beer cans, wine bottles, and other items in the room that violate policy. Officer Cave had already spoken to Josh, RA for the floor and member of the chapter. Josh insisted that it was not his fraternity brothers who made the mess and agreed to clean up the room before reporting to his opening day responsibilities. Jennifer immediately informed Amy, as this was not the first time Alpha Beta was in violation of policy, and following up from the incident may mean a possible suspension of the chapter.

It is important to note that while this incident occurred prior to the opening of residence halls, students belonging to special groups, such as fraternities and sororities, are allowed to move in a day early in order to assist with opening day. In exchange for the privilege of moving in early, these volunteers help students and parents unload their car and carry belongings up to their rooms. So while the academic year had not started, several brothers from Alpha Beta were already moved into the residence halls as members of this volunteer crew.

The day after move-in, Jennifer and Amy met with Josh to discuss the incident. Since they had not yet received the campus safety report, no official action was taken. However, they were anxious to find out what happened in the chapter room the previous night. Josh maintained his story that it was not members of Alpha Beta that had a party in the chapter room, but said he could not identify who was in the room. When asked who had access to keys to the room (besides himself and the members of his chapter), Josh could not say. After discussing with Josh his challenging role of being an RA and a brother, and their expectations of him in that role in the future, Amy and Jennifer were left to wait for the campus safety report in order to move forward.

Several weeks have passed and the campus safety report never was sent to the Department of Residence Life. As most campus safety reports are sent to

Residence Life within 24–48 hours of the incident, the pattern of this report not appearing after multiple requests has now caught the attention of many people on campus, including the Director of Residence Life, Director of Judicial Affairs and Vice President of Student Affairs. Unable to provide a reason for the report not being delivered, a reluctant Officer Cave personally delivered the report to Amy with a message of "we told you that you wouldn't want to see this" as it was being handed to her.

Upon reading the report, Amy discovered that Alpha Beta was not involved in the party that occurred in their chapter room the night before opening. Instead, she learned that the students attending the party were almost all of the RAs who were on staff in Jennifer's buildings. Every RA was named in the report, with the exception of two. Josh was one of the RAs who attended. Upon calling each RA into an individual meeting to hear their report of the night, it was confirmed that two RAs chose not to socialize with their fellow staff members that evening. The remaining RAs decided to have a beginning of the semester celebration, with Josh volunteering Alpha Beta's chapter room as a location. Each RA confessed to there being alcohol present, each knowing that alcohol is not allowed in the campus residence halls and that several of the students on staff were not of legal drinking age.

As with most drinking incidents, the campus safety report was then delivered to Matt, the Director of Judicial Affairs. The Residence Life office decided that the incident would need to be resolved first as a judicial case and then a decision would be made as to the continued employment of the RAs. That year the college had established a choice in judicial proceedings. The first was the traditional judicial process either with a hearing officer or judicial review board. The second was a mediation-based process meant for groups who admitted that they were responsible ahead of time. The RA staff fit the second scenario so Matt decided that the staff would participate in a group-based mediation process instead of the traditional judicial hearing. The entire RA staff gathered with a trained mediator to discuss the reasons they made the decision to have the party, the impact their choices had made on their residential communities, and the impact it has made on their area staff and others who were involved in the incident. When asked why they made this decision, the answer was a resounding "we didn't think the entire staff could get fired or held responsible."

As part of the mediation process, the group as a whole decided what would be the best sanction for their actions. A separation was made between the result of the judicial process and a second, and separate, process of deciding whether they should keep their positions as RAs. As part of the judicial process, each student was required to create alcohol education opportunities for their residential floors as well as lead a meeting with their fellow RAs in their residential area so that they understood the situation and their choices.

While the RAs were asked to keep the judicial procedures and employment meetings confidential, a growing conversation was happening on campus as stories were sent through the campus rumor mill. The RA handbook clearly stated that any RA found in violation of the alcohol policy would be immediately terminated from his/her position. Before employment discussions began, there were rumors and assumptions about the fate of the RAs. As the rumors grew, residents became more involved in the process. Many of the RAs were returning to their floor for a second year, were members of fraternities and sororities, and had strong connections to their residence hall floor community. As a show of support, residents created a poster and sidewalk chalk campaign saying "Save the RAs," in support of their RAs not being terminated from their positions. This took an incident that was primarily affecting three small residence halls and spread it to a campus-wide discussion.

By the end of the mediation process and in the midst of the student campaign, Amy and Jennifer had a decision to make. If the RA employment policy was followed, it would leave Jennifer with a staff of two (out of 15) RAs and the need to hire and train new RAs in the middle of the semester. In addition, it would have a strong impact on that residence hall, with the floor communities needing to say goodbye to their beloved RAs and accepting a new RA into the community. Accepting a new RA into the community was a particular concern because of the "Save the RAs" campaign. Finally, the RA staff for Amy's area would also be impacted by the need to help cover duty hours and programming needs until new staff could be hired. To not follow the policy means setting precedence for current and future RAs in relation to drinking on campus. In consultation with the Director of Residence Life and Director of Judicial Affairs, they leave the decision to Amy and Jennifer and ask for their recommendation in the morning.

As Amy, what would be your decision? As Jennifer, what would be your decision? What are the differences between the two points of view? What do you believe should be the ultimate decision?

CAMPUS CLIMATE AT OCEANSIDE UNIVERSITY

Benjamin Gillig and Shaila Mulholland

Setting

Oceanside University (OU) is a 100-year-old large public land-grant university on the West Coast, with close to 30,000 students enrolled in undergraduate, graduate, and professional programs. Located in a quiet, upper-middle class suburban community, the institution has been nationally recognized for excellence in biomedical sciences, engineering, the humanities, and education, and boasts high research productivity and world-renowned faculty. Approximately three-quarters of the students attending OU are undergraduates and one-quarter of students are enrolled in graduate or professional programs.

For the past two decades, and before the elimination of affirmative action policies in the mid-1990s, an ongoing issue at OU has been the low enrollment of underrepresented students, in particular African American students. Even through periods of strong enrollment growth at the state's public universities and improvements in high school graduation rates, OU continued to experience a dearth of African American applicants. The situation was further complicated in the mid-1990s, when state voters passed an initiative constitutional amendment that banned the use of race or gender in the admissions process. Oceanside University has since used a "total review" admissions process intended to evaluate *all* aspects of an applicant's file. However, admissions officers are under pressure to admit the "best" students, and ensure each entering class represents the most elite high school graduates. Over the past ten years, the total enrollment of African American students has remained under 2%.

Two years ago, OU's president announced the "Quest for Excellence" initiative, an eight-year campaign to enhance the prestige of the institution and its endowment. Citing competition from other research universities in the region, the president proposed a realignment of institutional priorities and strategy, which included: reinvestment in the campus's ambitious facilities improvement plan; enhanced funding for research; and significantly increased resources for faculty recruitment and retention. In the second year of the initiative, students began paying a "merit fee," which raised undergraduate tuition by 12%. Funds generated from the fees were utilized to pay for additional course offerings and to hire more faculty. The merit fee received strong support from the Faculty Senate, but several student groups raised concerns with the administration and posited that although the fees could support the proposed enhancement of academic programs and facilities, it would make OU unaffordable for many students.

Characters

Dr. Jackie Martin is Vice President of Student Affairs and Dean of Students, responsible for overseeing all student conduct matters.

Dr. Julius Gilbert, Oceanside University's eleventh president, is a distinguished faculty member from the School of Engineering.

Abigail Moyes is a senior majoring in linguistics and is the president of the Undergraduate Student Government Association.

Terry Vivas is a junior majoring in accounting and serving a first term as the president of the Black Student Union.

Evan Hawkin is a fifth year senior majoring in computer science and president of the Sigma Omicron Fraternity.

Wendell Wells is the Director of University Communications.

Case

During the first week of February, an OU fraternity began advertising a party for the following weekend. The fraternity, Sigma Omicron, has been a chartered Greek organization at OU since 1981, and with approximately 100 active members, is the campus's sixth-largest fraternity. Sigma Omicron owns and operates a chapter house, which is located a quarter mile from campus in a residential area occupied predominantly by OU students. The house is adjacent to three other fraternity houses, and the four chapters alternate throwing weekend parties that are attended by several hundred Oceanside students, mostly from the Greek community. These fraternity parties usually have a theme, and students often dress according to that theme.

You are the Vice President of Student Affairs and Dean of Students for OU. You have been closely involved with monitoring the safety and appropriateness of the theme parties. Over the past three years, campus police who patrol the neighborhood have been called to the vicinity with increasing frequency. Police calls usually involve reports of public intoxication, fights, or alcohol poisoning. Last November, a female student was transported to the Emergency Room from one of the fraternity houses after allegedly consuming a drink laced with GHB, a date-rape drug, during a party. Police were unable to find a suspect.

Sigma Omicron has decided to call its upcoming party "Culture Night." By university policy, fraternities are required to gain approval for any large-scale events or parties from the Greek Programming Board, a student committee that governs the social events sponsored by campus fraternities and sororities. In official proposal forms, Sigma Omicron leaders present Culture Night as a "celebration of members of our Greek community" and "fun event for all involved." In an open meeting held five days prior to the Culture Night party, the Programming Board unanimously voted to approve the program without discussion.

Advertisements for the party begin to circulate on Facebook and other social networking sites. On the party's Facebook page, Culture Night is described with the tag-line "in celebration of Black History Month." Several photographs of African Americans with the caption "black gangstas" are posted on the site, as is a description of what partygoers should wear: baggy clothes, golden front teeth, "bling," and "any other ghetto gear."

The party occurs as scheduled on Saturday evening, and is attended by roughly 80 to 100 students. Most of those in attendance are members of Oceanside Greek organizations.

The next day after the party, the Facebook page has been posted and re-posted with enough frequency that it catches the attention of several members of Oceanside's Black Student Union (BSU). BSU leadership is informed, and a special meeting of the BSU executive officers is called for Sunday evening. The BSU vice president of communication also happens to be on the editorial board of Oceanside's campus newspaper, and emails the paper's editor-in-chief with a link to the party's Facebook page. The BSU executive officers meet and agree to write a letter condemning the party as racist for publication in the campus newspaper. They also decide to pen a letter to the university president expressing their outrage, and desire that Sigma Omicron be sanctioned by the university. They decide to meet again the following day.

On Monday morning, a front-page article runs in the campus newspaper with the headline "Some Find Weekend Frat Party Offensive." The short story, which is placed below the fold, recounts information from the party's Facebook page and has a quote from the BSU president expressing outrage over the party. During the course of the morning, the electronic version of the story receives over a thousand hits on the newspaper's website.

By the afternoon, the University Communications Office begins to receive calls from local news outlets. At first, the director of communication dismisses calls from print and TV journalists as "fishing for a story," but when the lines start to light up he decides to call the president's chief of staff. The director explains that he only knows what the journalists have told him: the party took place over the weekend, appears to have mocked Black History Month, and has offended students. The communication director tells the chief of staff, "We need President Gilbert to weigh in" and the chief of staff agrees.

At 5:30 p.m., the president sends an email to the Oceanside campus expressing "sadness and concern" over the party. He states that "Oceanside University finds acts of prejudice and racism reprehensible," but says, "a full investigation must be completed before conclusions can be made." The text of the email is released to media outlets. Later that night, local TV news programs broadcast stories about the Culture Night party. The following morning, the local newspaper's lead headline is: "Black students allege racism at Oceanside," all six local morning-news TV programs have stories on the incident, and the regional newspaper runs a small front-page story. The Communications Office is inundated with inquiries from journalists, including reporters from all major news stations and national networks. The president, who is on a flight back from a conference in Washington, DC will not be on campus until the afternoon and has asked you to help field inquiries from the key stakeholders. So far, the governor and the chairman of the Board of Trustees have called.

On Tuesday morning, the letter from the BSU executive board runs on the front page of the campus newspaper, which is flying off newsstands. Campus newspaper reporters have also managed to interview the president of the Sigma Omicron chapter. In the story, which runs under the headline "'It was just for fun,'" the chapter president states, "I don't understand what people are so upset about, it was just a party." He adds: "people who think this was racism are just wrong. They shouldn't take themselves so seriously." Letters to the editor from the faculty condemn the party. In one letter, a seasoned faculty member in History argues that the problems of the party had less to do with the racist culture of the fraternity and more to do with structural problems that have long existed at OU. These problems include a need to address the underrepresentation of students and faculty of color and improve the campus climate. Some faculty also argue a need to revisit the admissions process at the university, to ensure that it was indeed in line with the values of the university to assess students in a holistic manner.

At 11:30 a.m., you attend a meeting organized by the BSU executive board and when asked by the BSU president to introduce yourself, you explain: "I'm here to express the university's solidarity with you. What has happened is unfair, and I want to acknowledge that." Explaining that the university president has requested a full investigation of the party, the session quickly becomes a question and answer exchange. When asked about who will conduct the investigation, you respond "that isn't clear yet. According to policy, the president can assemble a committee, or can request the Faculty Senate do so." When asked if the BSU will be consulted, you are unable to answer. The session grows tenser as the questioning continues. In response to students' questions about what policies the party may have violated, you reply: "I'm afraid it hasn't violated any of our behavioral policies. Because the party took place off-campus, I'm afraid the university is powerless to enforce the code of conduct." At this point, BSU leaders become enraged and the session is ended.

At 1:30 p.m., the president arrives back on campus. He calls for an immediate meeting in a large auditorium in the new student center. He plans to deliver a statement recently prepared by the communications staff. The statement describes the Culture Night party as "despicable," and promises that "the university will use any and all resources at its disposal to right this wrong." The statement is kept purposely vague. Once the communications staff prepares the revised statement for the press, the president heads to the student center. At 2:45 p.m., the president takes the stage before approximately 350 students, staff, and faculty. The BSU executive board is in attendance, and they sit together in the second row. The senior leadership of the university is also present, sitting in the first row. The university president begins his statement with an explanation of why he has only just returned to campus, and that he was away at a scholarly conference. To his shock, he is cut off by yells from members of the audience, some of whom begin shouting "No excuses!" He speaks louder, and continues his statement.

A few minutes in, the president reads, "we must fully investigate this incident to ensure that we ascertain the facts of the matter." At this point, the uproar from the audience becomes too loud to speak over and one student stands and shouts "If the administration isn't going to do anything about this, then we have to take action! If you agree that these problems have gone ignored on this campus for too long, stand up right now and join me as we walk out!" As the president looked out to the entire room, the shouting and chanting continued and students began exiting the auditorium. As they did, the president picked up his notes, left the stage and exited the auditorium through the stage door, followed by the university administrators.

Back in your office a few minutes later, you log onto Facebook to try and locate the Culture Night party's webpage, but instead find numerous posts with videos of the exchange that has just taken place in the student center. Something needs to be done and needs to be done soon. You believe that it is imperative that the university respond and look further into the Culture Night to "ascertain the facts of the matter," which aren't yet clear to you.

Feeling that the university is powerless to sanction the fraternity members through student conduct procedures, you ponder what should be done first.

HIRING IN THE VALLEY

Diane Cardenas Elliott and Audrey Loera

Setting

Valley Community College (VCC) is a comprehensive two-year college serving Valley and Bedford counties in the Northeast. VCC currently offers 80 associates degrees in career and transfer programs. The range of degrees run from liberal arts (Associates of Arts), sciences (Associates of Applied Science and Associates of Science), and fine arts (Associates of Fine Arts) to a full range of certificate offerings in career programs, business, technology, and information systems. The student population is approximately 8,500 each semester, with 65% of those attending on a part-time basis. VCC also offers a wide variety of personal enrichment and professional development courses which enroll an additional 3,000 students each semester.

The majority of VCC's students are Caucasian and live in the bi-county area served by the college. In the last five years, the student demographic has begun to change with increasing numbers of African American, Latino, and Asian students enrolling; these culturally diverse groups of students now comprise 15% of the overall student population. A recent analysis of student surveys and student focus groups conducted by the Director of Student Life reveal that involvement in student clubs and organizations has helped to promote a high level of camaraderie among students (often lacking at a commuter campus), higher levels of diversity awareness and sensitivity, and a higher retention rate overall for students who participate in student life and student activities programming.

Despite changing student demographics at VCC and in both counties, Valley and Bedford counties continue to be comprised of a significant number of wealthy citizens. Both counties are ranked in the top five income-producing and asset-holding counties in the country. The high per capita income has been driven by the high salaries at the large number of U.S. pharmaceutical firms, many of whom have their headquarters in Valley county. In addition, Valley and Bedford counties are political strongholds for a local conservative party.

The VCC Board of Trustees is comprised of 15 members, most of whom are appointed by the local county commissioners. Twelve of the 15 board members are Caucasian, closely mirroring the college and county demographic. Each member initially serves for a one-year term, however, appointments can be renewed thereafter for three years and there are no limits to the number of three-year terms a board member can serve. In fact, due to the conservative political climate that has been a mainstay of county politics for decades, there has been little turnover in trustee members over the last ten years and the Chairman of the Board has remained in that position for over 20 years.

Characters

Mary Lawrence has been the Dean of Student Services for the past four years. She reports to the Vice President of Student Affairs.

Charles Chester is the Vice President of Student Affairs and was only recently hired into that role in the past year.

Myra Smith has been the Assistant Director of Student Life for the past eight years. She reports to the Director of Student Life, a position which is currently vacant. Myra is an internal candidate for the Director's position.

Eve Jackson is a resident of a nearby county, and is an external applicant for the Director of Student Life position.

Janet Anderson is a well-known citizen of Bedford county and works as a mid-level manager at a local pharmaceutical firm that is relocating its headquarters to the Southwest. Janet is also an external applicant for the Director of Student Life position.

Pamela Thomas, **DeShawn Rogers**, and **Juanita Lopez** are presidents of the Student Government Association, the Phi Theta Kappa Honor Society, and the Orgullo Latino Club respectively.

Jack Kudless is a tenured History faculty member.

Case

As Mary Lawrence, the Dean of Student Services, you have been charged with overseeing the hiring of a new Director of Student Life which includes making the final hiring recommendation to the president of VCC. In accordance with Human Resource policies, you formed a search committee chaired by Jack Kudless. The search committee reviewed applicants and from a large pool selected seven potential candidates to interview. In addition to being interviewed by the search committee, the seven candidates also met with a student focus group consisting of Pamela Thomas, DeShawn Rogers, and Juanita Lopez. Based on the interviews and feedback from the student focus group, the search committee has selected three finalists.

Eve Jackson is an external candidate who spent the last five years working at a nearby community college as an Assistant Director of Student Life. She is young, energetic, and comes highly recommended by her current supervisor. As the Assistant Director of Student Life at her current institution, she was, along with her supervisor, responsible for successfully lobbying her college's administration to have a larger percentage of the student activity fees directed to the student life budget. With this budget increase, she was able to expand programming and activities to include many new student clubs that students had been asking to form since her arrival five years ago. In addition to this singular accomplishment, Eve brings academic qualifications to the table with a master's degree in Higher Education Administration and she is also currently pursuing her Ed.D. in Education Administration in her spare time from a local state university.

Myra Smith is the current Assistant Director of Student Life. Myra has held this position for the past eight years and has been instrumental in growing student life and improving student involvement at VCC. She is well liked by the students and able to meet the demands of the very busy student affairs office. However, you also are aware that Myra's former supervisor has had numerous issues with her performance. Specifically, on two prior occasions Myra allowed student club presidents to obtain cash advances on anticipated club expenses in violation of the college finance policy on reimbursement-only expenditures for student clubs. Since the cash advances did not follow protocol, there was no mechanism for tracking the return of funds. As a result, the Office of Student Life's financial account went into arrears and a dispute about whether the cash advance was reimbursed ensued. On the first occasion, Myra indicated that because she was new to the college, she was unfamiliar with the nuances of the college finance policy, and consequently she was only given a verbal warning. On the second occasion, Myra's supervisor felt she had had enough time to be aware of college finance policy, and because of the first incident, she was given a written warning that was placed into her employee file. The warning indicated that another violation of college finance policy could result in her termination.

Janet Anderson is an external candidate and a resident of Bedford County. She has served as an adjunct Business professor for the past three years and has frequently volunteered in the tutoring center. In addition, she has served as a co-advisor to the Business Club and currently chairs the Business Advisory Committee, a group of local industry professionals who provide advice to VCC's Business faculty on job-specific skills needed for program graduates and curriculum updates for degrees and certificates. Although Janet is an active member of the community and has received good teaching reviews from students, she has no experience in higher education administration.

The day before the final recommendation is due to the president of VCC, Jack Kudless stops by your office asking to speak to you privately. He indicates that the committee has put forth three finalists for your review, however, the search committee's top candidate by unanimous vote, is Eve Jackson, the external candidate from a nearby college. As a second choice they would endorse Myra who is currently fulfilling the job responsibilities and appears to be well liked by the students, despite the two warnings in her file.

In this conversation you also learn that Janet's application included a letter of recommendation from a prominent and vocal board member who was familiar with her volunteer time in the tutoring center and her contributions to the Business Advisory Committee. Jack also tells you that at a recent campus event, he ran into this board member. Knowing Jack was the chair of the search committee for this position, the board member took Jack aside and reinforced the case for Janet's candidacy, stating openly that she is a good fit for the position, given her service to the college, and that he doesn't want to see her leave the area. Both Jack and the search committee had already discussed Janet's candidacy, and no one on the committee felt she was qualified for the director position. Because the board member sought Jack out, and had a conversation about Janet, Jack felt pressured to advance her as a distant third finalist. Jack hopes that you will oblige the search committee's wishes that recommend Eve as the top finalist for the position, given Myra's somewhat problematic record, and Janet's nebulous qualifications for a position in higher education.

Later that day you are meeting with your supervisor, Charles Chester, who wants an update on the Director of Student Life search. As you are giving your update, Charles mentions Janet is a personal friend of one of the board members and this board member has personally called the president to offer his recommendation on Janet's behalf. You mention that the search committee has recommended her as a distant third finalist and her credentials in comparison to the other candidates are inferior. Charles is very unpleased to hear this. He suggests you think carefully about who you will put forth as the final recommended candidate and advises you to be sure you substantiate your final decision in writing after reviewing each candidate's overall record.

You return to your office to find a group of students including Pamela Thomas, DeShawn Rogers, and Juanita Lopez who were part of the focus group. They have recently learned that the search committee put forth Eve Jackson as their top finalist and are livid. They feel Myra is a better candidate and are threatening to boycott student club activities and some college-wide events for the rest of the academic year in protest. The students clearly express to you they don't want an outsider, and will refuse to work with anyone other than Myra. The students tell you that Myra has been an ally who has helped them along their path to become student leaders. You have been in Myra's position at another college, and understand that it is common for students to form a strong bond with student life personnel, and you are grateful the students have that connection here at VCC. Knowing this, you are still surprised the students have such strong opinions about personnel matters, and didn't expect them to want to have such influence over a search process.

What would you do?

FIGHTING WORDS AT CARPE DIEM

John P. Downey

Setting

Carpe Diem University is a medium-sized, private, non-sectarian institution in the Northwest. Founded in 1892 as a Methodist College for men, Carpe Diem University now boasts a diverse undergraduate population of 10,000 students (8,000 undergraduate and 2,000 graduate). The university has a large on-campus population, with 5,000 undergraduate students residing in the residence halls and 1,500 upper division students living in on-campus apartments. Carpe Diem prides itself on the diversity of its student body, with 42 states represented in the student body, over 30% coming from minority backgrounds and 5% from other countries.

As a comprehensive university, Carpe Diem offers over 50 undergraduate majors and five master's degree programs. The Music program is nationally recognized and has produced many world-class performers. Carpe Diem has always maintained above-average academic standards. Average SAT scores are 1280, and 85% of students graduated in the top 20% of their high school classes. In addition to academics there is a long history of student activism and involvement in out-of-class activities.

Characters

Carl Peters is a White junior Political Science major who had been written up by his Resident Assistant (RA) on two occasions last year for consumption of alcohol and disruptive behavior. The RA was supportive of him during this time because Carl's brother had been killed in Iraq the summer prior to his transfer to Carpe Diem. In addition to his disciplinary struggles last year he was placed on academic probation.

Khalid Abdullah, a junior from Saudi Arabia, is in good academic standing with no prior disciplinary record. He was recently elected to Student Senate. He is accused of posting comments on Facebook calling Carl a "racist redneck" and "skinhead" in retaliation for vandalism of his door that he believes Carl committed.

Joe Jackson is the RA for the 2nd floor of Chaplinsky Hall, where both Carl and Khalid reside. Joe is an African American senior and this is his third year on staff. He also serves as a senator on SGA and attends Carpe Diem

University on a full academic scholarship. He considers the comments posted on Facebook by Khalid to be a violation of the university's fighting words anti-harassment policy.

Professor Miles Coltraine has been the faculty-in-residence for Chaplinsky Hall for the past four years. He is a full professor of Music and has been at Carpe Diem University for 20 years. He lives in the apartment with his wife, a professor of law at another institution and part-time consultant to Carpe Diem University. Professor Coltraine is African American and is noted for his commitment to students. He is well known for holding "jamming" sessions in Chaplinsky lounge until late in the evening and has been doing so for many years. He encourages students to bring their instruments and engages them in music playing and in discussion, at times contentious, of current events. He has won several awards for his teaching and scholarship. He has heard about the incident in his hall and is concerned that such harsh words were used but is equally concerned that "the archaic speech policy has been used again."

Barbara Garcia is in her first year as the Director of Residence Life. She is Hispanic and feels she has found a home at Carpe Diem University. The dean, who was impressed with her administrative and management skills, heavily recruited her. She met with Joe Jackson, the RA, and supports his decision to document the Facebook incident using the fighting words anti-harassment policy.

Jerry Hart has been the Dean of Students and Vice President for Student Life for ten years. Dean Hart is known for his sense of humor and commitment to students. As a White administrator, he has worked hard to bring a diverse staff to Carpe Diem University, a fact that has not gone unnoticed by the minority community. He is concerned to hear the fighting words anti-harassment policy has been implemented and calls a meeting with Barbara Garcia.

Roberta Dylan has been President of Carpe Diem University for four years. Dr. Dylan was an undergraduate at Carpe Diem many years ago, before going on to a prestigious career as a professor of European History, stints as an academic dean and vice president, and eventually the "opportunity of a lifetime" to become president of her alma mater. She is known for her fundraising prowess and her focus on strong public relations with key people, both inside and outside the state, who can help raise the profile of the university. Although an award-winning teacher, she is less comfortable dealing with issues of diversity and student conflicts and relies heavily on her team to handle such matters.

Case

1. On October 1 at 12:30 a.m. Carl Peters was perusing Facebook when he noticed a comment from one of his residents, stating, "Carl Peters is a racist redneck and skinhead." The comment had just been posted by Khalid Abdullah, whom he had recently "friended" despite his general disdain for him. Carl walked down the hall to confront Khalid in his room. When he arrived, Khalid's door was open and he had several friends in his room. Khalid was on the computer. Before Carl could say anything Khalid jumped up, ran to the door, and showed him what had been written on the door in black magic marker. A note had been scribbled in large print that read, "Terrorist go back to your own country." Khalid immediately accused Carl as the culprit. Carl said "I agree with the sentiment but that is not my writing." Khalid said he was "sick of the racist crap" he got from Carl. An argument erupted and Joe Jackson, the RA, came out to break up what he thought was about to become a fistfight. Joe separated Carl and Khalid and met first with Carl and then with Khalid.

2. In his meeting with Carl, Joe listened carefully as Carl denied writing on Khalid's door and was outraged at being referred to as a "redneck racist" and "skinhead." He showed Joe the Facebook posting and in just 10 minutes there had already been 15 replies, most favorable to Khalid's posting. Several of the postings were from residents who were sitting in Khalid's room and lived on the floor. He claimed others on the floor, including Khalid, had called him these names before because he had "more conservative opinions." Carl claims he and Khalid did not get along because his brother was killed in Iraq fighting against "people of his kind." Joe rebuked Carl for referring to Khalid in this manner but allowed him to continue. Carl said he had been avoiding Khalid since their latest argument two days ago, following one of Dr. Coltraine's jamming sessions.

3. Joe left his meeting with Carl and went to his room to review the Code of Conduct he had received as part of his RA training. He read the "fighting words anti-harassment" policy, which reads as follows:

> The University prohibits conduct that prevents free academic interaction and opportunities or creates an intimidating, hostile, or offensive study or living environment. Thus, any written or verbal behavior beyond reasonable expression of opinion, such as a disparaging comment, epithet, slur, insult, or other expressive behavior, which is likely to cause another person humiliation, stress or psychological harm is strictly forbidden. Such words include, but are not limited to, those terms widely recognized to be derogatory references to race, ethnicity, religion, sex, sexual orientation, disability, and other personal characteristics.

4. Joe met with Khalid, who had calmed down considerably and apologized for causing a disruption. Khalid claimed, "I know Carl did this to my door and I am not going to take it." Joe listened as Khalid described how Carl had made statements against "Islam" claiming they were "known terrorists committed to the destruction of our great country" during one of Dr. Coltraine's jamming sessions in the lounge two nights ago. Khalid said when he tried to talk with Carl he was belligerent. Khalid claims he knows that Carl's brother was killed in Iraq but that does not excuse his behavior. Joe had heard from other students about Carl's comments but he had always had friendly relations with Carl so he did not give it any further thought. Joe expressed sympathy for what happened to Khalid's door, told him he would document it and have it investigated by police, but he would also have to document Khalid for his posting on Facebook. Khalid became outraged that he was being written up when it was his door that had been vandalized. He also asked, "Are you checking everyone's Facebook postings or just mine?" His final words to Joe were "I cannot believe you, of all people, are protecting this guy."

5. The next morning at 10:00 a.m. Joe met with Barbara Garcia, director of Residence Life. Joe showed her the Facebook posting, which by that time had over a hundred responses, most of which were favorable to Khalid's position. He also described the vandalism to Khalid's door, explained how he had contacted the police, who were investigating the incident, and then described the argument between Khalid and Carl. He explained that he does not agree with Carl's politics but "if we allow Khalid to use Facebook as a weapon to harass Carl, what will stop another student from using it against me?" Barbara agreed with Joe's analysis and his decision to document the vandalism and Khalid's violation of the fighting words anti-harassment policy. She promised to call Khalid in as soon as possible to discuss the vandalism and would tell the area coordinator for Chaplinsky Hall to handle the judicial case with Khalid.

6. At 1:00 p.m. Dean Hart met with Barbara Garcia and expressed frustration that she had not contacted him prior to agreeing to pursue the incident through the judicial system. She indicated that she had many years of experience and did not consider this to be an incident she needed to clear with her supervisor. Dean Hart told her that the fighting words anti-harassment policy had not been used in ten years, his first year on campus, because the faculty were against it. In fact, he had already received a call from Dr. Coltraine, who expressed concern that this policy is "being used as a tool against free speech and social media." Dr. Coltraine asked, "If we are not safe to express ourselves on a college campus using social media, where are we safe?"

The previous incident occurred ten years ago during one of Dr. Coltraine's jamming sessions when two students, one White and the other Black, engaged in a heated verbal exchange. At one point the Black student referred to the White student using a racial slur and the White student retaliated with his own racial slur. Everyone present agreed that Dr. Coltraine handled the incident very well, although the next day both students were brought before Dean Hart for violation of the fighting words anti-harassment policy. Dr. Coltraine was outraged that someone had reported the incident. He asked that the charges be dropped and that this policy be abandoned because "it has no place on a college campus." Dean Hart did drop the charges and agreed to a more strict interpretation of the policy, but insisted that the fighting words anti-harassment policy remain in place and be enforced because "students have a right to be free from harassment and if we do not enforce this policy it is useless to have it in our Code of Conduct."

7. At 3:00 p.m. President Dylan's Office called Dean Hart after she was informed by the University Relations Department that a video had been put on YouTube satirizing Carpe Diem as a "terrorist cell loyal to the Taliban." The video had a catchy song altering the lyrics of their football fight song. When Dean Hart viewed it he had to admit it was funny and was amazed it was produced in such a short period of time. By 4:00 p.m. the video had gone viral. His father-in-law from Florida had viewed it and called to ask, "Is this some sort of PR thing from your president?"

8. The faculty senate was scheduled to meet the next morning at 10:30 a.m. during common hour and Dr. Coltraine asked to be placed on the agenda to discuss the fighting words anti-harassment policy and the university's handling of this recent incident. He made it clear in an email to Dean Hart and Barbara Garcia that he had lost confidence in their abilities as leaders.

9. The local newspaper, the *Constitutional Observer* (a Pulitzer Prize-winning publication), and the local CBS television affiliate called the University Relations Office asking for a statement concerning "the racial incident that took place last night." The editor plans to run a front-page story on the local section of the paper on the incident and has been interviewing students from Chaplinsky Hall via email and with the assistance of a Carpe Diem student interning with the newspaper. The CBS affiliate plans to put a copy of the video on their web page and run a story tonight, with or without comment from Carpe Diem administrators.

10. President Dylan has asked to meet with Dean Hart at 5:00 p.m. in her office.

You are Jerry Hart, the Dean of Students. In the next hour you must prepare for your meeting with Dr. Dylan. You will be expected to explain the actions of your staff, have an outline for an appropriate response to the media, and a preliminary response for the president justifying the existence and use of the fighting words anti-harassment policy. Over the next 24 hours you will be expected to develop a more detailed and nuanced plan to respond to the emerging issues on campus, off campus, and in the social media.

INTERCOLLEGIATE ATHLETICS AT CLAYTON COLLEGE

Ginelle John

Setting

Clayton College is a private college located in the Southwest. Clayton College is in a suburban area in a town also named Clayton and has an enrollment of approximately 22,000 students. The majority of Clayton's student body is full-time and the ratio of women to men is 3 to 2. Clayton College's intercollegiate athletic programs are extremely popular among the college community, locals and especially among the alumni. There are eight men's teams (baseball, basketball, football, soccer, swimming, tennis, track and field, and wrestling) and seven women's teams (basketball, bowling, soccer, softball, swimming, track and field, and tennis).

The college and community are rallying behind a project to renovate the college's aging athletic center. With the generous support of alumni and community members, the college has raised over $900,000 toward the renovation of its athletic center. The estimated cost of the renovations is about $3 million. The renovations are scheduled to begin next year.

Characters

Patrick Williams has been Executive Athletic Director of Intercollegiate Athletics for three years. He reports to President Hampton.

Wallace Hampton has been president of Clayton College for three years and has worked to bring alumni "Back to Campus."

Douglas Matthews has served as Director of Development for one and one-half years.

Wayne Spears is an alumnus of Clayton College. He owns several successful businesses in the Clayton and neighboring communities.

Sophia Marshall is a 19-year-old sophomore. She wants Clayton to have an intercollegiate women's volleyball team.

Mark Harper is a 20-year-old sophomore who plays baseball at Clayton. If a women's volleyball team is created he will lose his athletic scholarship.

Case

Sophia Marshall has played volleyball on her high school team since she was
a freshman, however, by her senior year she was not sure if she wanted to
play competitive volleyball in college. Wanting to eventually pursue a law
degree, Sophia decided to attend Clayton College because of its strong history
and philosophy departments. Since her desire to play volleyball has waned,
it initially did not matter to Sophia that Clayton did not have an intercollegiate women's volleyball team.

By the end of Sophia's freshman year at Clayton, Sophia decided she
wanted to be more involved in extra-curricular activities. She was confident
that the extra-curricular activities would not interfere with her academics
and she believed it would look good on her law school applications. After
speaking with women who play intramural volleyball at Clayton, Sophia and
some of the women decided they want Clayton to offer a women's intercollegiate volleyball team.

With support from the Women's Student Association and over 3,000
student signatures, a letter was sent to Mr. Patrick Williams, Executive Athletic
Director, requesting that an intercollegiate women's volleyball team be
created and that athletic scholarships be offered to members of the women's
volleyball team. In the letter, Sophia and her supporters cite Title IX stipu-
lations that there be equitable opportunity for women to participate in sports
and that women receive athletic scholarship dollars in proportion to their
population.

You are Patrick Williams. You are all too familiar with Title IX, a federal
law prohibiting sexual discrimination at educational institutions that receive
federal funds. Specifically, this law forbids sexual discrimination in all aspects
of academic programs and student services, and this includes athletic
programs.

While the proportion of female athletes to female students is low, you have
always ensured that that female athletic scholarship dollars are proportionate
to their participation and that there is equal treatment (between men and
women) on any issues related to athletics, which includes, but is not limited
to scheduling of games and practice time, coaching, recruitment of student
athletes, equipment and supplies, and support services.

You realize that the creation of a women's volleyball team would be a
contentious issue. Although there is support for the volleyball team, you know
that funds will have to be diverted from some men's athletic teams to support
the women's volleyball team.

Born and raised in Clayton and coming from a working-class family, Mark
Harper and his parents were ecstatic and relieved when they found out Mark
was awarded an athletic scholarship to play baseball at Clayton. Mark has
played baseball at Clayton for two years. He is a sophomore business major

and received a scholar athlete award in his first year at Clayton, and with a GPA of 3.4 is expected to receive another one this year.

At the end of the season Mark was called into the coaches' office and informed that his athletic scholarship will not be awarded to him the following year, his junior year. Asked why, he was informed that a women's volleyball team is being created and that several men's scholarships from various men's teams had to be cut to fund the volleyball team athletes. After further investigating, Mark found out that scholarships from the men's soccer, swimming, and wrestling teams will also be cut. Mark quickly mobilized other male student athletes and got signatures from over 4,000 students asking that funding to men's sports program not be cut. In addition to the initiating petition, Mark wrote a letter to you informing you that without his scholarship, he will not be able to remain at Clayton and will have to transfer to another school.

Having played soccer and baseball when he was at Clayton, Wayne Spears has been a major supporter of Clayton's athletic programs for years and frequently attends the college's sporting events. Mr. Spears is also an active member of Clayton's Alumni Association and hosts an annual fundraising event on behalf of the college. Mr. Spears's annual event has always been one of the most successful for the college.

For the past two months, Mr. Spears has been in talks with Patrick Williams and Douglas Matthews about raising funds to renovate the athletic training center. Mr. Spears mentioned that he would personally donate $100,000 of his own money to the project and through a number of alumni events, will help raise additional capital for the project. However, upon learning that a number of scholarships from several men's teams will be cut to support a women's volleyball team, Mr. Spears wrote a letter to the president, you, and the director of development, threatening to withdraw his donation if scholarships to the men's teams are cut.

Within weeks of Mr. Spears threatening to withdraw his support for the athletic center project, Douglas Matthews has gotten several phone calls and letters from angry alumni upset with the prospect of funds being cut to men's athletic teams.

The president is concerned that donations will go down, support for the athletic center is in jeopardy, and that a major supporter of the college, Mr. Spears, is threatening to withdraw his support for the athletic center's renovation project. President Hampton has called you into his office to ask how you intend to handle this situation.

What do you do?

A CASE OF RELIGIOUS INTOLERANCE AT GREENWICH UNIVERSITY

Shadia Sachedina

Setting

Greenwich University is a mid-sized, four-year, public institution located in the heart of a city in the northwestern part of the United States. The university boasts a very diverse population of approximately 16,000 students. Since the population is so diverse, the university does little by way of diversity development or building of multicultural relationships within the campus community. Campus constituents believe that the diversity of the campus and the success of its students are indicative that the student body is tolerant of all differences.

As a nod to the diversity of the campus, the office of Student Activities is home to over 100 different clubs and organizations on campus, including a thriving number of various religious organizations. The office handles the co-curricular development of the student body and is responsible for developing and implementing a smorgasbord of culturally diverse and multicultural-rich programs as a testament to the diversity at the institution.

All students at Greenwich University pay a student activity fee which is used to fund the co-curricular life of the student population. A thriving Student Government Association oversees the dissemination of a portion of the student activity funds toward club and organization planning and development. Clubs that are registered through the office of Student Activities are also allotted a club space on campus. However, there are very limited spaces and all clubs share a room with other clubs, often resulting in some interpersonal conflicts.

Characters

Ann Morris has been the Director of Student Activities for the past 15 months. She reports to the Dean of Students who oversees the Division of Student Affairs. Ann's responsibilities include the supervision of campus activities, overseeing the advising of clubs and organizations, multicultural affairs, and working with Campus Ministry.

Tom Hastings is a junior and an active student on campus. He is a member of the LGBT (Lesbian, Gay, Bisexual, and Transgender) group on campus and has worked with various clubs and organizations to help increase LGBT awareness.

Simon Law is a faculty member who serves as the advisor to the LGBT group on campus.

Susan Jones is the office of Student Activities event coordinator and has worked in Student Activities for the past five years.

Sarah Dawson is the Assistant Director of Student Activities and has worked in Student Activities for close to eight years.

Joan Roberts is the Dean of Students and oversees the Division of Student Affairs. She has worked at Greenwich University for ten years.

Case

Silence finally reigns in the office of Student Activities as the door quietly shuts behind the last student assistant who has closed up shop for the night. It is 9 p.m., and you as the Director of Student Activities heave a big tired sigh and stare morosely at the proposal submitted by the Muslim Student Organization. It has been a long week, and you have been challenged from every corner on campus on your diplomacy and political aptitude. How is it possible that a subject that universally preaches peace and harmony becomes so fraught with anger and non-tolerance? You close your eyes and begin to mull over the incidents from the past few weeks. How did it all begin?

This past summer, the Development office had contacted you about a potential donor that they had been courting for some time. The donor was promising $100,000, but it was attached to some requirements. They insisted that $10,000 of that money must be used to develop a special suite for the campus Hillel Center. The suite of rooms was currently being occupied by members of the Campus Ministry which included the Muslim as well as Catholic chaplains. The college in their haste to secure the funding erected a glass wall that cordoned off the suite and summarily relabeled it the "Hillel Suite." They left it to you to inform the Campus Ministry staff that they were being relocated to a small room further down the hallway which they would now need to share. The fall semester starts with its usual rush of intensity, and pretty soon you began to hear murmurings among some of the students about the new Hillel suite. The campus newspaper approaches your office and requests an interview asking about the erection of the new Hillel suite. "What does this mean for the other religious organizations on this campus?" is just one of the questions posed by the reporter who emails you a spate of searching questions that demand answers within the week. You push the email into your overflowing pending file and decide to tackle it later.

The next day you attend a panel discussion on "Homosexuality and Religion." The panel is being hosted by a group of students and faculty who have banded together to help promote LGBT awareness on the college campus. On the panel you notice a diverse group of people, some of whom are spokespersons for nationally known Gay Jewish and Muslim groups. Also on the panel are students from the college LGBT association as well as the Muslim Imam (chaplain) who works with the Muslim students on campus. During the panel the Imam notes that he often meets with students who profess confusion on their identity and think they might be gay. He says "I tell them that this is not something that is allowed in our religion. You must pray and not focus on these feelings. They will go away in time." There are audible gasps from the audience and some students boo and hiss. However, you hear some students at the back of the audience loudly cheering and whistling. You recognize these students as part of the Muslim Student Organization.

Later that day, you are approached in your office by some students from the LGBT group. Tom, a vocal and active member of the group, says "what are you going to do about what that Imam said? It's not right. He is meeting with other students and telling them that being gay is a sin." Also in the room with you is the advisor to the LGBT group, Simon Law, a faculty member at the college and a close colleague. He concurs with the student and turns to look at you, "Really Ann. That was not acceptable. How can we sit by and let this Imam advise our students? Surely we have a responsibility to ensure that he is giving our students the right resources and help when they express their confusion about their identity?"

As you begin to head out of the office that evening one of your staff, Susan, who handles event registrations, stops by to see you. "What do you want me to do about this?"—she waves a piece of paper in front of your face. "It's a table reservation form for the main floor by the Jewish Student Association. They are asking for the use of the space to celebrate Hanukkah." She says.

"What is the description of the event?" you ask.

"They want to do a prayer reading and light the menorah. There will be singing and food." Susan responds, reading from the sheet.

"Why do they want to do it in the main hall?" you ask. "That's a very public space. Students are going to be headed to class at that time and it's not as if other religious groups hold functions in that area."

"They have always done it there" is the rejoinder. "Remember last year it raised questions with some of the other religious groups, so this year we let the Catholic Ministry disseminate ashes on Ash Wednesday in the space to keep them quiet."

You recall this with a sinking feeling. "We can't do this. It's not appropriate." You mutter out loud.

"Well precedence has been set," responds Susan. "What do you suggest?"

"Let's talk about this later. I have to go home." You respond.

The next morning, you are greeted by a lengthy email from Sarah, the Assistant Director of Student Activities. The email recounts an incident which occurred in one of your event spaces on campus at a student program the previous night. The Indian students were celebrating "Holi" an event that traditionally welcomes the start of spring. However, the students decided to get a jump start on their celebration this year and had proceeded to spray colored dye all over the floor and walls of the room. Sarah and you meet with Rani, one of the students who was coordinating the event. "We were just celebrating" protested Rani. "What's the big deal? You certainly don't say anything when the Jewish students are lighting their candles in the main hall of campus. Isn't candle lighting illegal on campus?"

Two days later you are sitting in your office when you get a call from Joan, the Dean of Students, who is also your supervisor. Joan sounds tired. "So I just got a call from the president's office regarding a proposal submitted by the Muslim Student Association. I am sending it your way. Please read it over and let's talk." On reading the proposal you notice that it is written very politely and with great respect. The proposal requests that the college provide space for the Imam on their campus. "We are not asking for anything that is not done for other religious organizations on this campus" the proposal notes. "Right now we have to go through a selection process to get space to pray our necessary five times a day" the proposal continues. "Is it not possible for us to get a space on campus that can be a prayer space designated for Muslims?"

What should you do?

IT'S NOT JUST THE WEATHER: A CHILLY CLIMATE FOR WOMEN AT CARLFORD COLLEGE

Rachel Wagner and Tracy Davis

Setting

Carlford University is a mid-size, private university in the Midwest with a strong liberal arts foundation. The schools of business and engineering are well supported by research grants and enjoy the largest percentage of undergraduate majors. Men make up 49% of the total undergraduate enrollment of 9,000. Over 95% of the undergraduate population is between the ages of 18 and 24. International enrollment is less than 5%, and the undergraduate population is 92% White. Carlford is largely residential; 75% of its student population live in campus housing and surrounding neighborhoods. Students are active in organizations: intramural and club sports and service organizations are the most popular. Greek letter organizations represent the smallest number of student organizations. However, the combined population of this category is over 1,000 members. A majority of students on campus are active in more than one club or organization.

Recently, the university's Board of Directors has set a new, strategic, five-year goal for first year student retention to exceed 92%—a 3% increase over the historical average. A cross-section of campus leaders from Enrollment Management, Academic Affairs, and Student Affairs were appointed to a university retention team to meet regularly with the provost. Among other high-profile activities of the group is a new grant program targeting innovative retention programs and interventions.

Retention rates at many universities are lower for men than women, particularly for African American and Latino men. At Carlford, however, the four-year graduation rates for men and women are 67% and 51%, respectively. Sexual assault and harassment cases make up an alarming portion of the judicial cases, and many students and young professionals have complained about the competitive patriarchal culture in both Greek life and the residence halls. In fact, hall director John Seidelman recently met with the director of Residence Life about the unusual difficulty in recruiting female resident assistants, as well as the general "chilly climate" in the halls.

Characters

Kirsten Johnston has been the Coordinator of Fraternities and Sororities for the last three years. This is her first professional position after completing her master's degree.

Anna Torres is Executive Director of Campus Life and Programs and reports to the Associate Vice President of Student Affairs. She has been at the university for almost two decades and was instrumental in advocating for the establishment of a women's center on campus. She is the former co-chair of the President's Committee on Inclusion and has a campus-wide reputation for being an astute and level-headed administrator and advocate.

Jake Hoverton is a sophomore Small Business Management major and the in-take coordinator for Zeta Theta Theta.

Karen Reeves is a Resident Assistant (RA) in Kirkland Towers and a junior Sociology major with a minor in Gender Studies.

Jordan Kirkland is the president of Zeta Theta Theta and a senior Applied Mathematics major.

Darren North is the Senior Vice President for Student Affairs and Enrollment Management and has been at the university for the last seven years.

John Seidelman has been the Hall Director for Kirkland Towers for seven years. He is a doctoral candidate in Educational Leadership.

Casey Shimmelman is a popular junior, former "Miss Western State," president of the Pan-Hellenic Organization and Teacher Education major.

Dr. Julie Weingarten is Professor of Feminist Theory and the Women's Center Director.

Ashland Simpson is Director of Residential Life.

Case

As Kirsten Johnston, you have had an active semester, overseeing the spring in-take process for both fraternities and sororities. Carlford University does not allow new students to rush Greek letter organizations during their first semester, and as a result the spring class tends to be large and predominantly first year students. Your main responsibilities include advising the Intra-fraternity Council, the Pan-Hellenic Council, and the National Pan-Hellenic Council, instituting and enforcing minimum standards, and oversight of the new membership processes for all Greek letter organizations on campus.

The new membership process went well with few complaints or problems. After a significant hazing-related case that was investigated prior to your arrival on campus, new response protocols and an awareness campaign seemed to have a chilling effect on overt hazing practices that had previously characterized student organizations. The most recent hazing case did not fall in your area of responsibility, but involved members of the men's club soccer team. You have investigated the few rumors that surfaced over the last semester, and all but two of the investigations were dismissed. The remaining two incidents were fairly minor and were addressed through campus judicial programs and representatives from the national organizations. Today is a campus study day in preparation for exams, and you are looking forward to the approaching end of the year. You return from lunch to find three messages on your voicemail. You have messages from the Executive Director, a hall director from Kirkland Towers, and the president of the Pan-Hellenic Council.

With the second message you learn that earlier today, Karen Reeves, who is an RA in Kirkland Towers, was conducting student check-outs. Several students who did not have exams were already moving out for the summer. After checking out a few students with scheduled appointments she went to the front desk to retrieve a key in order to check out Room 1907, the former residence of Jake Hoverton. Carlford's Residence Life department offers express check-outs for residents who are leaving at odd hours of the day or night. Jake, one of her favorite residents and a community leader who had been instrumental in planning several successful programs in the building, approached Karen earlier in the week to notify her that he was leaving on study day. He had no exams because he was on internship this semester at a local small business. His flight was at 6:00 a.m., and he agreed to sign the express check-out waiver and incur any housekeeping or damage charges that were determined by staff after his departure. When Karen entered his room, she saw that Jake's room was in generally good condition, but she noticed that he had left some trash in the room. Determining there were no items of value, she decided to gather up the trash in order to avoid charging him.

As she was gathering up a stack of handwritten papers, she noticed a sheet with the phrase "because tri nu snatch is the best" written in large scrawl. Karen looked closer and realized that she held several copies of a fraternity's questionnaire. Each sheet had a name, major, class year, GPA, and the responses to a series of questions:

- Why do you want to be a Zeta Theta Theta?
- What do you do for fun?
- Where is the best place to party?
- How often do you masturbate?

- What is your dream weekend?
- Consider the following three people: Hilary Clinton, Rihanna, and Casey Shimmelman. Who do you sleep with, who do you marry, and who do you kill?
- What's your theme song?

After reading through a couple of sheets, Karen gathered them up, locked the door and took the stack of over 30 papers to her hall director, John Seidelman.

John read through the pages and quickly realized that you, the Coordinator of Fraternities and Sororities, needed to see these documents. In addition to the offensive questions, the worksheets were filled with vulgar humor and misogynistic and racist comments. John immediately also walked over to his supervisor's office (Ashland Simpson), and shared the materials. Ashland contacted the Executive Director who picked up the worksheets that same morning.

Disturbed by the questionnaire, Karen walked over to the Women's Center to speak to her professor in Feminist Theory, Dr. Julie Weingarten. While telling Julie about her experience, a student worker, Callie, overheard them talking and piped in, "Oh, yeah, the fuck, marry, kill game. Some of my guy friends talk about that a lot, it happens all the time." Concerned about this, Dr. Weingarten called Anna Torres and explained that a student brought the situation to her attention. Dr. Weingarten announced that this transgression should clearly result in immediate and permanent suspension of the students implicated and a suspension of the fraternal chapter. She stated that there was no need for due process or an investigation. She felt the university had clear and compelling evidence as well as the names and identifying information of the perpetrators in the organization. Furthermore, she stated that this should result in an immediate review of all fraternal organizations and their intake processes. In addition, she believed no organization should be allowed to continue to meet, sponsor or conduct any business or social programming until their processes have been deemed void of similar practices. If these organizations pass the investigation, she also believed there should be a mandatory education program on the history of misogyny in the United States and its deleterious effects on women's health, safety, and well-being.

You call Anna first and she briefs you on the situation, including Professor Weingarten's concerns and the initial reaction of Vice President North— who is profoundly discouraged by the conduct of some students. However, he questions the idea of suspending such a large number of students.

John Seidelman wanted to let you know that he is deeply concerned about the incident and wants to offer himself as a potential resource. He offers assistance with conducting masculinity and gender workshops with Greek men as you see fit. He has an interest in gender role socialization and thinks that among other ramifications, some mandatory education that invites the students to interrogate social messages about masculinity may be in order.

Casey Shimmelman is almost incoherent when you reach her. As the president of the Pan-Hellenic Organization and the young woman named in the questionnaire, several tweets and Facebook messages have already brought the incident to her attention. She feels vulnerable and is particularly upset with the president of Zeta Theta Theta, a member of the Interfraternity Council, with whom she has frequently collaborated.

Given both the specific immediate incident and the more deeply seated issues, what steps would you take to address the problems? Who will you involve and how will you involve them as you address the personal as well as institutional issues?

About the Editors

Frances K. Stage is Professor of Higher and Postsecondary Education at New York University. She earned her B.S. at the University of Miami and her M.S. at Drexel University, both in Mathematics. Her Ph.D. is from Arizona State University in Higher Education. She was previously professor and associate dean of the College of Education at Indiana University (1986–2000), and a National Science Foundation Senior Fellow and a Fulbright Specialist at the University of West Indies, Mona, Jamaica and at Cave Hill, Barbados. Her research interests include college student access, learning, and achievement, particularly in mathematics and science, and research methods. Recent books include *Answering Critical Questions Using Quantitative Data, Theoretical Perspectives on College Students,* and *Research in the College Context: Approaches and Methods* with K. Manning. Stage began her professional career as a mathematics instructor in the Maricopa County Community College System in Arizona.

Steven M. Hubbard is Clinical Assistant Professor and Director of Student Affairs at New York University's McGhee Division and Adjunct Professor of Higher Education where he teaches and conducts research in higher education and college student development. His research focus includes faculty development, student learning, assessment, and LGBT college students. He is currently working on several projects on the development of women and minority scientists. He also consults with other organizations in higher education leadership and professional development. Hubbard has over 15 years experience in student affairs administration at the University of Iowa, Hamline University, and New York University. He earned his Ph.D. in Higher Education from New York University in 2006. Dr. Hubbard started his professional career as a city planner for local governments in rural southwest Iowa.

About the Case Study Authors

Marissa E. Amos, a lifelong resident of New Jersey, lives and works in Camden. She is a graduate of Rutgers, the State University of New Jersey, and currently a full-time graduate student in the College Student Affairs program at Rutgers.

Melissa Boyd-Colvin, student affairs professional and adjunct faculty at the University of Rhode Island, oversees the university's Leadership Center and the minor in Leadership Studies. Her research interests include teaching effectiveness, supervision, and strengths-based organizational development.

Katie Branch is an associate professor in the Department of Human Development and Family Studies and the director of the College Student Personnel graduate program at the University of Rhode Island. Her research interests include adult development and learning for diverse students in collegiate settings, environmental theory and assessment in higher education, and college student retention and educational attainment.

Diane Cardenas Elliott is an AERA postdoctoral fellow at Educational Testing Services. She earned her doctorate in Higher Education Administration at New York University, her Juris Doctorate at Rutgers University, and her B.A. from Villanova University.

Lakshmi Clark-McClendon is a Senior Disability Specialist for the Moses Center for Students with Disabilities at New York University. Lakshmi received her B.A. in English from Hunter College of the City University of New York, an M.A. in Learning Disabilities from Columbia University Teachers College, and an M.A. in Higher Education and Student Affairs, with a specialization in International Education, from New York University.

Katherine M. Conway is an associate professor of Business at Borough of Manhattan Community College, City University of New York. She has an M.B.A. in Finance and a Ph.D. in Administration, Leadership and Technology, both from New York University.

Lynn Ceresino Neault is Vice Chancellor, Student Services for the San Diego Community College district, which serves more than 100,000 students in credit and non-credit programs annually. She has extensive experience providing leadership for a variety of programs and services focused on student access, equity, and success at both the local and state levels. Her administrative responsibilities also include Institutional Research, student information systems, legislative oversight, and compliance.

Tracy Davis is Professor in the Department of Education & Interdisciplinary Studies at Western Illinois University. He is founding Director of the Center for the Study of Masculinities and Men's Development and recently co-edited the book *Masculinities in Higher Education: Theoretical and Practical Considerations*.

Megan E. Delaney is the Grants Coordinator for the College of Education and Human Services at Montclair State University, New Jersey, where she helps faculty organize and submit research and grant proposals. Megan has an M.A. in Counseling from Montclair State University and a B.A. in Anthropology from Connecticut College and is currently pursuing her Ph.D. in Counselor Education at Montclair State University. Her research interests include feminist approaches to counseling and leadership development.

Paul S. DeStefano is a second year candidate for an Ed.M. in College Student Affairs at Rutgers University. He currently serves as a graduate assistant with the Center for Social Justice Education and LGBT Communities. Paul is a graduate of Pace University where he received a B.A. in Communication Studies.

Erich Dietrich is Assistant Dean for Global and Academic Affairs at New York University, Steinhardt. He is an historian with a specialization in race, globalization, and higher education. He teaches Global Perspectives in Higher Education: Brazil, and has taught Twentieth Century African American History, U.S. History since 1865, and Culture Wars in America. Dietrich earned his B.A., *magna cum laude*, at Carleton College, his M.A. at the University of Wisconsin–Madison, and his Ph.D. at New York University.

W. Houston Dougharty is Vice President for Student Affairs at Grinnell College in Iowa. He holds degrees from the University of Puget Sound, Western Washington University, and UC–Santa Barbara. He is active in NASPA and ACPA.

John P. Downey works as the Dean of Students at Queens University of Charlotte in North Carolina. He has over 25 years' experience in higher education, in various capacities including both academic and student affairs.

Michael J. Dumas is an assistant professor in the Educational Leadership graduate program at the Steinhardt School of Culture, Education, and Human Development, New York University.

Catrina Gallo is currently a master's student in the College Student Affairs Program at Rutgers University. She earned her B.A. in Human Development and Mathematics/Computer Science from Boston College.

Benjamin Gillig is a Ph.D. student in Higher Education and Student Affairs at the University of Iowa. Gillig completed his master's degree in Postsecondary Educational Leadership at San Diego State University while serving as a graduate assistant in residential education. Gillig currently works in the Center for Research on Undergraduate Education at the University of Iowa. His research interests include college student learning and access to postsecondary education.

Steven Goss is the Director of Online Education at Bank Street College of Education where he teaches Information Design and Online Education. He earned his Ed.D. in Instructional Technology and Media from Columbia University Teachers College, an M.A. from New York University and a B.S. from Pennsylvania State University in Art Education. His research interests include online learning theory, new media arts, and web design.

Bart Grachan has worked at New York University's Steinhardt School of Culture, Education, and Human Development for four years, and with community college transfers for nearly ten, and has served as president of the New York State Transfer & Articulation Association. He has master's degrees in teaching and history, and is currently working on a doctorate in higher education administration, with research focusing on the senior institutional role in community college transfer success.

Florence A. Hamrick is a Professor at Rutgers, the State University of New Jersey, where she teaches in the College Student Affairs program. Her research agenda centers on higher education equity, access, and success for members of historically underrepresented or non-dominant groups. She earned graduate degrees at Indiana University (Ph.D.) and the Ohio State University (M.A.).

Daniel Holub is the Department Administrator for Morse Academic Plan in the College of Arts & Science at New York University. Daniel has over 15 years' experience in student affairs and worked at the American Musical and Dramatic Academy, the University of Iowa, and the University of Wisconsin–Milwaukee.

Mark Hummell is a student life advisor in the Office of Spiritual Life (OSL) at New York University Abu Dhabi. He provides interfaith programs for students, staff, and faculty, and works closely with OSL student interest groups, the NYU New York Chaplains, and a variety of spiritual affiliates on and off campus. He earned a B.A. in Psychology and Theology from the University of Notre Dame, a Master of Social Work from Arizona State University, and a Master of Divinity from Yale University.

Ginelle John works as an enrollment administrator for the Department of Occupational Therapy at New York University. Ginelle earned her Ph.D. in Higher Education Administration from New York University. Her areas of interest include college access and retention and college athletics.

Jillian Kinzie is Associate Director, Indiana University Center for Post-secondary Research and NSSE Institute. She conducts research and leads project activities on effective use of student engagement data to improve educational quality, and is currently co-principal investigator on the Spencer Foundation-funded project, *Learning to Improve: A Study of Evidence-Based Improvement in Higher Education.* She earned her Ph.D. from Indiana University in Higher Education with a minor in Women's Studies.

Sara Klein is the Associate Dean of Campus Life at Wagner College. She earned her Ph.D. and her master's degree in Higher Education Administration at New York University, and her B.A. from Washington University in St. Louis.

Audrey Loera is currently the Assistant Dean of Academic Programs and Partnerships at Raritan Valley Community College. She holds a doctorate in Education Administration from the University of Phoenix, a master's in Public Administration from Andrew Jackson University, and a B.A. from Villanova University.

Valerie Lundy-Wagner is an assistant professor and faculty fellow in the Higher & Postsecondary Education program within the Steinhardt School of Culture, Education, and Human Development at New York University. Her research interests relate primarily to bachelor's degree completion, with an emphasis on engineering students, minority-serving institutions, and academic advising.

Teboho Moja is a Professor of Higher Education at New York University in the Department of Administration, Leadership, and Technology. She teaches courses on globalization, internationalization, and reform. She also teaches a number of study abroad courses in South Africa, Turkey, India, and Israel. She is a visiting professor at the University of Johannesburg and has held visiting positions in Norway and Finland.

Shaila Mulholland is an assistant professor in the Department of Administration, Rehabilitation, and Postsecondary Education in the College of Education at San Diego State University. Her research and teaching interests focus on the history and development of state postsecondary education systems, access and equity for underrepresented students, and creating inclusive learning environments. She earned her Ph.D. from New York University in Higher Education Administration.

Patricia A. Muller is Associate Director and Senior Research Scientist of the Center for Evaluation and Education Policy at Indiana University. There, Dr. Muller conducts statewide, national, and international research and evaluation of the impact and effectiveness of K–12 and higher education programs and initiatives.

Julie R. Nelson, M.F.A., NCC, has been an academic advisor for 12 years and currently works in the Transition Program at North Carolina State University where she helps first year students who are academically underprepared. Julie earned her Ed.S. and M.A. in Counseling at George Washington University, and is currently chair of the Academic Advising Workgroup in the Student Affairs Partnering with Academic Affairs knowledge community within NASPA.

Kathleen M. Neville is the special assistant to the Dean of Graduate Studies at Salem State University. With over 20 years of experience in student affairs, Kathleen's research agenda examines the influence of diversity on the students' collegiate experience and learning outcomes.

Kim C. O'Halloran is Associate Dean of the College of Education and Human Services at Montclair State University in New Jersey. She teaches in the department of Counseling and Educational Leadership. Her research focuses on student learning, retention, and student and academic affairs collaboration. O'Halloran earned her Ph.D. in Higher Education from New York University, and her M.A. in Education Administration and B.A. in English from Rutgers University.

Tara L. Parker is an associate professor of Higher Education at the University of Massachusetts Boston. Her research examines higher education policy issues related to equitable college access and outcomes, particularly for historically underrepresented groups.

Shadia Sachedina has worked in Student Affairs for almost 18 years and is currently the Director of Student Life at Baruch College. She is completing her doctorate in Higher Education at New York University. Her dissertation focuses on transfer student success.

Samantha Shapses Wertheim currently serves as the Director of the Office of Graduate Student Life at New York University. She is currently pursuing an Ed.D. in Higher and Postsecondary Education at New York University; her research interests include cross-racial interaction among students, student development theory, and social justice education.

Kristen Sosulski is Director of the Center for Innovations in Teaching and Learning and Clinical Assistant Professor of Information, Operations and Management Sciences at New York University Stern School of Business. She is the co-author of *Essentials of Online Course Design: A Standards-based Guide* (2011). She worked for the Columbia University Center for New Media Teaching and Learning as a project manager, and taught computer programming in the Math, Science and Technology department at Columbia University Teachers College. She earned her Ed.D, Ed.M., and M.A. from Columbia University Teachers College and a B.S. from New York University Stern School of Business.

Paula Steisel Goldfarb is the Executive Director of MBA and EMBA Admissions and Graduate Financial Aid at New York University Stern School of Business. She is a doctoral candidate in the Higher and Postsecondary Education department at New York University, where her research interests focus on enrollment management, educational policy, and economics and financing of higher education. She earned an M.A. from Columbia University and a B.A. from Haverford College.

William Tobin is Director of Institutional Research at DePauw University in Indiana. His research interests include strategic planning, institutional policy and decision making, and student persistence. He is currently studying the adaptation of business intelligence processes to the academic sector. He earned his Ph.D. in Higher Education from Indiana University.

Rachel Wagner is Assistant Director of Residence Life at the University of Dayton and a doctoral candidate in the Social Justice Education program at the University of Massachusetts Amherst. Rachel has presented on men and masculinities, and anti-racist and social justice education at a number of campuses and national conferences.

Sandi M. Wemigwase is a student in the master's program in Social and Cultural Analysis of Education in the College of Education at California State University, Long Beach.

Ronald C. Williams is an assistant professor in the Department of Education & Interdisciplinary Studies at Western Illinois University. Dr. Williams also serves as Chief Diversity Officer for Academic Affairs and engages in enrollment management and student retention.

Kim Yousey-Elsener serves as an assessment consultant with Campus Labs, working with campuses across the nation on their assessment work. She also serves as Chair of ACPA's Commission for Assessment and Evaluation as well as adjunct faculty at Buffalo State College. She earned her Ph.D. from New York University, a master's from Kent State University and a Bachelors of Music Education from Baldwin-Wallace College.

Case by Case Index

Categorical Index

General Index